A POPULAR DICTIONARY OF

Buddhism

A POPULAR DICTIONARY OF

Buddhism

CHRISTMAS HUMPHREYS

NTC *Publishing Group*
NTC/Contemporary Publishing Company

Library of Congress Cataloging-in-Publication Data

Humphreys, Christmas, 1901–.
    A popular dictionary of Buddhism / Christmas Humphreys.
       p.   cm.
    ISBN 0-8442-0419-6 (paper)
    1. Buddhism—Dictionaries.   I. Title.
  BQ130.H85   1997
  294.3′03—dc21   97-24605
                                            CIP

Cover design by Kim Bartko
Cover photograph by Sharon Hoogstraten

This edition first published in 1997 by NTC Publishing Group
An imprint of NTC/Contemporary Publishing Company
4255 West Touhy Avenue, Lincolnwood (Chicago), Illinois 60646-1975 U.S.A.
Copyright © 1984 by The Buddhist Society, London
Manufactured in the United States of America
International Standard Book Number: 0-8442-0419-6

15   14   13   12   11   10   9   8   7   6   5   4   3   2   1

PREFACE

THIS work is presented as a Popular Buddhist Dictionary.
As such it is a compromise between a true Dictionary, which
is largely concerned with derivations and synonyms, and an
Encyclopædia, which sets out a few terms at considerable
length. It is therefore more of a Glossary, and is based upon
that originally compiled thirty years ago by A. C. March and
later expanded for inclusion in *A Buddhist Students' Manual*,
published by the Buddhist Society. It attempts to cover the
entire field of Buddhism, but this field is enormous, and terms
have had to be chosen from seven languages spoken in ten
countries in at least ten major Schools of Buddhism. Bearing
in mind that many of these terms have developed and changed
in meaning during the 2,500 years of Buddhist history, it will
be seen that the task has not been easy, and as the chosen
words and phrases had to be compressed into a book of modest
size, principles of choice and treatment had to be devised which
it is only fair to the reader to make clear.

As the work is not scholarly but 'popular', I have had to
create and hold in mind the type of reader for whom the work
is intended. Here he is: an English-speaking student of Buddhism who on the one hand is more than a casual reader of one
or two volumes, and on the other is not a trained scholar.
The former will not need this volume; the latter will have his
own Sanskrit, Pali and other dictionaries for reference, and
a background of knowledge far greater than can be accurately
included in the few lines here devoted to each term.

The test, therefore, is: what foreign terms, or English terms
of special meaning, is such a reader likely to find today, or
during the next few years, in the books on Buddhism which
he is likely to read? By such a test has every term been included or excluded. Much follows from this standard of choice.

THERE CAN BE NO CONSISTENCY

I consider myself bound by the present situation in popular Buddhist literature, wherein some terms are better known in Sanskrit than in Pali, and vice versa; some spellings have clearly come to stay, however unsupported by any scholarship; certain items in a list are well known while others, to the scholar far more important, are never mentioned. Few lists, therefore, are complete. From the Tibetan pantheon, for example, I have mentioned perhaps a dozen out of hundreds, and the same applies to the technical terms of the Abhidhamma system of mind-training, and that of Zen.

The selection of people, places, scriptures, and terms will seem arbitrary. Nevertheless, all those given are frequently mentioned, and the rest I think not.

I have included some Hindu, Taoist and similar terms because they are frequently mentioned in Buddhist literature, such as *Yoga* and *Wu-wei*.

Many terms are substantially different in form when they appear in translation, and often very different in meaning. For example, the Sanskrit *Dhyāna* has a different meaning in its Pali form of *Jhāna*, and the Japanese reading of the Chinese ideographs produces an utterly different sound. Thus the famous Chinese artist *Wu-Tao-tsu* appears in Japanese as *Godōshi*. As between the Sanskrit and Pali versions of a word I have chosen the better known to put first, and often omitted the little known equivalent.

I have included English words of specifically Buddhist meaning, like *Enlightenment* or *Soul*, and phrases such as the *Wheel of Life* which are now well known.

The treatment of each term is in accordance with the picture of the reader for whom the book is intended. The length, for example, varies from one word to a page, but the average is about fifty words for each. Facts are easier to describe in this length than doctrines, and I must apologize for the necessary air of dogmatism when saying so much in so little space.

I have added few derivations. To the reader I have in mind they are but a hindrance, for in many cases they bear no resemblance to the present meaning. I have, for example, because it is unusual, added that the Japanese *Kōan* (Chinese *Kung-an*) means a public document, but this has no relation to its meaning in Zen.

Finally, I have had to face and overcome six difficulties inherent in the premises, and make decisions, however inconsistent, in each case.

Where does 'Buddhism' end and, say, interesting words in Japanese, or terms of Chinese art, or of Indian philosophy, or mere travelogue, begin? Is *Tatami*, the Japanese mat, a Buddhist term? Or *Garuda* or *Wabi*?

How much cross-referencing should be included? In the space available I have had to use my discretion, leaving clues for further study but attempting no more. In the difficult matter of bibliography I have seldom given more than one book, and for the Scriptures have usually referred to 'A.P.C.', an Analysis of the Pali Canon in the Buddhist Society's *Buddhist Students' Manual*, or to my own 'W. of Bsm.', *The Wisdom of Buddhism*, an anthology published in 1960.

Words have levels of meaning, and the difficulty of choosing the level at which to describe a term was often considerable. This applies above all to the same term used in the Theravada and Mahayana Schools, the former being on the plane of moral philosophy and the latter of mystical metaphysics of universal significance. Thus *Buddha* has many levels, *Anattā* rises to the cosmic plane in the supreme doctrine of *Sūnyatā*, and *Compassion* in Theravada, where it is but one of the *Brahma-Vihāras*, becomes in the later School the inseverable partner of Wisdom itself.

Right spelling has puzzled more learned heads than mine, and there is still no adopted system for all the languages covered in this work. Pali is definite; so is Sanskrit, apart from the difficulty of diacritical marks, of which more later. Japanese, now that the post-war change has been abandoned, is once more clear, but Chinese is extremely difficult. I did not, for example, recognize Huien-tsiang, the great Chinese pilgrim, under the guise of Chuang-sang. Tibetan is worse. Amid all the variations of *Tulku*, in Tibetan and Mongolian, I have clung to the simplest, but the reader must be ready to face eleven. The slow change in a term in the course of centuries is often illuminating, as in *Stūpa*, *Thūpa* (not helped by the English archaeologists' invention of *Tope*), then *Dagoba*, *Dagaba* and *Pagoda*. In Japan one has at times to choose between a man's real name, his later Buddhist name and his posthumous title of honour. But at least the spelling of each is clear. What, then, of the *v* and *w* of Sanskrit? The actual sound is between the two. Ceylon has moved in the last forty years from the *w* to the *v*, but both will be found, confusingly.

And so to the use of diacritical marks. The West will in time discard them all, as it has with *Nirvana* and *Mahayana*. Meanwhile the marking helps pronunciation, and sometimes distinguishes the same word of different meaning according to the marks it bears. The greatest difficulty is with Sanskrit, a most precise language, where the removal of habitual marks may mutilate a word, as if one were to remove the accent from a word of French. I have compromised by marking the long A, the long I, the long U, and the mark over the N. All E's and O's are long, so need not be marked. The real difficulty is with the letter S, of which Sanskrit has three. The plain S has been left as such, but where the dash over the S means that it must be pronounced as SH, I have used an invention of my own, clumsy though it is, for the spelling of the word itself, yet not repeating it in the text. Thus *Sūnya*, void, is pronounced *Shūnya*, and I have presented it as S(H)UNYA. The vowels in all these languages are continental in pronunciation; the C is always CH, and the sound TH never in the English way. Every H, anywhere, is sounded. Thus Dhamma is pronounced D-h-amma, and Tathatā is Tat-h-atā.

I have used no marks in Chinese, and in Japanese the long O and the long U only. The modified O, as in Bön (Tibetan) or Körös (Hungarian), is used but rarely.

Finally, I must deeply thank those scholars who, from their non-existent spare time, have found it to help me in my own considerable problems. In particular, that great authority on Sanskrit Buddhism, Dr Edward Conze, has helped me enormously; in matters Tibetan both he and Mr. Marco Pallis have been of great help. For Japanese problems I turned to Dr Carmen Blacker of Cambridge University and Dr R. D. M. Shaw, and made inquiries from Dr Irmgard Schloegl in Japan. Mr Maurice Walshe was most helpful over Pali terms, assisted when necessary by Miss I. B. Horner. But the errors must still be many, and for all of them I am alone apologetically responsible.

For research I am grateful to the Buddhist Society's Archivist, Miss Marianne Winder, and for typing to Mrs Mary Anthony. But the patience of my wife, as in searching through forty volumes for a vaguely remembered reference, and of the publishers with the manner of the MSS. turned in, was inexhaustible, and I am grateful to the latter for the loan of Mr Nicholas Cowan who, with remarkable skill, turned a mass of material into this book.

T. C. H.

St. John's Wood

PREFACE TO THE SECOND EDITION

N o Glossary which includes living people and institutions can stand still, and this new edition of a work first published in 1962 needs appropriate revision. Where persons have died I have indicated the fact. Where an author has published important further works I have chosen the most appropriate titles to fill up available space. I have given changes of address where known.

The most troublesome change has been caused by the disintegration of B.S.M. (*A Buddhist Student's Manual*) into its constituent parts. *The Development of Buddhism in England* has reappeared in *Sixty Years of Buddhism in England* which I published in 1968. *A Brief Glossary of Buddhist Terms* is the basis of this present work, and a new and better *Analysis of the Pali Canon* by Russell Webb, published in Kandy, is appearing this year, fortunately with the same initials, A.P.C.

Two new entries appear on page 24 relating respectively to Mme David-Neel and A. P. Sinnett, both of whom have been mentioned in the text. Inclusion of these references rectifies an omission in the original edition.

For the rest, I have made three corrections to known errors and have improved cross-referencing. May the net result be of value to the persons for whom it was compiled.

T.C.H.

INTRODUCTION

HERE is a jumble of words translated from ten languages, themselves the voices of as many racial cultures, between them covering terms and people, places and doctrines culled from a dozen countries in which Buddhism has been developing for 2,500 years. In all this time it has never known the word authority, and differing schools of thought have developed with no more regard to orthodoxy than lies in a common acceptance of the Buddha's Enlightenment and the Way by which he gained it. The tolerance which flows from this absence of authority, though rare in the field of religion, has enabled doctrines and practices to flourish which may at first sight seem to be far from the original Teaching.

In the result the present held of Buddhism, itself a Western term for the Teaching of the Buddha and all that has grown up around it, is unique in range, depth and complexity, and no man is expert in all of it. The difficulty of compressing a thousand terms which are current in its Western literature into 50,000 words is therefore obvious. Vast themes must be set out in a few lines, and matters still the subject of dispute must be set down in a form too brief to be accurate. Meanings have changed, even in one school, in the course of centuries, and the same term may be used very differently and at different levels in, say, Ceylon, Japan and Tibet. It follows that accuracy and consistency are impossible, and the total picture given must be obscure. The reader therefore deserves some help in using the book to advantage and this, in the ideal, would be a mental map in which the terms described had each their place and meaning. This, however, would involve an Introduction as long as the book, and there is room for no more than a few notes on the divers factors which make up

THE FIELD OF BUDDHISM

The component parts of the whole are partly visible and objective, and partly invisible because subjective. Each part must be viewed in relation to the dozen major schools of Buddhism which later developed, and each of these has affected and been affected by conditions, physical and mental, in its own locality. Yet bearing all these factors in mind, the following may be helpful as a tentative sketch-map of the enormous field.

The visible parts would seem to be (A) the *History of Buddhism*, its genesis and spread, geographically and doctrinally; (B) the *Geography of Buddhism*, complementary to (A), showing the countries covered and affected by the ebb and flow of the schools of Buddhist thought and art and culture; (C) the *Races and Cultures* already existing in these countries, in which the ferment of Buddhist doctrine operated or which it produced; (D) the *Languages* in which Buddhism was taught, and into which the Teaching was translated and written down; (E) the *Literature, Arts and Crafts* in which Buddhist principles were made visible, and the cultural practices which flowed from, or were affected by, its coming; (F) lastly, the dispersion of the Buddhist *Monastic Ideal*, and the different forms which it took in the countries in which it was established.

The Invisible factors may be divided into (i) Doctrine and (ii) the Practice of Meditation.

(i) *Doctrine*

The East is concerned with Truth and the mind which seeks it, but it has never cut up the total field of the search for Truth and the means of finding it into the tight compartments of Western scholarship. Yet from the Western point of view a minimum of ten such categories of the mind's activities must, however briefly, be considered:

12

(*a*) **Buddhology** From a human being who, as the guerdon of a thousand lives on earth, achieved the mind's Enlightenment to, let us say, Vairocana, the Sun God of a Japanese school of ritual, is a long step, and the process a field of research on its own.

(*b*) **Metaphysics** The distinction between these is a
(*c*) **Philosophy** fine one. The Buddha deplored any time spent on 'unprofitable' speculation on ultimates, yet Buddhist achievements in metaphysics and philosophy have rarely been equalled and never surpassed.

(*d*) **Religion** Buddhism itself is not a religion, for it lacks the distinguishing features of such a term, yet certain schools of it can fairly be so called. Japanese Shingon and Shin, and much of Tibetan Buddhism, is clearly within the field of religion.

(*e*) **Mysticism** The mystic appears in all times and places, growing from all types of spiritual soil. And all mystics talk the same language, using the same symbols, whether Christian, Sufi or Taoist, ancient Buddhist or modern Hindu. Much of the finest literature of Buddhism must be classed as such, whether devotional writing or the incomprehensible sayings of the masters of Zen.

(*f*) **Psychology** Psychology is not a new science, as some unwisely think. The Abhidhamma, the third division of the Pali Canon of the Theravada School, contains a complete system of mind training based on analysis of consciousness taken to a degree not yet surpassed in the West, while in the Mahayana, the Yogacara or Mind-Only school is itself a system of psychology founded on spiritual experience.

(*g*) **Morality** Morality is common to all religions and ways of life and the basis of all true spiritual development. Sila, Buddhist morality, is in range and quality second to none, and the Theravada itself may be described as a system of moral philosophy.

(*h*) **Ritual and Magic** Both play a large part in man's

13

development, and though in a sense 'visible' are expressions of and intended to influence the performer's mind. The Shingon School of Japan and most of those of Tibetan Buddhism are filled with ritual, and some kind of Service in the temples is common from Theravada to Zen.

(*i*) **Compassion in action** If the power of compassion is little emphasized in Theravada Buddhism, it is of the essence of the Mahayana, wherein the Bodhisattva's vow to work for humanity's salvation without thought for his own is the very purpose of all activity.

(*j*) **Spiritual Achievement** It may be argued that this is the goal of all spiritual endeavour, but in Buddhism it is also a class of its own. The mystic achieves his vision in flashes; so does the man of Zen, but only in the Zen School is there a long and strenuous training designed to make this 'break through' repeatedly, until an enlightened state of consciousness is attainable and usable at will.

(ii) *Meditation*

All Buddhist schools agree that regular meditation is sooner or later an essential exercise in the attainment of spiritual manhood. The various methods and technique are manifold, but the necessity for it is a powerful factor in the field of Buddhism, and can never be ignored.

As already pointed out, these factors deeply affected each other in their development. Some of this interchange is visible, as in art and literature; some is less obvious for it took place subjectively. Yet the pattern of all teaching follows the pattern of the human mind. In Japan, for example, the distinction of Jiriki, salvation by self-effort, and Tariki, by the help of Another, reflects a basic antithesis. Again, the Theravadin, rational, practical-minded, of cold morality, in-turned upon the Arhat ideal, is only one part of the picture; another is the warmly-compassionate, mystical, more religious follower of the Bodhisattva ideal. Yet another part portrays the ritual-

14

magic of Tibet and schools of Tantric origin in China and Japan. Another is Zen, the hunger in the mind to exceed the limitations of thought, and to know Reality as thought can never know.

And even now we are learning about Buddhism. The Tun-huang caves have been known in China for fifty years, but the vast array of its pictures and sculpture and Buddhist books are only in the course of study, and MSS. revealed after a thousand years of darkness have not yet been translated in their entirety, any more than the yak-loads of Scriptures brought from Tibet by Aurel Stein, Sven Hedin, Tucci and a dozen more. By the translation of new texts, examination of *objets d'art*, excavation of Buddhist sites and the reassessment of early theories, we are daily learning more and more about the enormous field of Buddhism.

Let us then look briefly at some of the components above listed, and first at the history and geography of Buddhism. We begin at Lumbinī, in South Nepal, in 563 B.C. when a boy is born to the Rajah of the Sakya clan and Maya, his wife, of Kapilavastu. They are Hindus of the Kshatriya caste. The child grows into a young man of brilliant mind and attainment. He marries Yasodhara and has a son, Rahula. Yet his heart is set on the fact of suffering, its cause and cure, and the way to that cure for all mankind. Family ties cannot hold this great Bodhi-sattva. He leaves the palace and for six years leads a solitary life in the forest in search of Reality. Finally he wins through to Enlightenment, and under the Bo-tree on the full moon of May becomes Buddha, the All-Enlightened One, the latest of his line.

He moves across India to the Deer Park at Sarnath, near Benares, and there preaches his First Sermon, setting forth the Buddhist Middle Way between all extremes, the Four Noble Truths and the Noble Eightfold Path which had led him to his own Enlightenment. He founds the Sangha, the Order

15

of Bhikkhus, and sends them forth to proclaim the Dhamma. Princes and merchants, criminals and courtesans, soldiers, philosophers and seekers like himself, all came to hear the Message of the Way. He is given Retreats in which to spend the rainy season. He preaches to all by parable and story, in cities and villages, to groups beside the way. He returns to his father's home, Kapilavastu, where his wife and son enter the Order. Great men proudly serve him, Moggallana, Sariputta, Mahakassapa, and his cousin Ananda. Another cousin, Devadatta, strives to create division in the Order, and even to kill him, but the movement spreads and grows. And so for forty-five years he proclaimed the Dhamma until at the age of eighty, at Kusinara, he ended his last rebirth and entered Nirvana. His ashes were enshrined in numerous Stupas from one of which have been taken a few to rest in the Buddhist Temple of the Maha Bodhi Society in Calcutta.

The message spread; to Ceylon by the hand of Asoka's children, Mahinda and Sanghamitta, who in 252 B.C. planted a slip of the Bo-tree which may be seen today. To Burma and Thailand, and down the archipelago to Cambodia and Java. Then east, along the trade routes to China, Korea and Japan, and west to the Hellenic-influenced tribes of Afghanistan. Then north to Tibet and thence Mongolia. But by A.D. 1000 the movement had ceased. In India the great University of Nalanda still flourished, but soon with the rest of Buddhism it went down before the sword-point of Islam.

But that which arrived and developed in the lands about India was not any more one Buddhism. No Teaching which expressly allows its followers to explore all aspects of the mind is likely to remain of one school only, and in the long years of its history Buddhism has happily flowed into a dozen or more channels of thought and practice. Yet all retain three factors in common; the Buddha, as the All-Enlightened One; a large body of doctrine and practice; and a quite remarkable tolerance of differing points of view. There has never been a Buddhist war, nor has any man been killed or even injured for holding a different point of view.

Let us, then, look briefly at these schools of Buddhism, their scriptures and the men who wrote them.

The earliest school on record is the Hinayana which, by the third century B.C. had split into eighteen sects. Of these only one has survived, the Theravada or doctrine of the Elders, found today in Ceylon, Burma, Siam and Cambodia. Its Canon is complete, much having been written down in the first century B.C. All of it is available in English, thanks to the work of the Pali Text Society. Lying as it does on the fringe of the Buddhist world, this school was unaffected by development elsewhere, and is still, in doctrine and practice, built about the Sangha. But early in the history of Buddhism there was dissension at the great Councils called from time to time to settle and preserve the Doctrine, and already in the second century B.C. we find in two other schools of the Hinayana the seeds of the later views and practices which together formed the magnificent palace of thought which we know as the Mahayana.

Great scriptures continued to be written in India for centuries after the Theravada had found its home in Ceylon. A group of great importance was the Prajna-paramita literature, concerning 'the Wisdom which has gone beyond'. Two famous summaries are the Diamond and the Heart Sutras. All are concerned with Sunyata, the doctrine of the Plenum-Void, which is the Theravada doctrine of Anatta carried to its ultimate limits. About the same time appeared the Maha-Parinirvana Sutra, with the developed teaching of the Bodhisattva, the famous Lotus of the Good Law Sutra (Saddharmapundarika), about which two entire schools, the Tendai and Nichiren, were later founded, and the two Sukhavati Sutras which developed the teaching of the Pure Land, later to become the largest school in Japan. All these themes and ideas developed from seeds already visible in sects of the Hinayana School, and all were eagerly debated in the great University of Nalanda, where for nearly a thousand years the greatest minds of the East taught and debated the doctrines of Buddhism.

From this mass of learning there slowly crystallized out two major schools of Mahayana Buddhism. One of the greatest minds of India, Nagarjuna, in the second century A.D., founded, or at least systematized, the Madhyamika School as a 'Middle Way' between the prevailing views of Existence and Non-existence concerning visible and invisible phenomena. To solve the problem an Absolute and Relative Truth were admitted, but behind both lies the Sunyata of the Prajna-paramita literature. Later, in the fifth century these metaphysical doctrines were transferred to the field of psychology by the brothers Vasubandhu and Asanga, who between them crystallized the views of the Yogacara or Vijnanavada School of Mind-Only. In their foremost Scripture, the Lankavatara Sutra, the Buddha becomes a cosmic principle of Buddhahood; the doctrine of his three Bodies (Trikaya) is displayed, and in the Alaya-Vijnana, the 'Store-consciousness', appears the forerunner of the Unconscious of Western psychology. Another great Scripture is the vast Avatamsaka Sutra, but better known is the Awakening of Faith, thanks to the early translation by Dr Suzuki (1900).

These doctrines and schools took a long time to develop, but for a thousand years (300 B.C. to A.D. 700) they had the benefit of Buddhist rulers, such as the Emperor Asoka, King Kanishka of the Kushans in the north-west, and of King Harsha in the north-east, in whose shadow to grow. Buddhist art was able to thrive; the semi-Hellenic art of Gandhara in the north-west, the lovely art from the Mathura School under the Gupta Dynasty, and the spiritual faces of the Rupas of north-east India produced under the Pala kings. Groups of cave-dwellings were slowly carved out through the centuries, from mere Stupas, or relic-mounds, to lecture halls with rock-cut Viharas for the monks. In Bhilsa, Barhut and Sanchi, and later at Ajanta, Ellora and Karli, we can trace in existing ruins the lives and longings of the Bhikkhus and laymen of that day. Still the great names appeared, and great Scriptures were written, by Santideva in the seventh century, in the dialogues we know as the Questions of King Milinda, and in the Surangama Sutra, which may be of Chinese origin. Meanwhile the Abhidhamma of the surviving Theravada School was being slowly developed, and the Sutta Nipata and the Dhammapada, early works now famous the world over, were written down and made the subject of commentaries. But the sun of Indian Buddhism was setting. Whatever the causes of its decline in India, the swords of Islam destroyed the monasteries and those who lived in them, and when the Sangha went the Teaching followed.

But Indian thought was not a closed circuit. The trade routes to the East carried more than merchandise; they carried ideas. Early in the second century Buddhism arrived in China, perhaps with the Sutra of 42 Sections, a Hinayana work. By the time of Kumarajiva (fifth century) the task of translating the Indian Sutras was in full swing, and schools were founded about them. A curious blend of the old and the new took place, and out of the mixture came purely Chinese schools. The Tientai (Jap. Tendai) centred about the Lotus Sutra, while about the Avatamsaka Sutra was gathered a group of minds which, in the Kegon-Shu of Japan, produced some of the greatest philosophy of the world. The Pure Land teaching of the Sukhavati Sutras formed the heart of the Jodo School, which in Japan was carried to its limits in the Shin-Shu, while the uncompromising directness of Bodhidharma founded, with the aid of his great followers of the Ch'an tradition, the Sudden School of direct enlightenment known today as Zen.

Meanwhile a series of Chinese pilgrims, Fa-hsien, Hiuen-Tsiang and I-Tsing, brought back an increasing quantity of Indian texts, all of which were translated, studied and in turn applied in methods of self-enlightenment. Between them they encouraged and produced some of the world's greatest art, that

19

of the T'ang Dynasty (seventh to tenth century), which in the view of many has never been surpassed.

The message spread to Japan. First in the seventh century, when Buddhism was adopted by Prince Shotoku at his capital of Nara, and then in Kyoto which, from the eighth century onwards, produced some of the greatest schools, scriptures and minds in the field of Buddhism. All the Chinese schools were brought over and new ones were founded. Ch'an became Zen, in its two forms, Rinzai and Soto; Jodo was developed into Shin; Tendai and Kegon developed from their Chinese counterparts, and Nichiren founded the movement of his name, to adore the Lotus Sutra as Wisdom incarnate in words. The Tantric beliefs and practices of India passed through the Mantra School of Peking to become the Shingon of Japan, and in the Ritsu School even the Vinaya discipline was practised for centuries. Japanese art and culture developed accordingly, the Samurai preferring Zen, the people preferring Shin; the scholars developing the schools of thought of Tendai and Kegon. From these and the Japanese love of beauty came the Tea-Ceremony and Flower-Arrangement; Judo and Kendo and Bushido adopted the cult of Zen. Today the Shin sect has the greatest numbers, but Zen is the spiritual strength which reflects the virility of the nation and has power to affect as well the Western mind.

Meanwhile the Message was carried north, into Tibet in the eighth century by Padmasambhava and those who followed him, and thence into Mongolia. Three strains of Buddhism were taken in, the Vinaya discipline, the principles of the Yogacara School and the Tantras of Bengal. All were blended in the Tibetan mind, which also had the Prajnaparamita scriptures to study and apply. Schools were founded, reformed and allowed to die, as in the other countries where Buddhism had spread. Then the Gelug-pa, the Reformed movement of Tsongkha-pa became dominant, and includes today the Dalai and the Panchen Lamas. The pantheon grew under Tantric influence; heights of spirituality in pure experience were attained by some, even as the lowest ranks of the people were sunk in sorcery and psychic practices but little removed from the indigenous religion of Bön. Here again, the art of the country is Buddhist, the Thankas and images alike conforming to a rigid ecclesiastical discipline.

So, by the fifteenth century the picture is reasonably complete. In Ceylon, Siam, Burma and Cambodia, the Theravada with its Sangha of yellow-robed Bhikkhus and its complete Canon in Pali. In Tibet, a Tibetan Buddhism, a blend of many schools, and an Order which, having much in common with the older Sangha, is yet more of a Church. In Japan, the Order as such never claimed the authority which obtains in the Sangha proper. The monks are more teachers than priests; many of them marry and return to the world. In doctrine there is vast variety, including all those factors set out earlier herein. None alone is 'Buddhism'; none claims to be. Much is at the heart of Buddhism, the group of doctrines common to all schools. But at the edge of the circle, as it widened through the centuries, are beliefs and practices which seem remote from the centre. What would the Buddha have said to Tantric ritual, or to the pure faith of Shin? But that, says the Buddhist, is not the question, for the attitude to the Buddha himself has changed. Nowhere have the 'accidents of history' less importance than in Buddhism. Buddhism would not today be troubled if some great mind should prove that the Buddha as a man never lived at all. Buddhism is a Way, and so long as there are men who seek a Way from sorrow to Enlightenment, it will exist for those who tread it.

Buddhism came west. Back to India whence it had been expelled in the tenth to twelfth centuries. In the work of the Maha Bodhi Society, which has centres in all the great cities, and in the work of the late Dr Ambedkar among the 'untouchables', there are signs of a movement which may yet profoundly affect the face of India. But Buddhism continued west, to Europe and the U.S.A. A great range of Buddhist Scripture is now available in English; text-books on every corner of the field are appearing every year. There are societies large and small all over Europe; in England the movement began in 1907 and has since grown steadily. The same applies to the U.S.A. which, though behind in literature, is now catching up. As a factor in the field of Western thought Buddhism has come to stay.

ABBREVIATIONS

A.F.M.   Awakening of Faith in the Mahayana (Suzuki).
Ang. N.   Anguttara Nikāya
A.P.   Abhidhamma Pitaka.
A.P.C.   Analysis of Pali Canon.
B.E.   Buddhism in England.
B.L.B.   Buddhist Lodge Bibliography.
B.R.   Buddhist Review.
B.S.M.   *A Buddhist Students' Manual. See* page 10.
Bsm.   Buddhism.
Bst.   Buddhist.
B.T.   *Buddhist Texts,* compiled and edited by Edward Conze.
Buddhism   The Book *Buddhism* (Penguin Books) by Christmas Humphreys.
Burm.   Burmese.
Chin.   Chinese.
Dhp.   Dhammapada.
Dial.   Dialogues of the Buddha.
Dig. N.   Dīgha Nikāya.
E.R.E.   Encyclopaedia of Religion and Ethics.
Jap.   Japanese.
Jat.   Jātakas.
J.P.T.S.   Journal Pali Text Society.
J.R.A.S.   Journal Royal Asiatic Society.
Khu. N.   Khuddaka Nikāya.
Maj. N.   Majjhima Nikāya.
M.   Mahāyāna.
Nanjio   Nanjio's Catalogue of Chinese Tripitaka.
o.p.   Out of Print.
P.   Pali.
P.E.D.   Pali-English Dictionary.
P.T.S.   Pali Text Society.
Q.K.M.   Questions of King Milinda.
q.v.   (*quod vide*) which see.
Rh. D.   Rhys Davids.
S.   Sutta.
Sam. N.   Samyutta Nikāya.
S.B.E.   Sacred Books of the East.
Siam.   Siamese.
Sk.   Sanskrit.
S.P.   Sutta Pitaka.
Taisho   Taisho edition of Chinese Bst. Scriptures.
Tib.   Tibetan.
V.P.   Vinaya Pitaka.
W. of Bsm.   *The Wisdom of Buddhism* (Ed. by Christmas Humphreys).
Warren   Warren's *Buddhism in Translations.*
W.E.S.   Wisdom of the East Series.

SUPPLEMENTARY ENTRIES

David-Neel, Mme Alexandra. Famous French traveller and explorer in Tibet, and authority on Tibetan Buddhism. The first European woman to reach Lhasa. *See* her *My Journey to Lhasa* (1927). Further works included *With Mystics and Magicians in Tibet* (1931), and with Lama Yongden (q.v.), her disciple, *The Secret Oral Teachings in Tibetan Buddhist Sects.* For a while lived in Kum-bum monastery, in quarters specially built for her. Spent later years in Digne, France, and died there in 1969 aged 101.

Sinnett, A. P. English editor of *The Pioneer*, at Allahabad, in 1879 when H. P. Blavatsky (q.v.) reached India. Through her put in communication with the Masters 'M' and 'K.H.' by whom she had been trained in Tibet for the presentation of Theosophy to the West. Between 1880 and 1884 received some 130 letters from these Masters, later published as *The Mahatma Letters to A. P. Sinnett* (1923). The originals are now in the British Library. From the *Letters* Sinnett compiled *Esoteric Buddhism* (1883) and *The Occult World* (1881). Later wrote many books on Theosophy and played an active part in the movement in London. Died 1921.

A POPULAR DICTIONARY OF BUDDHISM

A (Sk. and P.) The prefix meaning 'not', the negative. Before another vowel it may be followed by a supplemental consonant for euphony: e.g. a(n)-attā, not Attā.

Abhaya (Sk.) Fearless. As a gesture in an image of the Buddha is that of protection. (*See* **Mudrā** *and* **Buddha Rūpa** for description.)

Abhāyagiri Famous monastery and surviving Stūpa at Anurādhapura (q.v.), once the capital of Ceylon.

Abhidhamma (P.) Lit. Higher Dhamma. The third division of the Canon of the Theravāda School (q.v.). (*See* **Tipitaka**.) It is largely a commentary on the Sutta Pitaka, the Sermons, and subjects them to analysis. Philosophical and psychological, it contains an entire system of mind training. (*See* **Satipatthāna**.) The Burmese Sangha specializes in the study of Abhidhamma. *See* Nyanatiloka, *A Guide through the Abhidhamma Pitaka* (1957).

Abhijñā (Sk.) or **Abhiññā** (P.) Super-knowledge. Modes of Insight attained by the practice of Dhyāna (q.v.). A high state of consciousness when six spiritual powers have been developed. They are (1) Power to see what one wills to see, anywhere; (2) Power to hear and understand all languages; (3) Power to read thoughts; (4) Knowledge of former lives (one's own); (5) Knowledge of former lives (those of others); (6) The deliverance of mind from passions. (*See* **Iddhis**.)

Abhishekha (Sk.) Lit. sprinkling. Baptism; hence consecration or initiation. A term in the Bst. Tantras of Tibet. *See* Snellgrove, *The Hevajra Tantra*, Vol. I, pp. 131-3 (1960).

Absolute There is no one Bst. equivalent to the Hindu Parabrahman, the indescribable Ultimate. The nearest is Dharmakāya, a philosophic term. Psychologically this is the Ālayavijñāna of the Yogācāra School. Ontologically Sūnyatā is the absolute Void, even void of voidness, of which a positive concept is Tathatā, the Suchness or Thusness of things. For relationship *see* Suzuki, *Essays in Zen Buddhism* Third Series, p. 295-8 (1939).

Acala (Sk.) The immovable. A stage in the Bodhisattva's career. 'A Nirvana which is not extinction' (Suzuki). In Jap. art is Fudō, the most important of the five Myōō, minor gods who are earthly agents for the five Nyorai (q.v.).

Ācārya (Sk.) Suffix meaning master or teacher, e.g. Sankarācārya.

Acintya (Sk.) Inconceivable. Beyond the power of mentation.

Ādi-Buddha (Sk.) The primordial Buddha of Tibetan Bsm., the self-existent, unoriginated source of Universal Mind. Its creative power is symbolized under form of five Dhyāni Buddhas (q.v.), whose active aspects are personified under the Dhyāni Bodhisattvas, these in turn being represented on earth as the Manushi or human Buddhas of the seven Root Races of humanity. There are seven Dhyāni Buddhas, but names of five only are generally given. Avalokitesvara (q.v.) is the Dhyāni Bodhisattva of the present age and the Buddha Gautama his earthly reflex.

Advaita (Sk.) Hindu term meaning non-dual, not two. The Indian doctrine taught by Sankara of a Non-duality beyond the Pairs of Opposites which is more than One, One being only the Opposite of Many. Cp. Zen which strives for the immediate inner experience of such a Non-duality. (*See* **Vedanta**.) Some Buddhist writers use the form Advaita.

Āgama (Sk.) Tradition. The Āgamas are Chinese transla-tions of the Sūtras or Sermons as collected by the Sarvāsti-vādin School of the Hīnayāna. They vary little from the corresponding Sutta Pitaka of the Theravāda Canon of today.

Agati (P.) The wrong path as distinct from the right path (to Enlightenment). Not to be confused with Āgati, rebirth.

Agnosticism The doctrine that man can never know the nature of Ultimate Reality. Bsm. differs from agnosticism in that it asserts an innate transcendental faculty in man (*buddhi*) which by elimination of all elements of 'defilement' (*āsavas*) may contemplate Reality and attain perfect know-ledge and enlightenment—Nirvāna (q.v.). (*See* **Intuition**.)

Ahamkāra (Sk.) The false belief of individuality, that the self contains some immortal and unchanging faculty or soul (q.v.).

Ahimsā (P.) Not hurting; compassion, especially for animals. Both Buddhist and Jain lay great stress on virtue of *ahimsā*. First Bst. precept enjoins negative compassion by not taking life, and second of Four Sublime Moods (*see* **Brahma Vihāras**) inculcates positive compassion for all life. (*See* **Karunā**.)

Ajantā Series of rock-cut caves in the Deccan containing world-famous Bst. frescoes, mostly of sixth century A.D., and Bst. sculptures. Caves cut for Viharas and halls for worship between second century B.C. and seventh century A.D. and show a corresponding development in style.

Ājīva (P.) Livelihood. Right Livelihood is the fifth step on the Noble Eightfold Path (q.v.). (*See* **Livelihood.**)

Ākāsha (Sk.) Space, as the spiritual essence of Space. The primordial Substance. Without cognizable attributes it is the plane of manifestation in which lies inherent the Ideation of the Universe. It lies beyond differentiation and therefore beyond description. In esoteric Bsm. the Akasic records hold 'nature's memory'.

Akshobhya (Sk.) The Imperturbable. One of the Dhyāni Buddhas (q.v.), 'pairing' with Amitābha (q.v.) even as Amoghasiddhi and Ratnasambhava are another pair, with Vairocana (q.v.) in the centre.

Akusala (P.) Unwholesome, used of those volitions which are accompanied by Greed, Hate or Delusion and thereby cause undesirable Karmic results. Cp. *Kusala*, wholesome.

Ālambana (Sk.) Ārammana (P.) Object of consciousness.

Alamkāra (Sk.) Adornment, as a rhetorical figure of speech.

Ālāra Kālāma The recluse to whom the youthful Prince Gautama first went for spiritual help on leaving his father's home to save mankind.

Ālaya-vijñāna (Sk.) The central or universal consciousness which is the womb or 'store' (*ālaya*) consciousness. A term introduced by the Yogācāra School of Indian Bsm. (q.v.) For comparison with the Unconscious of Western psychology *see* Suzuki, *Zen Buddhism and Psychoanalysis* (1960).

Amarāvati Site of magnificent specimen of Buddhist art, near Madras. Sculptures formed decorations of a Stūpa (q.v.) 138 feet in diameter, and an inner and outer rail surrounding

28

it. Most of the sculptures were destroyed before the Stūpa was discovered, the specimens rescued being now in British Museum and Madras Museum. The work dates from 200 B.C.—300 A.D. and represents the intermediate stage between ancient Buddhist art and that of the Gandhara period (q.v.), both symbol and figure being used to depict the Buddha.

Ambapālī A courtesan in the city of Vaisali who gave a mansion to the Buddha for the use of the Sangha. He graciously accepted.

Ambedkar, Bhim Rao, PH.D., Barrister at Law (1891-1956). Indian Bst. who founded a movement in India for converting millions of the Scheduled Castes ('Untouchables') to Bsm. Horrified with the conditions in which they lived he dedicated his life to their redemption. Became a Member of the Bombay Legislative Assembly and Law Minister to the Central Government, where he helped draft the present Constitution. On 31 October, 1956, at Nagpur he and his wife with half a million followers formally renounced Hinduism and took Pansil (q.v.) from a Bst. Thera. Already a sick man, he died soon after. His work is being carried on by the Indian Bst. Society he founded, under the inspiration of the English Bhikshu Sangharakshita (q.v.) *See, The Buddha and his Dhamma* (1957).

America, Buddhism in Although there have been thousands of Japanese Bsts. on the West Coast for many years, and although there have been well-founded Bst. organizations in various States for the past thirty years, there is as yet no central Bst. organization in the U.S.A., and the position of Bsm. fluctuates too fast for accurate assessment. The Japanese have formed The Buddhist Churches of America in San Francisco, but the oldest established Bst. society for

29

Westerners is the First Zen Institute of America (q.v.) in New York. Theravada interests are catered for in the American Buddhist Academy of Riverside Drive, New York. The oldest periodical is probably *The Golden Lotus*, published in Philadelphia.

Amida (Jap.)   *See* **Amitābha.**

Amis du Bouddhisme, Les   The Buddhist Society in Paris, founded in 1929 by Miss Constant Lounsbery (q.v.) under the inspiration of the late Tai Hsü of China while on a visit to Europe. For long headquarters of Buddhism in France. Address: 4 Square Rapp, Paris 75007. *See* **France, Buddhism in.**

Amitābha (Sk.) **Amida** (Jap.)   The Buddha of Infinite Light. As Amitayus, the Buddha of Infinite Life. The Fourth of the Dhyāni Buddhas (q.v.). The personification of Compassion. In the Pure Land sects of China and Japan, *Amitābha* is the intermediary between Supreme Reality and mankind, and faith in him ensures rebirth in his Paradise (*Sukhāvatī* q.v.). Esoterically, *Amitābha* is Higher Self, and rebirth into his paradise is the awakening of the *Bodhicitta* (q.v.) in the heart of man. For Scriptures *see* **Pure Land.**

Amoghasiddhi (Sk.)   One whose achievement is not in vain! One of the five Dhyāni-Buddhas (q.v.) of Tibetan Bsm.

Amrita (Sk.) **Amata** (P.)   Immortal, deathless, a name for Nirvāna. Lit., and in mythology, the ambrosia of the Gods.

Amritānanda, Thera   Nepalese Buddhist who became a Bhikkhu in Ceylon and then returned to become the leading Bst. in Nepal. Founded his own Theravāda Centre and School on the hill of Swayambhūnāth (q.v.), near Katmandu. Organized fourth Congress of World Fellowship of Buddhists

30

at Katmandu in 1956, and has since travelled extensively in Europe, the U.S.A., the U.S.S.R. and Japan.

Anābhoga (Sk.) Purposeless. Effortless, unaware of conscious striving. (*See* **Purposelessness**.)

Anāgāmin (P.) 'Never Returner'; third of the four stages on the Path. The *anāgāmin* does not return to earth after his death, but is reborn in the highest formless heavens and there attains arhatship. (*See* **Fetters, Four Paths**.)

Anāgārika Lit. a homeless one. One who enters the homeless life without formally entering the Sangha. A term first adopted in modern times by the Anāgārika Dharmapāla (q.v.).

Ānanda I. The Cousin and 'Beloved Disciple' of the Buddha. It is said that at the Master's death he had not yet attained to Arhatship, and suffered intense grief at his passing. Later his very love for the Master enabled him to burst the bonds of self and so to enter Nirvana.
 II. A word originally meaning physical pleasure and later spiritual bliss.

Ānanda Metteyya The name given to Charles Henry Allan Bennett in 1902 when he was ordained in Akyab, Burma, as a Bhikkhu. In 1908 he led a Mission to England to establish Buddhism as a living religion in the British Isles. The Buddhist Society of Great Britain and Ireland (q.v.) was founded to assist him on arrival. A.M. returned to Burma after six months, but in 1914 was forced to return to England by ill-health. Author of *The Wisdom of the Aryas*. He died in March, 1923. *See* Humphreys, *Sixty Years of Buddhism in England*.

Ānapāna-sati (P.) Watching over the breathing, in and out. One of the fundamental exercises in 'Mindfulness', and the

31

development of higher states of consciousness. Of all subjects for concentration, and later meditation, the most common in all Schools. Analysed at great length in Bst. Scriptures (*see* **Sati-patthāna** *and* **Vipassanā**).

Anattā (P.) Anātman (Sk.)   The essentially Buddhist doctrine of non-ego. One of the 'Three Signs of Being' with *Anicca* and *Dukkha*. The doctrine of the non-separateness of all forms of life, and the opposite of that of an immortal and yet personal soul. As applied to man it states that there is no permanent ego or self in the five *skandhas* (q.v.) which make up the personality. The Buddha, however, nowhere denied the existence of an ego or soul, but taught that no permanent entity, not subject to *Anicca* and *Dukkha,* can be found in any of the human faculties. That which pertains to any human being is not immortal; that which is immortal and unchanging is not the possession of any one human being. The Reality behind the flux of *Samsāra* (q.v.) is an indivisible unity, and the separate possession of no part of it. (*See* **Attavāda, Ego, Sakkāya.**)

Angkor Complex of religious buildings in Cambodian jungle, dating from zenith of Khmer rule in twelfth century A.D. Most famous is Angkor Wat, one of finest religious buildings in the world. Partly Hindu and partly Bst. in style and decoration. The ruins of the Royal city of Angkor Thom nearby have the Bayon, a four-faced tower at centre. *See* Groslier and Arthaud, *Angkor* (1957).

Anguttara Nikāya Fourth of the five Nikāyas or collections of Discourses of Buddha into which *Sutta Pitaka* is divided (*see* A.P.C.). Trans. as Gradual Sayings, the subjects being grouped singly, then in twos, threes, etc.

Anicca (P.) Impermanence; one of the three characteristics of all existence; the others being *Dukkha* and *Anattā* (q.v.).

Bsm. teaches that everything is subject to the law of cause and effect, is the creation of preceding causes and is in turn a cause of after-effects. There is in existence, therefore, no unchanging condition of being, but only an ever-becoming flux.

Animal Rebirth as an animal is often recorded in the Bst. writings but should be accepted figuratively, in sense of displaying vices of stupidity, gluttony, etc. No actual rebirth in animal form exists for human beings.

Annihilation Misunderstanding of *Anattā* (q.v.), has led to idea of annihilation as goal of Buddhist endeavour. The only kind of annihilation taught by Buddha was that of the *skandhas* (q.v.) which form the evanescent part of man. When the Arhat enters Parinirvāna he passes 'beyond the vision of gods and men' (i.e. losing objective existence but retaining subjective being). *See* **Anattā, Nirvāna.**

Anshin (Jap.) Repose of mind. As used, e.g., in the famous question by the second Patriarch Hui–k'o to Bodhidharma, who sought repose of mind. *See* **Hui–k'o.**

Antara-bhava (P.) Condition between lives.

Antaskārana (Sk.) Lit. 'Making an end'. In the esoteric analysis of man's principles the path or bridge between the lower mind or personality and the higher mind or reincarnating compound of principles and faculties in which is inherent the power to achieve Enlightenment. *See* Blavatsky, *The Voice of the Silence.*

Anurādhapura One of the 'lost' cities of Ceylon, now largely uncovered. Founded 437 B.C., it was the capital of Ceylon until Tamil invaders drove Sinhalese to Polonnaruwa (q.v.) and thence to Kandy (q.v.). Once had five million inhabitants. Sights include Bodhi-Tree (q.v.), three famous Stūpas and the seated Buddha under the trees. *See also* **Mahinda**. *See* Mitton, *The Lost Cities of Ceylon* (1916).

Apabhramsa An Eastern dialect of India, in which was written, *inter alia*, Saraha's *Treasury of Songs*. (*See* B.T. No. 188.)

Apāya (P.) The four 'Lower Worlds', the animal world, ghost world, demon-world, hell. (*See* **Asura, Preta, Wheel of Life.**)

Appamāda (P.) Zeal in right doing. Unwearying mindfulness.

Apramāna (Sk.) Immeasurable. Used of the four Brahma Vihāras (q.v.).

Apsarā (Sk.) One of the many terms in the East for the nature spirits in female form which vary in importance from 'Angels' to 'fairies'. Cp. the Dākinīs of Tibetan Bsm. Also the Yakshinīs of India.

Aranyakas (Sk.) A forest dweller. One who leaves his home to seek Enlightenment. (*See* **Anāgārika, Homelessness.**)

Arhat (Sk.) **Arahat** (P.) In Chin. Lohan. In Jap. Arakan. A worthy one. One who has travelled the Noble Eightfold Path (q.v.) to the Goal and, having eliminated the ten Fetters (q.v.), attains Nirvāna (q.v.). The Arhat is the ideal of the Theravāda School, the Bodhisattva (q.v.) that of the M. School. *See* Horner, *Early Buddhist Theory of Man Perfected* (1937).

Arūpa (P.) Formless, Incorporeal. *Arūpalokas*: The highest meditative worlds, where form cognizable by the five senses does not exist, being purely mental. *Arūparāga*: attachment to the formless meditative worlds; the Seventh Fetter on the Path. (*See* **Fetters, Four Paths.**)

Aryan From Ārya (Sk.) meaning noble. In P. Ariya, e.g., the Aryan or noble Eightfold Path, or the four Aryan or noble Truths. Taken from the Aryan race, the word was used by the Buddha as worthy of the race, noble in conduct.

Āsana (Sk. and P.) Posture in meditation. For a list of those most common in Bsm. and Bst. art *see* Gordon, *The Iconography of Tibetan Lamaism,* p. 24 (1939). Dhyānāsana, the posture of meditation with the soles of the feet visible on either thigh, is used throughout the East. That with only one sole raised, sometimes called the half-Lotus (*see* **Lotus**), is found in some Rūpas, as in Siam. (*See* **Buddha Rūpas.**)

Asanga Brother of Vasubandhu (q.v.). Natives of Peshawar in fifth century. Founders of the Dharmalakshana or Yogācāra School of Mahayanist Idealism. Also known as the Vijñānavāda or Mind-Only School. Hiuen Tsiang (q.v.) was a follower of Asanga and founded the Hossō School on his teachings.

Āsava (P.) **Āsrava** (Sk.) Mental intoxication, defilement. The four *Āsavas* are: *Kāma*, sensuality; *bhava*, lust of life; *ditthi*, false views and *avijjā*, ignorance (of nature of life). Erroneous ideas which intoxicate mind so that it cannot contemplate pure truth and attain enlightenment. Total freedom from *Āsavas* is a sign of the Arhat (q.v.).

Asceticism As practised for gaining magical powers or propitiating gods is essentially selfish. In First Sermon Buddha condemned extreme asceticism as ignoble and useless, and taught Middle Way between self-mortification and allurements of senses. Only asceticism Bsm. permits is bodily self-control as aid to mental self-control: i.e., renunciation of temporary pleasure for permanent happiness. Rules governing laymen are Five Precepts (q.v.) always, three additional for special occasions. For Bhikkhus Ten Precepts plus 227 Vinaya Rules.

35

(See **Pātimokkha.**) Buddhist ideal is the Arhat or Bodhisattva, not the ascetic.

'As if' Bsm. teaches that all manifestation is in the last analysis illusion. Within this field of Māyā the imagination may be usefully directed to create in thought the condition of mind desired, and an effort made to behave 'as if' this condition had been achieved. Thus the Sōtō Zen monks are taught to 'act as Buddha', in meditation and in daily life, on the principle that they are Buddha already, and have only to become aware of it.

Asoka (the Great) Emperor of India (270–230 B.C.), grandson of Chandragupta, founder of the Maurya Dynasty. A great Bst. ruler, who was converted to Bsm. from Hinduism after long period of wars of conquest. He abolished wars in his Empire, restricted hunting or killing for food, built hospitals for man and beast, and engraved on rocks and pillars throughout the Empire his famous Edicts, setting forth the moral precepts of Bsm. He sent his son Mahinda and daughter Sanghamitta to Ceylon where they converted the ruler and people to Bsm. Also known as Dharmasoka and Piyadasi. See Vincent Smith, *Asoka* (1901); Mookerji, *Asoka* (1928) and for Edicts, *see* Nikam and McKeon, *The Edicts of Asoka*, Chicago (1959). (See **Ceylon, Lumbini, Nepal.**)

Āsrava (Sk.) *See* **Āsava** (P.).

Assaji (P.) The disciple of the Buddha whose simple declaration of the doctrine of causation converted Sariputta and Moggallana. *See* No. 25 in W. of Bsm.

Asura (Sk. and P.) The Sura were benevolent gods, the Asura those who fought against the former. Elemental forces, projections of the forces in man's mind. (*See* **Apāya.**)

Asvaghos(h)a A Buddhist writer and poet of the first century A.D. Author of the *Buddha-Carita Kāvya*, famous Life of Buddha in verse. There is a trans. from the Chin. version, the *Fo-sho-hing-tsan-king* in S.B.E. Vol. 19, and from the Sk. version in S.B.E. Vol. 49. The famous Shastra trans. by Suzuki as *The Awakening of Faith* was attributed by the Chinese to Asvaghosa, but it is now considered a fifth century Chinese work.

Atheism Bsm. is atheistic in that it does not recognize an absolute Personal Deity, but it is not philosophically atheistic as it does not deny Ultimate Reality. (*See* **Agnosticism.**)

Atīs(h)a (Sk.) Famous Indian scholar of profound learning (982-1054). Arrived in Tibet in 1038 and stayed till his death. Entirely reformed the prevailing Buddhism, enforcing celibacy in the existing Order and raised the level of morality. Founded the Kahdam-pa School, 'those bound by ordinance'. In the fifteenth century Tsong-kha-pa (q.v.) again reformed this School, re-naming it the Gelug-pa (q.v.). *See* Snellgrove, *Buddhist Himālaya*, pp. 193-8 (1957).

Ātman (Sk.) **Attā** (P.) The Supreme SELF; Universal Consciousness; Ultimate Reality. The Divine element in man, degraded into idea of an entity dwelling in the heart of each man, the thinker of his thoughts, and doer of his deeds, and after death dwelling in bliss or misery according to deeds done in the body. For Buddhist attitude to Ātman conception *see Anattā*. (*See* **Self, Soul.**)

Atonement Vicarious. Primitive Bsm. knows nothing of vicarious atonement; each must work out his own salvation. We may help each other by thought, word and deed, but cannot bear results or take over consequences of another's errors or misdeeds. In Mahāyāna the stress on compassion has produced doctrine of Bodhisattvas who help humanity by

37

renouncing benefit of their accumulated store of 'merit', and 'handing it over' to credit of bad karma of humanity. This has further developed into salvation by grace of Amida by calling on his name. If. however, atonement is understood as an 'at-one-ment' with the Law of the universe (*Dharmakāya* q.v.) then it may be called a Buddhist principle. (*See* **Amitābha, Parivarta, Tariki.**)

Attavāda (P.)   The false belief in the existence in man of a permanent soul, Attā (Sk. Ātman) which makes him separate from the other manifestations of the One Life. The false belief in an immortal soul. Cp. *Sakkāyaditthi*. (*See* **Anattā, Ātman.**)

Attha-sīla (P.)   Eight Sīlas. Some laymen take for a period eight of the Precepts (q.v.) instead of the normal five. Samaneras (q.v.) take them permanently. Bhikkhus take Dasa-Sīla, all ten.

A U M   The Prānava A U M, usually spelt OM (q.v.) is an invocation of multiple symbolic meaning and ritual uses. Each constituent letter has its own meaning of profound power. It precedes, pronounced as only an initiate knows how, the Tibetan formula *Om Mani Padme Hūm. See* Govinda, *Foundations of Tibetan Mysticism* (1960).

Australia, Buddhism in   Buddhist Societies have been founded in various parts of the continent, notably in New South Wales, and there is now a Buddhist Federation of Australia in Melbourne, G.P.O. Box 2568-W.

Authority   (1) There is no 'authority' in Bsm. in the sense of one who gives forth doctrine which must be accepted, or who gives authoritative explanation of doctrine. Each Buddhist is his own authority, in the sense that he must learn the

Truth for himself, by study, self-discipline and practice. (2) No written teaching or scripture is authoritative in the sense of binding. See Buddha's advice to Kālāmas. (W. of Bsm. No. 22.) (3) So-called 'authorities' on Bsm. are authorities only in the sense that they translate the *letter* of the teaching and comment upon it. They are not necessarily competent to expound its spiritual meaning.

Avalokites(h)vara (Sk.) Also called Padmapāni. 'The Lord who is seen.' The SELF as perceived by *Buddhi*, the faculty of intuition. The Bodhisattva of the Dhyani Buddha Amitābha (q.v.). Personification of the self-generative creative cosmic force. For feminine aspect *see* **Kwan-yin**.

Avadāna (Sk.) Stories or a collection of such stories to illustrate the life of a hero. Part of the surviving Canon of the Sarvāstivādins (q.v.) being tales of the Buddha and his former lives. For comparison with Jātakas (q.v.) *see* Appendix I of E. J. Thomas, *History of Buddhist Thought* (1933).

Āvarana (Sk.) An obstacle. In his trans. of the *Heart Sutra* Conze gives 'thought-covering'. Anāvarana, unobstructed.

Avatamsaka Sutra (Sk.) In Chin. Hua-yen. In Jap. Kegon. Part of the Sutra is separately known as the Gandavyūha (q.v.); all these terms mean flower decoration, or garland. Many Chinese scholars regard it as the highest development of Bst. philosophy in China. This enormous work of M. Bsm. has never been translated in full. For partial trans. *see* Vol. I *The Eastern Buddhist.* (*See* **Jijimuge, Kegon.**)

Avatāra (Sk.) A Manifestation or incarnation of the Hindu God Vishnu. The Buddha is regarded by many Indians as his ninth and latest Avatar, thus keeping the most famous of all Indian Teachers within the Hindu pantheon. (*See* **Kalki Avatāra.**)

Avici (Sk.) 'No waves.' Stagnation, therefore death. The lowest of the Bst. hells. Or 'no intermission', of suffering.

Avijjā (P.) **Avidyā** (Sk.) Lit. unwitting. Hence ignorance; lack of enlightenment. The fundamental root of evil, and the ultimate cause of the desire which creates the *dukkha* of existence. It is the nearest approach to 'original sin' known to Bsm. Its total elimination, resulting in perfect enlightenment, is Goal of Buddhist Path. Ignorance is first of the Twelve *Nidānas* or Links in the Chain of Causation; *first* because it is the primary cause of existence. It is the *last* of the Ten Fetters, *last* because until full enlightenment is attained there still remains some degree of ignorance. The final removal of the veil of ignorance reveals supreme Truth—Nirvāna. (*See* **Moha, Sin.**)

Awakening of Faith, The (Sk. Shraddhotpāda Shāstra. Chin. Ch'i-hsin-lun). Sk. original lost. Two trans. from Chinese are *The Awakening of Faith*, Suzuki (1900) and *The Awakening of Faith*, Timothy Richard (1907). A work of the Yogācāra (q.v.) School. One of the most famous Bst. Scriptures. Now held to be a Chinese work of fifth century A.D.

Āyatana (P.) Spheres. Used psychologically. The twelve bases or sources of mental processes. Six are the five sense organs and mind; the other six are the corresponding sense objects, conceptions or thoughts being objects of mind. (*See* **Indriya.**)

Ayodhya Important city in the kingdom of the Kosalas in north-east India in the time of the Buddha. Not to be confused with Ayuthia, equally important city in north of Thailand.

Ayudhyā (Ayuthiā) (Siam.) The Thai Bst. capital after Sukhodaya (q.v.) until sacked by the Burmese in 1767. The

Bst. school of sculpture followed that of Sukhodaya. Only notable change in head-dress. *See* Le May, *The Buddhist Art of Siam* (1938). Distinguish from Ayodhya in India.

Bala (P.) Powers. In particular, five of the twenty-two Indriya (q.v.). They are Faith (Saddhā), Energy (Viriya), Mindfulness (Sati), Contemplation (Samādhi) and Wisdom (Paññā. In Sk. Prajñā). For the ten Bala of the Bodhisattva *see* Suzuki, *Studies in the Lankavatara Sutra*, p. 425 (1930).

Bamboo Grove Famous place of retreat near Rajagriha given the Buddha by King Bimbisara of Magadha. (*See* **Retreat.**)

Bāmiyān Ruins of Bst. monastery in Afghanistan. Large range of Bst. assembly halls carved from face of sandstone cliff, but famous for two enormous images of Buddha as Lord of the World, one 120 feet high and one 175 feet. Gandhāra art, third to sixth century A.D.

Bardo Thödol (Tib.) *See* **Tibetan Book of the Dead.**

Bashō (Jap.) Famous Japanese poet (1643-1694). A great traveller and lover of nature, he was the founder of the modern school of Haiku (q.v.) in which he embodied, as few before or since, the spirit of Zen.

Beauty Bsm. is the only religion which recognizes a form of deliverance through the appreciation of beauty (*Subha*). *See* W. of Bsm. Nos. 51 and 52. In the pure contemplation of great beauty there is no sense of self, and completely to be free of self is a moment of enlightenment.

Begging-Bowl Bhikkhus of the Theravāda daily go round the neighbourhood getting their bowls filled with food at the choice of the householders, and this meal they eat according to their Rules before noon. Cp. *Takuhatsu*.

Belgium, Buddhism in   Various attempts have been made to form Bst. Societies in Belgium, that of M. Kière of Liège, with its periodical, *Le Sentier*, lasting the longest. The present group in Brussels centres round the lectures of M. Robert Linssen, author of *Living Zen*. A Summer School is held every year.

Belief   *Sammāditthi*, the first step on the Noble Path is often translated 'right belief'. More correct rendering is 'right view'. Belief in Bsm. must result from apprehension based on reason, not on mental obedience to the authority of another. *See* **Faith, Noble Eightfold Path.**

Bhagavad Gītā (Sk.)   The 'Lord's Song'. A complete treatise on spiritual development along the lines of Karma Yoga, the way of Right Action. Is included in the epic poem the Mahā-Bhārata. Date unknown. Trans. Radhakrishnan (1948).

Bhagavat   The Holy Lord, hence the Blessed One. A Hindu term used in the invocation to the Buddha which opens Pansil (q.v.).

Bhakti (Sk.)   Devotion to a spiritual ideal, from bhaj, to love or honour. Those using this way of development prefer to personify the Ideal and to reach Truth by its service. Bsts. who take the Bodhisattva Vow (*see* **Vow**) are at least in part Bhakti Yogins. The Bst. Bhakti schools include the Shingon and Shin of Japan.

Bhārhut   An early Bst. Stūpa of c. 150 B.C. Most of remaining carving removed to Calcutta Museum. Valuable to art historians as being pure Indian art before influence of Gandhāra felt, and before the first image of the Buddha had been made. *See* Cunningham, *The Stūpa of Bhārhut* (1879).

Bhatgaon One of the three cities lying near together in the plain of Nepal (*see* **Katmandu** *and* **Patan**). Famous for its wealth of carved buildings, for the great bell in the Darbar Square, and the golden doors of the old Palace, 'one of the finest specimens of metal-work in Asia' (Landan).

Bhava (Sk. and P.) Philosophical term signifying 'becoming'; a state of existence (all existence being states of 'becoming'), a life. In the Causal Chain (*see* **Nidānas**), *bhava* is the link between *upādāna* (clinging to life), and *jāti* (rebirth).

Bhāvanā (Sk. and P.) Lit. a 'making-to-become'. Self-development by any means, but especially by the method of mind-control, concentration and meditation.

Bhavanga (P.) The sub-conscious stream of becoming in which all experience is stored. Corresponds to Ālaya-Vijñāna (q.v.).

Bhikkhu (P.) **Bhikshu** (Sk.) A member of the Buddhist *Sangha* (q.v.); variously translated as monk, mendicant, friar, almsman, priest; all of which are alone inadequate. A *Bhikkhu* is one who has devoted himself to the task of following the Path by renunciation of the distractions of worldly affairs. He relies for his sustenance upon the gifts of the lay disciples, being under no obligation to give anything in return, but often devoting part of his time to secular and religious teaching. A *Bhikkhu* keeps the Ten Precepts (q.v.) and his daily life is governed by 227 Rules (v. *Patimokkha*). Feminine equivalent *Bhikkhuni* (P.) *Bhikshunī* (Sk.). (*See* **Sangha**.)

Bhilsā The Bhilsa topes is a generic name for a group of

Stūpas near Bhopal in India of which the most famous is Sanchi (q.v.). *See* Cunningham, *The Bhilsā Topes* (1854).

Bhūmi (Sk. and P.) Ground, as Bhūmisparsa (q.v.) A stage in progressive sense, as in Loka (q.v.). In the M., the ten or twelve stages in the career of a Bodhisattva. *See* E. J. Thomas, *History of Buddhist Thought*, ch. XVI.

Bhūmispars(h)a The earth-touching attitude in a Buddha-Rūpa (q.v.) in which the Buddha calls the earth to witness his sacrifices to attain Enlightenment. (*See* **Mudrā, Buddha Rūpa.**)

Bhūta (Sk.) (1) Real, Reality. Thus Bhūtatā, Reality, Bhūtatathatā, 'real suchness'. (2) The ghost or shell of the dead which exists for a while after the death of the body. It is these 'astral' remains (called starry because faintly visible to some) which are contacted and often unnaturally used in spiritualistic practices, whether in the Shamanism of Mongolia, among the Dug-pas of Tibet or in Western séances. Hence the Eastern term 'Bhūta-worship' applied to those in the West who indulge in these practices. (*See* **Cremation.**)

Bhutan A country in the Eastern Himalayas ruled by a Mahārajah of Tibetan stock. The natives are Bsts., mostly of the Dug-pa (q.v.) or unreformed school of Tibet.

Bhūtatathatā *See* **Tathatā**.

Bibliography, A Buddhist Compiled by Arthur C. March. 260 pp. medium 8vo. Published by the Buddhist Lodge, London, in 1935. Over 2,000 items detailed and classified under authors, with a detailed subject index. Referred to as B.L.B. (Buddhist Lodge Bibliography). Supplements were printed for the years 1936-40.

Bimbisāra King of Magadha at time of Buddha. Built city

of Rajagriha. Convert to Bsm. and presented Bamboo Grove to Buddha for use of Sangha. Was dethroned and murdered by his son Ajatasattu.

Birth   The arising of a state of being in any sphere of existence, the effect of anterior conditions. No coming of existence from previously non-existent: creation *ex nihilo* inconceivable to a Buddhist. (*See* **Gati.**)

Blavatsky, Helena Petrovna   Born Russia, midnight 30/31 July, 1831. Co-founder with Col. Olcott (q.v.) of Theosophical Society; author of *Isis Unveiled, The Secret Doctrine, The Key to Theosophy, The Voice of the Silence,* etc. Declared herself a Buddhist at Galle (Ceylon) in 1880 and inspired the Buddhist revival in Ceylon. d. 8 May, 1891, London. Accusations of deceit made by agent of S.P.R. were withdrawn. *See* W. Kingsland, *The Real H. P. Blavatsky.*

Blofeld, John   English Buddhist. A leading scholar in Chinese Bsm., having travelled widely in China. Translator for the Buddhist Society of works of Huang Po and Hui Hai. Author of *The Zen Teaching of Huang Po* (1958), *The Jewel in the Lotus* (1948), *The Wheel of Life* (1959), and *Beyond the Gods* (1974).

Blue Cliff Records   *See* **Hekigan Roku.**

Blyth, R. H.   English Buddhist who has spent most of his life in the Far East. For sixteen years studied Zen in Korean monasteries. Now lives in Japan with Japanese wife. Professor of English in the Peers' School, Tokyo. Author of *Zen in English Literature and Oriental Classics* (1942), of several volumes on the Haiku (q.v.), and a series on Zen and Zen Classics. [Died 1965.]

Bodhi (Sk.) Enlightenment. The spiritual condition of a Buddha or Bodhisattva. The cause of *Bodhi* is *Prajñā* (q.v.) wisdom, and *Karunā* (q.v.) compassion. *Bodhi* is the name given to the highest state of *Samādhi* (q.v.) in which the mind is awakened and illuminated. (*See* **Buddhi.**)

Bodhi-citta (Sk.) Wisdom-heart. The aspiration of a *Bodhisattva* (q.v.) for supreme enlightenment for the welfare of all. Nāgārjuna says that the Bodhisattva, by renunciation of all claim to results of individual meritorious deeds, practises compassion to the highest degree of perfection by working ever in the worlds of birth and death for the ultimate enlightenment of humanity. (*See* **Bodhisattva, Parivarta.**)

Bodhidharma (Sk.) Deeply learned Indian Bst. who arrived at the Chinese Court in A.D. 520. Known in China as Tamo, and in Japan as Daruma. For his famous interview with the Emperor *see W. of Bsm. No.* 118. Thereafter he meditated for nine years in silence and departed. The twenty-eighth Indian and first Chinese Zen Patriarch. (*See* **Patriarchs.**) The father of Zen Bsm., although it was left to Masters of the eighth century, led by Hui-neng, to consolidate his teaching and technique into a school of Bsm. (*See* **Zen.**)

Bodhisattva (Sk.) **Bodhisatta** (P.) One whose 'being' or 'essence' (*sattva*) is *bodhi*, that is, the wisdom resulting from direct perception of Truth, with the compassion awakened thereby. (*See* **Bodhi-citta.**)

In Theravāda, an aspirant for Buddha-hood: the Buddha is described in Jātaka accounts of his former lives as *the Bodhisatta*.

In Mahāyāna, the Bodhisattva is the ideal of the Path as contrasted with the Arhat of the Theravāda. Having practised the Six Pāramitās and attained Enlightenment, he renounces Nirvāna in order to help humanity on its pilgrimage. The

Bodhisattvas are often called 'Buddhas of Compassion', as love in action guided by wisdom is their aim.

The *Dhyāni Bodhisattvas* (q.v.) are hypostatic personifications of the attributes of the Dhyāni Buddhas, who are in their turn the objective aspects of the self-creative forces of the primal reality, Ādi-Buddha (q.v.). (*See* **Pāramitās.**)

Bodhi Tree (or Bo-tree)   The tree under which the Buddha attained Enlightenment at Buddha Gaya (q.v.). A fig tree, popularly called Pipal; scientific name *Ficus religiosa*. The cutting at Anuradhapura in Ceylon, planted by the son of Asoka (q.v.) is the oldest historical tree in the world.

Bodhnāth   Buddhist temple near Katmandu, Nepal. Date of foundation unknown, but may be contemporary with Asoka. Regarded as the holiest shrine of Bsm. outside India, it is a famous place of pilgrimage for Tibetans coming down from the North. The central Stūpa famous for the all-seeing eyes painted on the four sides

Bojjhanga (P.) Bodhyanga (Sk.)   Factors leading to Enlightenment. For seven of these, *see* **Sambodhi.**

Bön (Tib.)   Pronounced Pön. The indigenous, pre-Buddhist religion of Tibet. Little is known of it in detail, but it seems to have much in common with the Shamanism of Mongolia, a form of nature-worship mixed with psychic and sexual practices. At its best it has been influenced to the good by Bsm.; at its worst is has dragged down members of the Dug-pa school to its own level. *See* Hoffmann, *The Religions of Tibet* (1960).

Bonze (Jap.)   English variation on the term Bonzu or Bō-zu, meaning originally the chief monk in a Bst. monastery, but later used for any monk. The term now preferred is Bō-san, meaning literally one who lives in a Buddhist temple.

Borobudur Enormous Bst. structure in Java covered with fine reliefs of subjects from M. Bsm. A stepped pyramid on square base covering about 520 feet square. Begun about A.D. 850. Restored by Dutch. *See* Krom, *The Life of the Buddha* (The Hague, 1926).

Brahma (Sk.) One aspect of the triune God-head of Hinduism, with Vishnu and Shiva. But in the Bst. Scriptures the word is used as an adjective meaning holy or God-like, as in the Brahma-vihāras.

Brahma-Cariya The pure or chaste holy life, used of the monk. Also used of a layman who takes eight of the Precepts (q.v.) and interprets the third as a vow of chastity.

Brahma Vihāra *Brahma* in this connexion means lordly, or divine. *Vihāra* here means a state of mind. Hence the four 'Divine States of Mind' which are methods of meditation in which the mind pervades the six corners of the universe with concentrated thoughts of *Mettā* (love), *Karunā* (compassion), *Muditā* (sympathetic joy) and *Upekkhā* (serenity) (q.v.).

'British Buddhist', The Organ of the Maha Bodhi Society's Buddhist Mission in England. Founded October, 1926. Publication ceased December, 1934. *See Wheel, The.*

British Maha Bodhi Society Founded in July, 1926, by the Anagarika Dharmapala (q.v.) at Foster House, 86 Madeley Road, Ealing, as a branch of the parent Society founded by him at Calcutta in 1891. Published *The British Buddhist* in October, 1926, replaced by *The Wheel* in January, 1935. Moved to 41 Gloucester Road, N.W.1, in 1928. Closed 1939. *See* Humphreys, *Sixty Years of Buddhism in England.*

Buddha A title, not the name of a person. Derived from root *budh*, 'to wake', it means one who knows in the sense of having become one with the highest objects of knowledge, Supreme Truth. There have been Buddhas in the past and there will be others in the future. (*See* **Maitreya**.) Gotama, the historical founder of Buddhism (q.v.), was born at Lumbinī (q.v.). Date of his birth not entirely agreed, but according to modern historical research, 563 B.C. The birthplace is marked by pillar erected by Asoka (*see* **Lumbinī**). Birth, death and Enlightenment celebrated on Full Moon day of month *Vaisakha* (April-May) (*see* **Wesak**.)

The best Life is E. J. Thomas, *The Life of the Buddha* (1927) or Nanamoli, *The Life of the Buddha* (1972). The *Lalitavistara* (on which Arnold's *Light of Asia* is based), and *Fo-sho-hing-tsan-king* (S.B.E. 19) are overlaid with myth and legend. (*See also* **Fiction**.)

Buddhacarita The Sanskrit title of a poem by Asvaghosa (q.v.). It is a life of the Buddha with much legendary matter. For translation from the Sanskrit *see* E. H. Johnston (1936); for translation from the Chinese by Beal, vol. 19 S.B.E. (*Fo-sho-hing-tsan-king*).

Buddha Day *The World Fellowship of Buddhists* (q.v.) is working to secure the agreement of all Buddhist countries to observe as 'Buddha Day' the Full Moon day of the lunar month of *Vaisakha* (April-May) (in the West called *Wesak*) (q.v.). Thus, even though the Japanese keep 8 April as the Buddha's birthday, Japanese Buddhists may accord with the rest of the world in keeping 'Buddha Day'.

Buddha-Dhamma (P.) The teaching of the Buddha. The phrase most often used in Theravāda countries for what in the West is called Buddhism or Buddha Sāsana (q.v.).

Buddha Gaya (Bodh Gaya) One of the four Holy Places of Bsm. (q.v.); the place where Buddha attained Enlightenment.

Spot marked by Bo-tree and Temple, six miles from Gaya, Bihar, India. (*See* **Dharmapāla**.)

Buddhaghosa　A great Buddhist scholar born N. India early fifth century A.D., who translated Sinhalese Commentaries into Pali and wrote *Visuddhi Magga* (q.v.) and other works, including Commentaries on much of Pitakas. *See* B. C. Law, *Life and Work of Buddhaghosa* (Calcutta, 1923).

Buddha Jayanti (Sk.)　The year 1956-7 was observed with great celebrations in the Bst. world as the 2,500th of the Bst. era, and the celebrations were named Buddha Jayantī, from *jaya*, a victory, hence a banner, hence celebration.

Buddha Rūpa　An image of the Buddha. For 500 years the person of the Buddha was considered too holy to be depicted in the form of an image. At Sanchi, for instance, the symbols of the vacant throne or the footprint are used; at Amarāvati (second century A.D.) both symbolic and actual representation were used (*see* **Gandhāra**). Buddha *rūpas* represent the Blessed One as seated, standing, or recumbent (lying on the right side).

In the images found in the Theravāda School the four most common Mudrās (gestures) are: Bhūmisparsa, or 'Calling the Earth to witness'. Here the right hand is stretched down over the right knee; the Dhyāna, or Samādhi, with the hands folded in the lap in Meditation; the Abhaya, meaning fearlessness, the mudrā of Protection or Blessing. Here the right hand is raised, palm forward. Fourthly, the Dharmacakra, or Teaching mudrā, where the Buddha is 'setting in motion the Wheel of the Law'. Here the raised right hand has at least two fingers closed, or the two hands may be touching in more complex form.

In M. Schools a great variety of forms are used, especially in Tibetan Bsm. In iconography there are also Rūpas of Bodhisattvas and lesser members of the Bst. pantheon. (*See* **Mudrā**.)

Buddhi (Sk.) The vehicle of Enlightenment (*Bodhi*, q.v.). The faculty of supreme understanding as distinct from the understanding itself. The sixth principle in the sevenfold constitution of man taught in the esoteric schools of Buddhism, and as such the link between the Ultimate Reality and the Mind (*Manas*). Nearest English equivalent is the intuition.

Buddhism The name given by the West to the Teachings of Gautama the Buddha (q.v.), but usually called by his followers the *Buddha Dhamma* (*see* **Dhamma**). Buddhism is a way of life, a discipline; not a system of dogmas to be accepted by the intellect. It is a way to live Reality, and not ideas concerning the nature of Reality.

Buddhism in England *The Journal of Oriental Philosophy and Religion*, published by the Buddhist Lodge, London. Founded May, 1926, by A. C. March. In 1945 it was renamed *The Middle Way* (q.v.).

Buddhist Nominally, one born into the Buddhist religion, or one who accepts Buddhism as his religion by public recitation of *Pansil* (q.v.). Actually, one who studies, disseminates and endeavours to live the fundamental principles of the *Buddhadhamma* (q.v.).

'Buddhist', The Bst. monthly periodical published in Colombo. Founded 1888. Organ of the Young Men's Buddhist Association of Colombo.

'Buddhist Annual of Ceylon' Published at Wesak each year by Bastian and Co., Colombo, from 1920 to 1932. It was well illustrated, with reproductions of Buddhist architecture and works of art, and with portraits of notable persons in the Buddhist Movement. Largely succeeded by the Ceylon Daily News Buddhist Annual, published at Wesak.

51

'**Buddhist Review', The**   Journal of the Buddhist Society of Great Britain and Ireland, 1909-22. First Bst. magazine published in Europe. Distinguished list of contributors. Editors included Capt. Ellam, Francis Payne (q.v.), Howell Smith, Sir D. P. Jayatilaka and Ananda Metteyya (q.v.). *See* Humphreys, *Sixty Years of Buddhism in England* (1968).

Buddhist Society, The   The oldest Buddhist organization in Europe. Founded in London as The Buddhist Lodge in 1924 by Mr and Mrs Christmas Humphreys (q.v.), it seceded from the Theosophical Society in 1926, when its journal, *Buddhism in England*, now *The Middle Way*, was founded. Renamed 'The Buddhist Society, London', in 1943, and 'The Buddhist Society' in 1952 in deference to the request of provincial affiliated societies.

Its present premises at 58 Eccleston Square, S.W.1, include a lecture hall, a library of 3,000-4,000 volumes, a shrine room, a bookstall, an art collection, archives and offices. Vice-Presidents include Miss I. B. Horner (q.v.) and Dr E. Conze (q.v.). *See* Humphreys, *Sixty Years of Buddhism in England* (1968).

Buddhist Society of Great Britain and Ireland   *See* **England, Buddhism in.**

Buddhist Vihara Society in England   Founded in April, 1948, to expedite the opening of a Vihara (q.v.) in London. The founding Hon. Secretary was Mrs A. Rant. *See* Humphreys, *Sixty Years of Buddhism in England* (1968).

Buji (Jap.)   In Chinese Wu-shih. 'No thing (special)'. A term of Zen Bsm. A natural, unaffected attitude to life, seeing all things as they are and accepting them as such, without fixing the mind on any of them.

Bunko (Jap.)   A library. Thus, the Matsugaoka Bunko, the

Pine Hill Library opened by Dr. Suzuki at Kamakura for Japanese students interested in Western thought.

Burma, Buddhisi.1 in   Kanishkha (q.v.) introduced M. Bsm. c. A.D. 100, but when Buddhaghosa visited Burma c. A.D. 450 he established the Theravāda as the national religion. Burmese scholars have specialized in the Abhidhamma and the practice of meditation. For modern scholars *see* **Thittila.** In 1954-6 the Sixth Great Council was held in a specially built Cave near Rangoon designed to reproduce the Saptaparna Cave (q.v.) in which the First Council was held at the Buddha's passing.

Bushidō (Jap.)   The knightly cult of the Japanese Middle Ages which produced the finest swordsmen and some of the finest warrior minds in history. In the Kamakura period (1185-1335) the Japanese genius, says Suzuki, went either to priesthood or soldiery. From the blend of the two, the warrior trained in spirit as well as body in the service of his Lord, came the spirit of Bushidō.

Bu-ston (Tib.)   Tibetan scholar (1290-1364) who, as well as writing commentaries and histories, collected the existing translations of the Bst. Scriptures and arranged them into two groups. These later formed the two divisions of the Tibetan Canon, the Kanjur and Tanjur. Author of *History of Buddhism in India and Tibet*, trans. Obermüller (1932).

Butsuden (Jap.)   The building in a Japanese monastery which houses the principal Bst. image. The monastery's Shrine. Cp. *Butsudan*, a private shrine in a house. Cp. **Hondō.**

Caitya (Sk.) **Cetiya** (P.)   From *Cita*, a funeral pile. Any tumulus raised over the dead. In Bsm. synonymous with *Stūpa* (q.v.) though Caitya is a more religious term. It is, however, used by archaeologists for the rock-hewn temples found in India. (*See* **Chörten, Pagoda.**)

Cakra (Sk.) **Cakka** (P.)   A wheel. Used figuratively as in *the Wheel of the Law* and *the Wheel of Life* (q.v.).

Cambodia   Ancient seat of Khmer civilization. Buddhism, introduced about fifth century, completely subdued Brahmanism by twelfth century. Formerly tinged with Mahayanism, now pure Theravāda. Capital Phnom-Penh has 'National Institute for study of Buddhism of Lesser Vehicle', opened in 1930. Has many Buddhist ruins and temples, including famous *Angkor Wat.* (q.v.) *See* Brodrick, *Little Vehicle.*

Canon   Only Canon recognized by Theravāda School is the *Tipitaka* (q.v.) or Three Baskets in Pali. Not committed to writing until c. 100 B.C. Mahayana Schools have their own Scriptures in Sanskrit, Chinese, Japanese, Tibetan, etc. The Tibetan Canon (Kanjur) comprises the Sutras and Tantras. The commentary (Tanjur) is an encyclopaedia of 224 volumes, dealing with metaphysics, art, astrology, etc., with commentaries and' texts by Nāgārjuna (q.v.) and other Masters. (*See* **Tibet.**) *See also* A.P.C.

Caste   Class distinctions, dependent mainly on Aryan or non-Aryan birth or on occupation, prevailed at time of Buddha, but caste system a later development. No class distinctions in *Sangha* (q.v.): e.g., Upali the barber, one of the despised trades, was superior of Kshatriya nobles Ananda and Devadatta, superiority depending on length of time since ordination.

Catechism   There is no official Catechism for Bst. children, or for those entering Bsm., but Col. Olcott wrote *The Buddhist Catechism* in 1881 as part of his work in organizing Bst. schools in Ceylon, and Subhadra Bhikshu wrote *A Buddhist Catechism* in 1890, later reprinted as *The Message of Buddhism.*

Catena A chain. Beal's *Catena of Bst. Scriptures from the Chinese* is a famous early anthology (1871).

'Cat's Yawn' Periodical of the First Zen Institute of America, Inc. As a bound volume contains thirteen issues published 1940-41. Contains much of the work of Sōkei-an Sasaki (q.v.).

Causation For the so-called Chain of Causation see **Nidānas, Wheel of Life.** For Causation as a factor in the universal and human cycle of existence *see* **Karma.**

Cause *See* **Hetu, Nidānas, Paccaya.**

Cetanā (P.) Volition. A factor of consciousness. Nearest Bst. term for Will (q.v.). The Sankhāras (q.v.) have been called Karma-producing impulses or volitions. (*See* **Karma.**)

Cetasika (P.) An Abhidhamma term for a factor of consciousness. The fifty-two *cetasikas* are really the three *skandhas* (q.v.) of Feeling, Perception and the *Sankhāras.*

Ceylon Ancient names Taprobane and Lanka. Converted to Bsm. by son and daughter of Asoka (q.v.) (c. 252 B.C.). Stronghold of Bsm. for many centuries, but had periods of decline. The teaching became almost extinct on several occasions, being revived by Bhikkhus from Siam and Burma. Almost exterminated by forced conversions under Portuguese rule revived under Dutch and British rule, last revival being that by Col. Olcott (q.v.) in 1880. Always consistently Theravāda in doctrine. Present sects Siamese, Ramanya (rigid in doctrine and discipline), Amarapura (more liberal in views). (*See* **Anurādhapura, Mahinda.**) Now known as Sri Lanka.

Ch'an (Chin.) From the Sk. Dhyāna. In Jap., Zen. The Zen Bsm. of Japan derives from the Ch'an Bsm. of China, founded in the sixth century by Bodhidharma and formed into a School

55

by Hung-jen, Hui-neng and their followers in the eighth century. Ch'an Bsm. has been described as the Chinese reaction to the intellectual Bsm. of India. Zen Bsm. may be called Japan's reaction to Ch'an. Yet the Ch'an/Zen School is, even with the distinction of Rinzai and Sōtō Zen, unique as a School of spiritual development, and the word 'Zen' has in this work been used for both the Chin. and Jap. forms. For specific Ch'an Bsm. *see* Chang, *The Practice of Zen* (1959), Humphreys, *Zen Buddhism* (1949) and the numerous works by Dr D. T. Suzuki (q.v.). (*See* **Zen**.)

Chanda (P.)   A term approximate to will. Intention, desire, but desire which is still under some control and can be directed downward, becoming Tanhā (q.v.) or upward, to liberation.

Channa   The Buddha's charioteer, who drove him from his father's palace into the forest, where he entered the homeless life to seek salvation for mankind. A favourite subject in Bst. art.

Cha-no-yu (Jap.)   The Japanese Tea Ceremony. Lit. Tea and hot water. The ceremonial making and taking of tea in a mood which aims at *Satori* (q.v.). A form of Japanese culture which springs from Zen Buddhism. *See* Okakura Kakuzo, *The Book of Tea*.

Chela (Hindi)   The disciple or follower of a Guru, a spiritual teacher.

Chenresi (Tib.)   'The greatly compassionate.' The Tibetan name for *Avalokiteshvara* (q.v.). The supreme Protector and patron Deity of Tibet. The Bodhisattva who manifests in the Dalai Lama (q.v.).

China   Buddhism was introduced into China in A.D. 67 by two Indian Bhikkhus, Kasyapa Matango and Dharmaraksha; the White Horse Monastery built to accommodate them exists today. It made rapid progress, eventually becoming one of the 'tripod' of religions with Taoism and Confucianism. Many schools of Buddhist thought developed and flourished, but the two predominating schools were the Ch'an (Jap. Zen) and Pure Land (q.v.).

Best work is *Buddhist China*, by R. F. Johnston. *See also* Pratt's *Buddhist Pilgrimage*, and Blofeld, *The Jewel in the Lotus*. (*See* **Amitābha, Bodhidharma, Ch'an, Kwan-Yin, Patriarchs, Pure Land, Zen**.)

Chohan A Rajput term used by Indian writers to denote high spiritual rank. *See, Mahatma Letters to A. P. Sinnett* (1924) for references to the Maha-Chohan.

Chörten (Tib.) Tibetan name for Stūpa (q.v.). (*See* **Mani**.)

Chuang-Tzu (Chin.) Chinese Taoist writer and philosopher, who by his writing consolidated the teaching of Lao-Tzu and his *Tao-Te-Ching* and so founded Taoism (d. c. 280 B.C.) Taoism has strong affinities with Zen. *See, Chuang-Tzu, Mystic and Moralist*, trans. Giles (1926).

Chunda (P.) The metal-worker who invited the Buddha to the meal after which he died. The food is described as 'pig's flesh', but may mean truffles, on which pigs feed. But the whole story may be symbolic. *See* Humphreys, *Buddhism*, p. 41.

Citta (Sk. and P.) Mind. Consciousness. Cp. Manas. Also heart, as in Bodhi-citta (q.v.). (*See* **Citta-mātra**.)

Citta-mātra (Sk.) Nothing but mind. Hence All-Mind or Mind-Only.

Compassion Lit. 'to suffer with', compassion is the supreme Buddhist virtue, being based on the fundamental principle of the unity of all life. The second of the Four Sublime Moods—

karunā, identifying oneself with the suffering of others and so creating active affection (*mettā*)—is the only form of vicarious sacrifice known to Buddhism. (*See* **Bodhisattva, Brahma Vihāra, Karuṇā**.)

Conscience Buddhism knows nothing of an 'inner monitor' implanted by deity as an infallible guide to right conduct. 'Conscience' is a quality of the mind resulting from past experience. One's state of moral development depends on one's response to experience in past lives, and in the present life. There is no absolute right and wrong; there is gradual growth towards the highest morality—utter unselfishness. (*See* **Hiri, Sin**.)

Consciousness Consciousness in Bsm. is divided into two classes: Phenomenal (*manovijñāna*) and Transcendental (*ālayavijñāna*). The former is the relation between subject and object and the inferences drawn therefrom. It depends for its expression on the sense organs and mind, and is therefore personal. The latter is independent of sense organs and of the relation of subject and object. The action of the former is ratiocinative, of the latter intuitive. These two aspects are united in an ultimate identity which will be realized at the goal of the Eightfold Path. The dhyanic consciousness represents the union of the two aspects of consciousness, in which individual consciousness is not lost, but is transcended in the union with universal consciousness. (*See* **Ālayavijñāna, Dhyāna, Manas, Samādhi, Viññāna**.)

Conversion *See* **Parāvritti**.

Conze, Dr Edward, Ph.D. (Cologne) Born 1904. English Buddhist. Recognized authority on Sk. and Tib. Bsm. Specialist in the Prajñāpāramitā philosophy and literature. Vice-President of the Buddhist Society, London. Author of *Buddhism* (1951), *Selected Sayings from the Perfection of Wisdom* (1955),

58

The Buddha's Law among the Birds (1955), *Buddhist Meditation* (1956), *Buddhist Wisdom Books* (1958), *Buddhist Scriptures* (Penguin, 1959, *Perfect Wisdom* (1961), etc., and Editor of *Buddhist Texts through the Ages* (1954).

Council The First Great Council was held at Rajagriha immediately after the passing of the Buddha, the Ven. Kasyapa presiding. The Scriptures, as then agreed, were recited by all, Ananda leading with the doctrine and Upali with the Rules of the Order. The Second was held at Vaisali about 100 years later. As only a minority upheld the original teachings and Rules the majority seceded and held a rival Council, from which schism the 18 sects of the Hinayana School were later formed. The Third Council was held in the reign of Asoka (q.v.) at Pataliputra (Patna) about 250 B.C. Here the Canon was fixed, though not reduced to writing until the first century B.C. in Ceylon, when a Fourth Great Council was held. About A.D. 70 a Council was held in Kashmir under the patronage of King Kanishka, but as the doctrines promulgated were exclusively Mahayana it is not recognized by the Theravāda. The Fifth Council was held in 1871 at the instance of King Mindon of Burma, when the Tipitika was carved on 729 marble slabs and preserved at Mandalay. The Sixth Great Council was opened in Rangoon at Wesak, 1954, and sat until 1956 when Buddha Jayanti (q.v.) opened. Meetings held in enormous Hall built specially near Rangoon in imitation of the Saptaparna Cave (q.v.): 2,500 Bhikkhus took part in checking the entire Pali Canon.

Craving *See* **Desire.**

Cremation Cremation is the usual mode of treating the dead in hot countries, and the Buddha's body was cremated. The ashes were divided into ten parts, and Stūpas (q.v.) erected over each of them. It is from surviving Stūpas that undoubted

59

relics of the Buddha have been recovered. (*See* **Piprawa Relics**.) Cremation not only destroys the physical body but also certain finer 'bodies' which, if not destroyed, can be used for evil or unnatural purposes by those with the necessary knowledge. (*See* **Bhūta, Dug-pa**.)

Culla (P.)   Small, as opposed to Mahā, big.

Dagoba   More correctly spelled Dagaba. From the Sk. Dhātu-garbha, relic cavity. Used in Ceylon as co-terminous with Stūpa (q.v.), but the Dagaba is the actual relic-chamber, which is found apart from Stūpas, while many Stūpas have no Dagaba.

Dahlke, Dr Paul (1865-1928)   Pioneer German Bst. Prolific writer of books and articles, those in English including *Buddhist Essays* (1908), *Buddhism and Science* (1913) and *Buddhism and its Place in the Mental Life of Mankind* (1927). Editor of *Die Brockensammlung,* which he largely wrote. Built in the garden of his house at Frohnau, near Berlin, Das Buddhistische Haus, the first Vihāra (q.v.) to be built in Europe. Here he lived in ascetic conditions, observing the Rules of the Sangha. After his death the Haus fell into decay but is now in use again in Bst. hands. For Memoir *see* B. in E. vol. 3, pp. 50-53.

Dai Butsu (Jap.)   The Great Buddha at Kamakura. Erected in 1252 of bronze plates welded together, it is 52 feet high. A figure of Amida in meditation. The monastic building (Hondō) which once housed it was destroyed in a tidal wave, and the great image now stands amid the trees of the old monastery garden. (*See also* **Tōdaiji**.)

Daigo (Jap.)   Great Satori (q.v.).

Daitokuji (Jap.)   Rinzai Zen monastery in Kyoto founded by the great Zen master Daitō Kokushi in 1383. One of its sub-temples is Ryōsen-an (q.v.) of which Mrs Ruth Sasaki (q.v.) was 'Head Monk'. The monastery is famous for its gardens and its collection of Bst. Art.

Dākinī (Sk.) In Tib. Khadoma. A 'sky-walker'. The Dākinīs are female embodiments of intuitive knowledge as taught in the Tantras (q.v.). They act as female counterparts of the male divinities, and may appear in horrific form. In art they appear as naked female figures in hieratic attitudes. For classes of Dākinī *see* A. Gordon, *The Iconography of Tibetan Lamaism* (1939).

Dalada Maligawa The Temple of the Tooth at Kandy, Ceylon. Kandy is the scene of the annual Perahera (q.v.) at Wesak, the Full Moon of May.

Dalai Lama (Tib.) The spiritual and temporal Head of Tibet. Regarded as the earthly manifestation of Chenresi, the 'Precious Protector', the Tibetan term for Avalokiteshvara. The word Dalai, 'great Ocean' (pronounced Dālé, to rhyme with barley) is Mongolian, and was a title granted to the third Grand Lama of the Gelugpa School in 1587 by Gusri Kham, a Mongol prince whom the Lama had called into Tibet to help him quash rival attempts for supreme power. There have been fourteen Dalai Lamas, of whom the fifth and thirteenth are most famous. The Fifth (1615-1680), a great administrator and reformer, was the first to gain full temporal power of all Tibet in addition to being Grand Lama of its leading School, the Gelugpa. For Life of the Thirteenth (1876-1933) *see* Bell, *Portrait of the Dalai Lama* (1946). For method of choosing successor *see* **Tulku**. The present, Fourteenth, Dalai Lama was born in Amdo on 6 June 1935, and was approved, brought to Lhasa and enthroned in 1940. For his early life *see* his *My Land and my People* (1962). He visited India in 1956 for India's Buddha Jayanti (q.v.) celebrations, and then returned to Tibet.

In 1959 he was forced into exile by Chinese Communists. Pending his return he lives at Dharmsala in the Punjab.

Dambulla   A cave in the hillside near the centre of Ceylon containing an enormous reclining Buddha, first century A.D. The level of art in the figure and attendant painting is not high.

Dāna (Sk. and P.)   The virtue of alms-giving to the poor and needy; also, making gifts to a Bhikkhu or community of Bhikkhus. One of the three 'acts of merit', *dāna*, benevolence, *sīla*, moral conduct, *bhāvanā*, meditation. The first of the ten Pāramitās (q.v.).

Dars(h)ana (Sk.) **Dassana** (P.)   Seeing. Objectively, a display, a splendid sight, the reverence roused by that sight. Subjectively, the inward understanding. Cp. *Vipassanā*. In Hinduism may mean a philosophic view, a school of thought.

Dasa-Sīla (P.)   The Ten Precepts taken by all Sāmaneras and Bhikkhus. (*See* **Sīla**.)

Davids, Dr T. W. Rhys, LL.D., PH.D., D.SC. (1843-1922) Pioneer Pali Scholar. In 1864 entered the Ceylon Civil Service where he learnt Pali from the Ven. Sumangala Thera. Back in England he founded in 1881 the Pali Text Society (q.v.), and gave the rest of his life to it. President of the Buddhist Society in Great Britain and Ireland (q.v.) at its foundation in 1907. Apart from translations, author with Dr Stede (q.v.) of the *Pali-English Dictionary*, and three works on Bsm.— *Buddhism* (1878), *Buddhism, its History and Literature* (1896) and *Buddhist India* (1903). (*See* **Mrs. Caroline Rhys Davids**.)

Davids, Mrs Caroline Rhys, M.A. (1858-1942)   Pioneer Pali scholar. Worked all her life with her husband, Dr T. W. Rhys

Davids (q.v.) in the Pali Text Society (q.v.) which she carried on after his death in 1922 to her own in 1942. Prolific translator and writer. Interested in isolating in the Pali Canon the actual teaching of the Buddha, she wrote a series of polemic volumes, in particular *Gotama the Man* (1928) and *Sakya, or Buddhist Origins* (1931). Her numerous articles were in part collected in *Wayfarer's Words*, published posthumously in 1942. (*See* **Horner**.)

Dāyaka (Sk. and P.)   Lit.: Giver. A term used in both Theravāda and Mahayana countries to denote the lay supporter of a Bhikkhu or the Mahayana equivalent. The Dayaka undertakes to supply the Bhikkhu with his legitimate needs, such as food, new robes and medicine, and in modern times will often pay his travelling expenses.

Death (Sk. and P. *Marana*)   The last of the chain of the twelve Nidānas (q.v.). The abandonment of the body (Rūpa) and other sheaths or bodies which alike dissolve at death. To the Bst. a recurrent phenomenon. (*See* **Devachan, Rebirth**.)

Delusion   *See* **Avijjā-Avidyā, Māyā, Moha**.

Dengyō Daishi   *See* **Tendai**.

Dentō Roku (Jap.)   Japanese name for the Transmission of the Lamp (q.v.) written in 1004, the earliest Zen history extant.

Dependent Origination   A commonly accepted term for the twelve Nidānas (q.v.) or Paticca Samuppāda.

Depung (Tib.)   The 'Mound of Rice' monastery, or College of Lamas outside Lhasa, at one time containing eight to ten thousand students. Founded 1414. Wealthy and powerful, it has long exercised much influence on Tibetan Bsm.

63

Desire (Sk. *Trishnā*, P. *Tanhā*)   Thirst for separate existence in the worlds of sense. 'Desire' in itself is colourless, but selfish desire is the cause of suffering. The 'will to live' must be transmuted into 'aspiration' for the welfare and ultimate enlightenment of all beings. *Tanhā* is one of the twelve links in the chain of Causation (*Nidānas*) (q.v.). Its source is delusion (*Moha*) (q.v.) caused by attraction to the six objects of sense.

Detachment   *See* **Viveka**.

Deva (Sk.)   'Shining One.' Celestial beings, good, bad or indifferent in nature. The devas may inhabit any of the three worlds (*see* **Tiloka**). They correspond to the angelic powers of Western theology.

Devachan   'Dwelling place of shining ones', is the subjective 'heaven' state in which an individual lives between two earth 'lives' after the death of the gross physical bodies and the separation of the *Kāma-rūpa*.

Devadatta (Sk. and P.)   A cousin of Gautama the Buddha and his most persistent enemy. According to the Pali Canon he twice tried to kill him, as well as attempting to cause schisms in the Sangha. *See* Brewster, *The Life of Gotama the Buddha* (1926).

Devil   There are numerous classes of demons mentioned in the Buddhist scriptures. The personification of evil and the tempter of man is usually called **Māra** (q.v.). The allegory of the Buddha's temptation by **Māra** is related in the **Mahā vagga** (A.P.C.).

Devil Dances of Tibet   The so-called Devil Dances, in which the Devil in many forms is frequently portrayed, are in fact cognate to the Western Morality Plays, and are equally ways of teaching a populace of low education the basic principles of morality and some of the principles of Bsm. The costumes and masks are traditional, and like the Nō examples in Japan of high craftsmanship.

Dhamma (P.) Dharma (Sk.) The Pali form is generally used by the Theravāda School, the Sanskrit by the M. School. Dharma, in sense of 'the course of conduct right for a man at this particular stage of evolution', is now well known in the West through its use in Theosophical literature.

The Sk. form comes from Aryan root 'dhar', to uphold, sustain, support, and has been rendered in English as system, doctrine, religion, virtue, moral quality, righteousness, duty, law, standard, norm, ideal, truth, form, condition, cause, thing and cosmic order ; it may mean any of these according to the context. We may trace basic meaning in Eng. *form*, that which supports, that which gives state or condition to the orderly arrangement of parts which makes a thing what it is; from which comes Eng. 'good form', conduct appropriate to any given occasion.

Technical definitions come under five headings:

(a) *Dhamma*—Doctrine. Any teaching set forth as a formulated system; the guiding principles accepted or followed by a man, as applied to Bsm.: the Teachings of the Buddha. (*See* **Buddhism.**)

(b) Right, Righteous conduct or righteousness, Law, Justice. (*See* **Sammā.**)

(c) Condition. Cause or causal antecedent. Cause and effect being practically identical, *Dhamma* is here viewed from its causal side, as in (d) it is viewed from aspect of effect.

(d) Phenomenon. *Dhammā* as effect. It is used in this sense in first verse of Dhp.: 'All *dhammas* (phenomena) are mind-created'; and in the famous formula *sabbe dhammā anattā*—the whole of the phenomenal world is *anattā*, etc.

Application of word *Dhamma* to phenomena indicates orderly nature of existence; universe is expression of Law.

(e) Ultimate Reality. In Mahayana *Dharma* is sometimes synonymous with Tathatā (q.v.) or Ultimate Reality. (*See* **Dharma-kāya.**)

Dhamma-cakka-ppavattana-sutta (P.) The 'setting in motion of the Wheel of the Law', or Sermon on the Foundation of the Kingdom of Righteousness. The first discourse of the Buddha after his Enlightenment. Delivered to his first converts in the Deer Park at Benares. (*See* **First Sermon.**)

Dhammadūta (P.) A missioner, one who proclaims the Dhamma, the Teaching of the Buddha.

Dhammapada (P.) The Path or Way of the Buddha's *Dhamma* or Teaching. The most famous Scripture in the Pali Canon. A collection of 423 verses comprising a noble system of moral philosophy. There are many English translations from the Pali version. For a translation of the Chinese version, *see* Beal's *Texts from the Buddhist Canon commonly known as Dhammapada.*

Dhāraṇa (Sk.) Intense concentration upon one interior object to the complete exclusion of all else. In one sense can be practised throughout the day.

Dhāraṇī (Sk.) An invocation, usually longer than a Mantram (q.v.), which has magical powers in its recitation. 'The embodiment of a power in a sound' (Morgan). Lit.: 'supporters', they fix the mind of the meditator on an idea or vision. Can also be a by-product of meditation, the 'fixing of an experience'. *See* Suzuki, *Manual of Zen Buddhism.*

Dharmakāya (Sk.) The Body of the Law. The Buddha as the personification of Truth. In Mahāyāna, one of the triple aspects of Bhūtatathatā (*see* **Trikāya**). The Essence Body, 'Consciousness merged in the Universal Consciousness'.

66

Dharmapāla, the Anāgārika   Name used by D. H. Hewavitarne, the famous Buddhist propagandist. Born in Ceylon in 1865, he joined the Theosophical Society in 1884. Inspired by H. P. Blavatsky (q.v.) he studied Pali, and in 1891 founded the Maha Bodhi Society (q.v.). He then proclaimed himself as an Anāgārika, a homeless wanderer, and worked hard for the main object of the Society, the restoration of Buddha Gaya (q.v.) into Buddhist hands, which was only achieved in 1953. In 1893 he attended the Parliament of Religions at Chicago. In 1925 he founded the British Maha Bodhi Society in London. In 1931 he entered the Order as Sri Devamitta Dhammapāla, and died in 1933. Photograph in Humphreys' *Buddhism.*

Dharmasāla (Sk.)   A Rest-house for pilgrims, often provided by a rich man for those coming to a special place of pilgrimage.

Dhātu (P.)   Root, in sense of elements. Used in several senses in Bst. Scriptures, of the four elements, of the three basic planes of existence and so on. Dharmadhātu is the root, or seed, or conversely universal world of Dharma, Truth.

Dhyāna (Sk.); P., Jhāna (q.v.); Chin. Ch'an (q.v.); Jap. Zen (q.v.)   A term so fundamental in Bsm. that the above variations have four distinguishable meanings. A fifth is Dzyan (q.v.). Basic meaning, meditation. The practice of Dhyāna leads to Samādhi (q.v.); both are to be distinguished from Prajñā (q.v.) which is out of time and duality. Rinzai Zen, following Hui-neng, concentrates on Prajñā; Sōtō on Dhyāna, quiet meditation, though both are necessary. Prajñā, supreme Wisdom, is reached by Dhyāna; Dhyāna leads to Prajñā. For the Dhyāna posture in meditation and in art *see* **Āsana, Buddha Rūpa** *and* **Mudrā.**

Dhyāni - Bodhisattvas   The five Dhyāni - Bodhisattvas of Tibetan Bsm. are emanations from their respective Dhyāni-

Buddhas (q.v.). They are Avalokiteshvara (q.v.) or Padma-pāni, Samantabhadra (q.v.), Vajrapāni (q.v.), Ratnapāni and Visvapāni.

Dhyāni-Buddhas The personifications of aspects of the one Ādi-Buddha which appear in meditation. Hence name of 'Meditation Buddhas'. These and the Dhyāni-Bodhisattvas (q.v.) are part of the methods of Tantric Bsm. (q.v.). Their names are Vairocana, Aksobhya, Ratnasambhava, Amitābha and Amoghasiddhi. *See* A. Gordon, *The Iconography of Tibetan Lamaism* (1939), and Govinda, *Foundations of Tibetan Mysticism* (1959).

Diamond Sutra The Vajracchedikā Prajñāpāramitā Sutra, 'the Perfection of Wisdom which cuts like a Diamond'. One of the two most famous Scriptures in the vast Perfection of Wisdom (Prajñā-pāramitā) group of the M. Canon. The Heart Sutra (q.v.) is a still smaller epitome of this 'Wisdom which has gone beyond'. The Sk. original of the Diamond probably compiled in fourth century. A Chinese trans. in the British Museum dated 868 is the oldest printed book known to us. As the Kongō-kyō the work is immensely popular in Japan. The latest trans. from Sk. is in Conze, *Buddhist Wisdom Books* (1958), with commentary. For trans. from Chinese, *see* Price, *The Diamond Sutra* (1955).

Digha Nikāya The 'Collection of Long Discourses' is the first section of the *Sutta Pitaka* (q.v.). For analysis see A.P.C. *Dialogues of the Buddha*, vols. I-III contain whole of Digha.

Dipankara Buddha (Sk.) The Luminous. The only one of the predecessors in office of Gautama the Buddha of whom there are any details in the Scriptures. It was he who taught Gautama Siddhārtha in previous births, and prepared him for his future achievement.

Ditthi (P.)   Views. *Sammā-ditthi*, right view, is the first step of the Noble Eightfold Path (q.v.). An example of wrong views is *Sakkāya-ditthi*, the false belief that the *skandhas*, or constituents of personality, contain an immortal 'soul'. (*See* **Belief.**)

Dōgen (Jap.)   The Japanese Founder of Sōtō Zen Bsm. in Japan (1200-1253). Dōgen studied the teaching of the T'sao-tung School in China for four years before bringing it, in 1227, to Japan. He stands alone as the Founder of the Japanese School, and is by far its greatest name. He would have no dealings with the Court, but retired to the mountains where he founded Eiheiji, near Fukui. There he taught that moral training, meditation and enlightenment are three facets of one process. All *is* Buddha, and we have but to realize what we are. Dōgen was a very great man, and his school of Zen Bsm. should be far better known. Extracts from his writings appear in Masunaga, *The Soto Approach to Zen* (*see Shōbō-genzō*). For Soto and Rinzai Zen see *Middle Way*, May, 1960, pp. 14-17.

Dōjō (Jap.)   Any place where Bst. teaching is given or the Way practised. Hence a Bst. monastery, but used more particularly in Jūdō (q.v.) and Kendō (q.v.) for the room where that art is practised. Cp. *Sōdō*.

Dokusan (Jap.)   Private interview with Rōshi, or Zen teacher, in a Rinzai Zen temple. Cp. San-Zen, the name for the general practice of such interviews.

Dorje (Tib.) (Sk. Vajra)   The thunderbolt symbol used in art and ritual magic in Tibet.

Dosa (P.)   (1) Fault, (2) Hatred, anger, ill-will. One of the 'three fires' which burn in the mind until allowed to die for

69

want of fuelling, the others being Lust and Illusion. (*See* **Moha, Rāga.**)

Dōshin (Jap.) *See* Tao-hsin, the Fourth Chinese Patriarch.

Doubt As a factor of consciousness in the Abhidhamma analysis *see* Vicikicchā. For the 'Great Doubt' which precedes Satori in Zen Bsm. *see* I-ching. (*See* **Nivaraṇa.**)

Dug-pa (Tib.) Originally a sub-sect of the Kargyut-pa School (twelfth century), it remained unreformed by the work of Tsongkha-pa, and has largely sunk to the level of the indigenous Bön (q.v.). Now found mostly in Bhutan and Ladak. It claims three levels, the high, middle and low. The best is at Kargyut-pa level, the worst little better than sorcery. Sometimes known as the Black Hats. *See* Hoffmann, *The Religions of Tibet* (1960).

Dukkha (P.) Ordinarily translated as suffering or ill, but no word in English covers the same ground as *Dukkha* in Pali. Ordinarily set in opposition to *Sukha*, ease and well-being, it signifies dis-ease in the sense of discomfort, frustration or disharmony with environment.

Dukkha is the first of the Four Noble Truths (q.v.) and one of the three Signs of Being, or Characteristics of Existence, with *Anicca*, impermanence, and *Anattā*, unreality of self. *Dukkha* is largely the effect of man's reaction to *Anicca* and *Anattā*. It follows that existence cannot be wholly separated from *Dukkha*, and that complete escape from it is possible only by liberation from the round of birth and death.

Dukkha is the last link in the chain of Dependent Origination, *Jarāmarana*, old age and death, being characterized as inseparable from grief, lamentation, sorrow, distress and despair.

Dzyan Another corruption of the Sk. word Dhyāna (Cp.

Jhāna, Ch'an, Zen). *The Book of Dzyan* is a highly cryptic Tibetan work in the same series as *The Book of the Golden Precepts* (q.v.). On its Stanzas, H. P. Blavatsky compiled *The Secret Doctrine* (q.v). (*See* **Kiu-te**.)

Eastern Buddhist, The The Journal of the Eastern Buddhist Society, Kyoto. Published irregularly from 1921 to 1939. Founded and edited by Dr D. T. Suzuki and Mrs B. L. Suzuki. New series begun 1965.

Ego Bsm. denies an ego in the sense of a self in man ultimately separate from the self in every other man. The belief in an ego creates and fosters egoism and desire, thus preventing the realization of the unity of life and the attainment of enlightenment. (*See* **Anattā, Skandha**.)

Eisai (Jap.) Japanese Bst. (1141-1215) who brought Rinzai Zen from China to Japan. He made little headway in Kyoto, but among the warriors of Kamakura (q.v,) the new teaching of direct action immediately caught on. He also brought tea plants from China, and is known as the father of Japanese tea and all that it has come to represent.

Eka (Jap.) *See* **Hui-k'o**, the Second Chinese Zen Patriarch.

Ekacitta (Sk.) The 'one thought-moment' out of time, in which the Zen monk experiences Non-duality, that state before the One became the Many, before thought was born. Cp. *Ichinen, Kenshō, Satori.*

Ekāggatā (P.) One-pointedness of mind, rather in limiting sense of reducing other factors in consciousness. Cp. *Dhyāna, Manasikāra, Samādhi.*

Ekaks(h)ana (Sk.) The One Moment of eternal NOW. Cp. *Ekacitta.*

Ellora Group of buildings in the Deccan, some Hindu and some Bst., all carved from solid rock. Bst. group date from period when work at Ajantā (q.v.) ceased, about seventh century A.D. Bst. caves partly Vihāras and partly Halls for Worship, with Stūpa and Buddha-rūpa. (*See* **Karli**.)

Emerald Buddha A large image of the Buddha in jasper on the altar of the Temple of that name in the royal palace of Bangkok. It has a strange history of being stolen and recovered many times by rival would-be owners.

Encyclopaedia of Buddhism, An Scheme sponsored by Ceylon Government to coincide with Buddha Jayanti (q.v.) in 1956. Editor in Chief, Dr G. P. Malalasekera. National committees set up in many countries. A Volume of Specimen Articles published in 1957, and the First Fascicule in 1961.

Engakuji (Jap.) Famous Rinzai Zen monastery in Kamakura, founded in 1282 by Hōjō Tokimune for his Zen teacher, Bukkō Kokushi, who became the first Abbot. Built originally in the Chinese style, it commemorates the Mongolian as well as the Japanese dead in the unsuccessful invasion of Japan by the Mongols in 1281. Tokimune, who led the defending forces and was a pious Buddhist, is buried there. Imagita Kōsen, the first Rōshi of Dr D. T. Suzuki (q.v.) is also buried there, and Dr Suzuki lived for many years in Shōden-an, one of its sub-temples. He chose it for the photographs of the training of monks in a Zen monastery in his *Zen and Japanese Buddhism* (1958).

England, Buddhism in First Bst. Mission to England landed April, 1908, led by Bhikkhu Ananda Metteyya (q.v.). Received by Buddhist Society of Great Britain and Ireland, founded November, 1907, by Dr Ernest Rost and others, with Professor Rhys Davids as President. *The Buddhist Review*, founded 1909, ceased 1922. The Buddhist League was founded 1923, by Francis Payne, to replace moribund Buddhist Society of

72

Great Britain and Ireland, which was formally wound up 1925. The Buddhist Lodge was founded November, 1924, becoming Buddhist Lodge, London, in 1926, the Buddhist Society, London, in 1943 and the Buddhist Society in 1952. Its journal *Buddhism in England*, founded May, 1926, was renamed *The Middle Way* in 1945. The Buddhist Mission was founded by Anagarika Dharmapala (q.v.) at Ealing, July, 1926; removed 1928 to 41 Gloucester Road, N.W.1. *The British Buddhist*, founded as their journal 1926, replaced in January, 1935, by *The Wheel* (q.v.).

The London Buddhist Vihara was opened in Knightsbridge in 1954 with funds from Ceylon to serve as such in London. Now at 5 Heathfield Gardens, Chiswick, W.4 (*see* **Vihara**, From 1956 attempts have been made at 131 Haverstock Hill, N.W.3 to form an English Vihara, so far in vain. In 1966 the King of Thailand opened the Buddhapadipa Temple at East Sheen. In the following year Lama Trungpa Rimpoche opened a Tibetan Centre at Samye Ling, Dumfries, and the Ven. Sangharashita (q.v.) became Head of the Friends of the Western Buddhist Order, with headquarters in London. In 1972 the Rev. Jiyu Kennett opened a Zen training centre at Throstle Hole Priory, Northumberland. In 1973 the Lama Chime Rimpoche opened Kham Tibetan House, Essex, and in 1974 the British Buddhist Association was founded in Crowndale Road, N.W. under the Ven Vajiragnana. Many of these organizations have Groups in this country and elsewhere. The Buddhist Society (q.v.) has some forty.

Engo (Jap.) **Yuan-wu** (Chin.)   Chinese Zen Master (1063-1135). Famous for his comments and 'Introductory Words' to a hundred cases or sayings of earlier Chinese masters collected by Setcho (q.v.). Engo's pupils collected the total material and in 1125 published it as the Hekigan Roku (q.v.) or Blue Cliff Records. *See, The Blue Cliff Records* (1961), trans. **Shaw.**

Enlightenment   Buddhism rests historically on the fact that Gautama Siddhartha became *Buddha,* a word meaning (fully) enlightened or awakened. Both meanings imply freedom from the mind's limitations, and the expansion of this mind until one with All-Mind and commensurate with the universe. This is the goal of every Bst., to break through the barriers of thought to the Non-duality which lies beyond the One and the Many, and all others of the 'pairs of opposites'. But 'rare indeed is a Buddha, rare as the flower of the udumbara tree', and the Scriptures only attempt to speak of lesser stages of spiritual achievement, such as Samādhi, Prajñā and Satori (q.v.) (*See* **Nirvāna, No-Mind.**)

Enō (Yenō) (Jap.)   *See* **Hui-neng,** the Sixth Chinese Zen Patriarch.

Equanimity   One of the aims of meditation. (*See* **Samādhi, Samatā, Upekkhā.**)

Esoteric   (1) Secret; in the sense of teaching not revealed to those unworthy or unfit to receive it. Such teaching may refer to phenomenal or spiritual matters. (2) Symbolic; the inner or spiritual meaning underlying the literal surface meaning. Spiritual truths are apprehended by the intuition (*see* **Buddhi**) and cannot be revealed or explained except to those whose inner development enables them to grasp them. The 'Heart' doctrine, as opposed to the 'Eye' doctrine.

Esoteric Buddhism   A book written by A. P. Sinnett from material given him in letters from the Mahatmas M. and K.H. and first published in 1883. The letters themselves were published in 1924 as *The Mahatma Letters to A. P. Sinnett* (q.v.). H. P. Blavatsky said that the title should have been Esoteric Bodhism, for the teaching given is that of the esoteric school of Wisdom (Bodhi) which long antedates the religion founded by

Gautama the Buddha. The book is a basic text-book of Theosophy.

Essence of Mind Term used in Wong Mou-Lam's translation of the Sutra of Hui-neng for Hsin (Jap. Shin), an untranslatable term for the Heart/Mind which is behind the ephemeral personality or *skandhas*, and, being already enlightened, needs but awakening to that fact. (*See* **Mushin, No-Mind**.)

Ethics Buddhist ethics are based on the doctrine of *Anattā* (q.v.). Every quality encouraging altruism is therefore considered a virtue, and every opposite quality a vice. The Buddhist moral code is set forth in the Noble Eightfold Path and in the Precepts (q.v.).

Evans-Wentz, Dr. W. Y., M.A., D.LITT, D.SC.(OXON.) English writer on Tibetan Bsm. now living in U.S.A. Author of *The Tibetan Book of the Dead* (1927), *Tibet's Great Yogi, Milarepa* (1928), *Tibetan Yoga and Secret Doctrines* (1935) and *The Tibetan Book of the Great Liberation* (1954). [Died 1965.]

Evil Bsm. is not dualistic, and therefore does not divide phenomena into absolute 'good' or 'evil'. It recognizes 'evil' as limitation, and therefore purely relative. There is therefore no 'problem of Evil' as in theistic systems of thought. All evil is traced to desire for self. (*See* **Anattā, Dukkha, Ego, Sakkāyaditthi**.) The basic evil is the idea of separateness, and the Buddhist goal is the removal of evil by the eradication of all sense of separate Selfhood. (*See* **Kusala, Sin**.)

Experience Buddhism is not so much a religion as a way of life. Even the Scriptures have little value compared with actual experience of the doctrines they describe. This is why Bsm. claims no Authority (q.v.) for any doctrine and professes

complete tolerance for differing opinions. Satori (q.v.)
is described as a personal yet impersonal, direct, intuitive
experience of the non-relative. It is unmistakable and unforget-
table, but being beyond the plane of the intellect incommunicable in words. This experience, large or small, is the goal of
Zen training.

Extinction Early translators of the Bst. Scriptures wrongly
interpreted Nibbāna (Sk. Nirvāna) as extinction, without
explaining that it is the extinction of awareness of separate
self-hood. (*See* **Nirodha**.)

Eye Doctrine Name used for the exoteric teaching of the
Buddha, of the intellect, as distinct from the Heart Doctrine
or the 'true Seal', as handed down from Master to Master.
See Notes to *The Voice of the Silence*. Trans. H. P. B. (1889).

Fa-Hsien Chinese Buddhist pilgrim who in the early fifth
century travelled through India to collect information on Bsm.
He reached as far West as Afghanistan and then sailed home
from Ceylon, arriving in 414. At the request of Kumārajiva
(q.v.) published an account of his journey and the books he
had collected as *An Account of Buddhist Kingdoms*. The
account is doubly valuable when compared with that of Hiuen
Tsiang (q.v.) who travelled much the same journey in the
eighth century. *See, The Travels of Fa-Hsien*. Trans. H. A.
Giles (1923).

Faith In Bsm. faith (Saddhā, P.) is not the acceptance of
doctrinal beliefs, but confidence in the Teacher and his Teaching as a Way to a Goal desired. In Bsm. there is no reliance
on the authority of another's spiritual achievement, however
great, and the Buddha so taught in words. See his admonition
to the Kālāmas, W. of Bsm. No. 22 In the Mahāyāna faith
is in the power of the Buddha within.

Fetters The Ten Fetters are erroneous mental conceptions and desires which have to be cast off as the Path is followed to the Goal. For details *see* **Four Paths** *and* **Samyojanā.**

Fiction, Buddhism in There are yet few books which convey in fiction the essence and flavour of Bsm. The Lama in Kipling's *Kim* and in Talbot Mundy's *Om* are both good. Mrs Adam Beck's *Life of the Buddha* is the best Life in fiction form, and her *Garden of Vision* is still the best attempt to put the flavour of the Zen life into a story, though somewhat sentimental. Some of her short stories are more successful. Less known works are Mundy's *Ramsden,* a tale of black and white magic in Tibet, and *The Youngest Disciple,* by Edward Thompson (1938) also *Mipam,* by Lama Yongden (1938).

Finland, Buddhism in Buddhism in Finland is inseparable from the work of its founder, Consul Mauno Nordberg (1884-1956), who studied Bsm. while a Consul in Paris and founded the 'Friends of Buddhism' in Helsinki in 1945. Here he built up a Bst. Library, lectured and broadcast on Bsm., translated Bst. works into Finnish and Swedish. Represented Finland at Conferences of the World Fellowship of Buddhists.

Fire Fire appears in Bst. writings as the flames of undesirable forces in the mind. Thus the Three Fires of Hatred, Lust and Illusion which must be allowed to die for lack of fuelling. *See* the 'Fire Sermon of the Buddha' (W. of Bsm. No. 14). For the psycho-physical heat induced by special meditation in Tibet, *see* **Tum-mo.**

First Sermon After the Buddha's Enlightenment at Buddha Gaya he moved slowly across India until he reached the Deer Park near Benares (*see* **Sarnath**), where he preached to five ascetics his First Sermon. It sets forth the Middle Way between all extremes, the Four Noble Truths and the Noble Eightfold

77

Path. *See* W. of Bsm. No. 13. (*See* **Dhamma-cakka-ppavattana sutta.**)

First Zen Institute of America Founded in New York in 1930 as the First Zen Institute of New York, to replace the existing Buddhist Society of America, which had been formed round the teaching of Sokei-an Sasaki (q.v.), the first Zen Rōshi to make his home in the West. Name later changed to First Zen Institute of America. Publications, *The Cat's Yawn* (1947) and *The Development of Chinese Zen,* Dumoulin (1953). A Japanese branch has been opened at Ryōsen-an, Kyoto, by Mrs Ruth Sasaki (q.v.).

Five Houses, The Common term for the five lines of transmission or Schools of Chinese Ch'an (Zen) Bsm. existing at the end of the T'ang Dynasty (c. 900). Two of them, the Ikyō and Hōgen sects, did not long survive; the Ummon sect did not long survive its founder, Ummon, though it produced great men, and this left the two schools which, under their later Japanese names, are the Sōtō and Rinzai schools of today.

Five Precepts *See* **Pansil, Precepts, Sila.**

Five Ranks A doctrine constructed by Tōsan Ryōkai (807-869) (q.v.). Based 'not on the ontological-psychological analysis of Bst. philosophy but on the experience of enlightenment' (Dumoulin). The exercise involves five relations between the Absolute and the Relative, A later commentary by Sōzan Honjaku gives the fivefold analogy of the lord and vassal, or master and servant. *See* Dumoulin, *The Development of Chinese Zen* (1953), Chap. II.

Flag, The Buddhist Jointly devised by Mr J. R. de Silva and Colonel Olcott, founding President of the Theosophical Society (1875) to mark the revival of Bsm. in Ceylon which followed the arrival in the Island of Col. Olcott and H. P. Blavatsky in

1880, when they publicly took Pansil as Bsts. First used 1888 when Wesak (q.v.) celebrated as a public holiday. The six colours are those alleged in the Scriptures to have radiated from the aura of the Buddha. Flag consists of the six colours red, blue, yellow, white and rose in vertical stripes with 'a tint compounded of them all together', represented by these five colours in horizontal stripes at the end. Adopted by the World Fellowship of Buddhists, and now used widely in Bst. buildings and at Bst. celebrations.

Flower-Arrangement In Japanese, Ikebana. As great lovers of nature, the Japanese try to create miniature editions, as in their gardens, built of stones, trees and water; or stunted trees in small containers, and in flower arrangement so stylized that each symbolizes a message, frequently a Bst. message. Ikebana, like Cha-no-yu (q.v.) was born in the Silver Pavilion (q.v.) near Kyoto built in fifteenth century. Leading exponent in England, Miss Stella Coe, a qualified master of the art. *See* Gustie Herrigel, *Zen in the Art of Flower Arrangement* (1958).

Fohat (Chin.) Sk. equivalent, Daiviprakriti. Primordial Light. The intelligent vital force of the universe, forming or destroying perishable forms. The power of the One Life of the universe It has been called cosmic electricity. *See* Blavatsky, *Theosophical Glossary.*

Four Noble Truths The basic truths of Bsm., as set forth by the Buddha in his First Sermon (q.v.). They are: *Dukkha*: There can be no existence without 'suffering'; *Samudaya*: The cause of suffering is egoistic Desire; *Nirodha*: The elimination of Desire brings the cessation of Suffering; *Magga*: The Way to the elimination of Desire is the Noble Eightfold Path (q.v.).

Four Paths The Four Paths or Stages on the Path to liberation are (1) **Sotāpanna**: 'He who has entered the Stream'. At this stage he is free from the first three of the Ten Fetters (*Sam-*

yojanas), i.e. *Sakkāya-ditthi*; the illusion of being a 'self' separate from all other selves. (2) *Vicikicchā;* mental vacillation, doubt. (3) *Sīlabbata-parāmāsa*; belief in the efficacy of Rites and Ceremonies.

The second stage is (II) **Sakadāgāmin**: 'He who will return once only' to this world before attaining liberation. Such is nearly free from (4) *Kāmacchanda*, delusions of the senses. (5) *Patigha* or *Vyāpāda*; ill-will or aversion.

(III) **Anāgāmin**: 'He who will never return' to this world, being utterly free from these five Fetters.

(IV) **Arahat**: 'The Worthy One', who attains Nirvāna. Such a one has cast off the five higher Fetters of (6) *Rūparāga*, desire for existence in the worlds of form; (7) *Arūparāga*, desire for existence in the formless worlds; (8) *Māna*, Conceit or self-esteem; (9) *Uddhacca*, restlessness; and (10) *Avijjā*, ignorance. (*See* **Arhat.**)

Fourteen Fundamental Buddhist Beliefs   The Fourteen Points compiled at the Council organized by Col H. S. Olcott at Adyar, Madras, in 1891, and accepted by the representatives of Burma, Ceylon, Japan (nine sects), and Chittagong; and later by the chief Mongolian lamas. The points are set forth in the Appendix to Olcott's *Buddhist Catechism*.

France, Buddhism in   Les Amis du Bouddhisme (q.v.) was founded in Paris in 1929 by Miss Constant Lounsbery (q.v.) and is the only substantial Bst. organization in France. Famous French Bst. scholars include Bigandet, Poussin, Sylvain Lévi, Grousset, David-Neel (q.v.), Demiéville, Guénon, Benoit.

Freewill   Determinism, in the sense that human action is determined by forces independent of the will, is classed in Bsm. as an erroneous conception. It asserts that the will of man is not bound by external causes, but is free in the sense that all fetters are of man's own making, and may be by man himself cast off. In other words; will *per se* is free, but is limited by the results of its own previous acts. (*See* **Karma**.)

Fudō (Jap.) Jap. name for Acala (q.v.), a manifestation of Dainichi (Vairocana, q.v.). Popular subject for Jap. painting and sculpture, adopted into Bsm. as one of five Myōō, manifestations of the five Nyorai (q.v.).

Gahakāraka (Sk.) 'The builder of the house' of self, the self which holds together unreal components in an unreal unity and gives the illusion of being a compound thing. The analogy is from a house which, being taken to pieces, ceases to be—a house. An equally well used analogy is that of the chariot. But for an attack on these analogies as false *see* Sammitīya. *See* Dhp. 153-4, and for verse translation Arnold, *The Light of Asia*, Book Sixth.

Gampo-pa (Tib.) Tibetan saint and author (1077-1152). Regarded as a reincarnation of Srong tsan Gampo, hence his name. A pupil of Marpa (q.v.) and his successor. As such, one of the founders of the Kargyut-pa School (q.v.). His greatest work is *The Precious Rosary*, trans. Evans-Wentz as *The Supreme Path of Discipleship*. *See* 'The Precepts of the Gurus' in Book I of his *Tibetan Yoga and Secret Doctrines* (1935). *See* also the *Jewel Ornament of Liberation*, trans. Guenther (1959).

Ganda-vyūha (Sk.) Part of the Avatamsaka Sutra (q.v.). A name for the forty fascicles of the Sk. original of this great M. scripture, the rest only surviving in Chinese translation.

Ganden (Tib.) Large monastic college just outside Lhasa, founded in 1417 by Tsong-Kha-pa (q.v.) who is buried there. One of the three largest and most powerful monasteries in Tibet. (*See* **Depung** *and* **Sera**.)

Gandhāra The Sk. name for a district covering the modern Peshawar in India, and parts of modern Afghanistan. At one time a Bst. stronghold, it played an important part in evolution of the doctrines of the Mahayana School. Famous for its style of sculpture, which is a blend of ancient Indian modified by the Graeco-Roman styles of Asia Minor. Its period was A.D. 100-300. Ancient Indian Bst. art did not depict figure of the Buddha but symbolized his presence; Gandhāra art depicts the figure, the whole life history of the Buddha being drawn upon for scenes. *See* J. Marshall, *The Buddhist Art of Gandhara* (1960). (*See* **Buddha-Rūpa**.)

Garbha (Sk.) Womb, as Tathāgata-Garbha, the womb of Buddha-hood or the Ālaya-Vijñāna.

Garuda (Sk.) Figures of birds with human heads, the traditional enemies of Nāgas (q.v.). Popular in Hindu and by derivation in Bst. art, esp. in Siam.

Gāthā (Sk.) A set of verses. A stanza or song produced by a mind in a condition of spiritual insight. *See* the *Thera-* and the *Therīgāthā*, the Songs of the Brethren and Sisters, in the Pali Canon (*see* A.P.C.). The records of Zen Bsm. give many cases of men expressing their sudden flashes of enlightenment in Gāthā form.

Gati (P.) A course of existence, gate, entrance, way of going. The conditions of sentient existence. (*See* **Wheel of Life**.)

Gelong (Tib.) The general term for an ordained monk of a Tibetan Buddhist Order. (*See* **Trapa** *and* cp. **Bhikkhu**.)

Gelug-pa (Tib.) Lit. a virtuous one. A member of the School of Tibetan Bsm. founded in the fourteenth century by Tsong-kha-pa (q.v.) as a reformed school of the earlier Kah-dam-pa founded by Atisha in the eleventh century. On ceremonial occasions its higher ranks of lamas wear yellow hats, whereas the remaining Schools continue to wear red head-dress. The famous monasteries of Depung, Sera and Ganden belong to this School, as do the Dalai Lama and Panchen Lama. Its members are celibate. (*See* **Tibetan Buddhism, Schools of.**)

Gendun (Tib.)   The Tibetan generic term for the Bst. Order, in the Theravāda School known as the Sangha. (*See* **Tibetan Buddhist Orders.**)

Germany, Buddhism in   Germany is and has always been the only rival to England in its interest in Bsm. Apart from its own pioneer Bst. scholars, as Neumann and Oldenberg, German scholars have become famous in other lands, as Nyanatiloka (q.v.) and Govinda (q.v.). In 1903 a Buddhist Mission Society was founded at Leipzig, and held a Buddhist Congress in 1906. As early as 1888 the Bhikshu Subhadra (Zimmermann) published his *Buddhist Catechism*, while *Buddhist Essays* of Dr Paul Dahlke (q.v.) appeared in 1908. George Grimm's Old Buddhist Community was founded at Utting in Bavaria in 1921; the Gemeinde um Buddha worked in Berlin from 1928-33, and by the Second World War there were active centres also in Hamburg, Stuttgart, Munich, Düsseldorf and Cologne, some publishing their own journals. After the war Guido Auster founded a Bst. Secretariat in Berlin to reorganize the suppressed Bst. activities, and in 1955 a pan-German society was founded as the Deutsche Buddhistische Union, with headquarters in Munich (now Hamburg).

Gesar of Ling   A famous hero of Tibet. A very long poem of war and chivalry of the fifth century A.D. It has been called the Iliad of Central Asia. *See* David-Neel and Yongden, *The Superhuman Life of Gesar of Ling* (1939).

Geshe (Tib.)   Lit. a spiritual preceptor. A man learned in ecclesiastical law, 'a kind of Doctor of Divinity' (Tucci).

Ghantā (Sk.)   A hand-bell used in Tibetan Bst. ceremonies, usually with a Vajra (thunderbolt) handle.

Ginkakuji (Jap.)   *See* **Silver Pavilion.**

Gods   There are many Gods in the Bst. as in the Hindu pantheon, but none is absolute or beyond the Wheel of Life (q.v.). All that exist objectively, as Devas, or hypostatically, as projections from the human mind of aspects of the multiple Reality, are forces in Nature and the mind, and none is worshipped as having power to abrogate Karma (q.v.). All alike are part of manifestation, and with its disappearance at the end of a cycle will also disappear.

Golden Pavilion   *See* **Kinkakuji.**

Golden Precepts, Book of the   A series of ninety small treatises, some pre-Bst., of which H. P. Blavatsky translated parts of thirty-nine to form her work *The Voice of the Silence* (1889). The original is in Senzar (q.v.), for which language see Preface to the work. It belongs to the Yogācāra School of Tibet where the translator received her training.

Gompa (Tib.)   The Tibetan term for a Buddhist monastery.

Goroku (Jap.)   Enigmatic remarks or replies by Zen masters to their pupils, often collected into such works as the *Mumonkan* or *Hekigan Roku* for the use of later generations.

Gotama (P.) **Gautama** (Sk.)   Clan name of the Buddha. Cp. *Siddhārtha.*

Govinda, The Lama Anāgārika   German Buddhist born in 1898 as E. L. Hoffmann. Studied in three European universities before leaving for Ceylon and Burma, where he studied Pali Bsm. Then studied Sk. and Tibetan Bsm. in India; later, after further study, entered the Kargyut-pa School (q.v.),

84

of Tibetan Bsm., founded by Marpa. A painter of distinction, he has held exhibitions in India. His wife, Li Gotami, is a distinguished Parsi artist. Now lives in Almora, India. Recent publications include *Foundations of Tibetan Mysticism* (1959) and *The Psychological Attitude of Early Buddhist Philosophy* (1960).

Gradual School of Enlightenment The Zen School of Shen-Hsiu, pupil of Hung-jen, the Fifth Chinese Zen Patriarch, who founded this School in the North while Hui-neng (q.v.) founded the Sudden School in the South. For meaning of the distinction *see* **Sudden.**

Guilt The Bst. born has no feeling of guilt in the sense of fear of a God who will punish him for his wrong-doing. But he knows that he will by the law of Karma receive the effects of his wrong-doing and in this way suffer the effects of his sin (q.v.).

Guna (Sk.) The three Gunas pertain to Hindu philosophy. They are Sattva, here meaning spiritual happiness or bliss; Rajas, restless energy with the implication of violence, and Tamas, inertia.

Gunin (Jap.) Japanese name for the Fifth Patriarch of China, Hung-jen (q.v.).

Haiku (Jap.) Japanese verse-form of 17 syllables arranged 5, 7, 5. Modern school founded by Bashō in seventeenth century. In its brevity and sole concern with humble things of the moment the Haiku expresses much of the Japanese attitude to life. Yet the overtones are subtle and profound, and what is merely hinted at is more important than what is said. *See* Tanka, the larger form of 31 syllables and *see* Blyth, *Zen in English Literature* (1942). (*See* **Sabi, Wabi.**)

Hakuin, Ekaku (Jap.) Hakuin Zenji, the Zen teacher (1685-1768), was the father of purely Japanese Rinzai Zen Bsm., as

85

distinct from Chinese Ch'an Bsm. practised in Japan. From a humble life in a small temple he became the greatest Zen master of modern times. He believed in fierce, direct methods of training, and entirely remodelled the Kōan system. He trained a very large number of successors. A prolific writer, little of his work is yet published in English, but his 'Song of Meditation' appears in W. of Bsm. No. 137, and, with a long commentary by a modern master, Amakuki Sessan, in Leggett, *A First Zen Reader* (1960). Hakuin produced the famous Kōan, the 'sound of one hand clapping'. He was also a notable sculptor and artist.

Halo   A halo or nimbus, whether as circle behind the head or oval behind the whole figure, is widely found in Bst. art. It presumably represents the effulgence of light round the holy figure produced by his spiritual development. (*See* **Ūrna, Ushnisha**.)

Happiness   (In P. Sukha, the opposite of Dukkha, q.v.). To the Bst. happiness is a by-product of right living, and never an end in itself. The sense of happiness and unhappiness are both transcended in the course of mind-development (Bhāvanā, q.v.). Happiness should not be confused with spiritual states of consciousness such as Samādhi, or Prajñā.

Harsha   King Harshavardhana (606-647) ruled over all N. India as the last of India's great Bst. rulers. After years of fighting he ruled the country as Asoka (q.v.) before him, as a tolerant, enlightened and progressive monarch. A patron of the arts and an author of repute himself, he did his best to enforce Ahimsā, harmlessness, throughout his kingdom. Tolerant in religion, he allowed Hindus full liberty. After his death they gained full power again.

Heart Doctrine, The   The distinction between the Doctrine of the Eye and that of the Heart is basic to Oriental Wisdom.

The former contains the doctrines and practices of a teaching; the latter its Wisdom which cannot be written down. In the words of *The Voice of the Silence*, 'The Dharma of the "Eye" is the embodiment of the external and non-existing. The Dharma of the "Heart" is the embodiment of Bodhi, the Permanent and Everlasting'. (*See* **Eye-Doctrine, Seal.**)

Heart Sutra, The   The Prajñāpāramitā Hridaya Sutra, one of the smallest and, with the Diamond Sutra (q.v.) the most popular of the many Scriptures contained in the vast Prajñā-pāramitā literature. As the Shingyō it is recited daily in count-less Bst. monasteries in Japan. It is the most remarkable epitome of the 'Wisdom which has gone beyond', and one of the greatest scriptures in the world. For trans. *see* Suzuki, *Manual of Zen Buddhism* (with Chin. text, 1935), and Conze, *Buddhist Wisdom Books* (with commentary, 1958). *See also* Suzuki, *Essays in Zen Buddhism, III*, 'Essay V'.

Heaven   *See* **Devachan, Sukhāvatī, Tushita.**

Hekigan Roku (Jap.) or **Hekigan Shū**   In Chinese, Pi-yen Lu or Pi-yen Chi. The Blue Cliff Records or Blue Cliff Collection of 100 stories of previous Masters made by Setchō (q.v.) with his own comments on each in verse. The collection was used by a later Master, Engo (q.v.) who added his own comments and Introductory Words. Engo's pupils published the whole material in 1125 as the Hekigan Roku. In the thirteenth century the work was translated into Japanese and has been ever since one of the most popular such collections. Trans. into English as the *Blue Cliff Records* (1961) by R. D. M. Shaw. *See* also D. T. Suzuki in *The Eastern Buddhist*.

Hell   There is no hell in Bsm. in the sense of endless torture. The hells described and depicted in Bst. countries are temporary states of purgatory (*apāyas*), of which Avīcī is the lowest. The period of suffering is measured by the acts of the sufferer in the previous life. *See* B. C. Law, *Heaven and Hell in Buddhist Perspective* (1925). (*See* **Heaven.**)

Heruka (Tib.) A type of Tantric divinity in Tibetan Bsm. which appears under many names. Another is Hevajra. The 'fierce' manifestation of the Buddha-nature. *See* Snellgrove, *Buddhist Himalaya,* pp. 202-211.

Hetu (Sk. and P.) Cause, antecedent condition. Important term in Bst. doctrines of causation. Nearly synonymous with Pratyaya (q.v.). Must be considered with background of accumulated Karma (q.v.). Looking forward, Hetu is in one sense motive, as the producing cause.

Hiei, Mount (Jap.) A high hill to the N.E. of Kyoto chosen by Dengyō Daishi early ninth century to establish his Tendai (q.v.) (Chin. T'ien-tai) School of Bsm. Scores of other temples were later built on the mountain-side, and the monks in them played a considerable part in the turbulent politics of Kyoto in the fourteenth century.

Himālaya (Sk.) From Ālaya, the abode of Hima, snow. The range of mountains which spread across India, Ladakh, Tibet, Nepal, Sikkim and Bhutan. *See* Snellgrove, *Buddhist Himalaya* (1957).

Hīnayāna Lit. small or lesser career or vehicle (of salvation). A term coined by Mahayanists to distinguish this school of Bsm. from their own *Mahā-yāna,* or great vehicle. The early Hinayana sects of Bsm. numbered 18, and included the *Sarvāstivādins* (q.v.) and the *Mahāsanghikas* (q.v.) as well as that known today as the *Theravāda* (q.v.). The Theravāda, being well established in S. India and Ceylon at the time of the Moslem invasion of India, survived the extermination of the other schools of Hīnayāna, and alone today represents the earliest school of Bsm. (*See* **Mahāyāna, Theravāda.**)

Hindrances *See* **Nivarana.**

Hiri (P.) Moral shame, in sense of being ashamed to do wrong. (*See* **Conscience, Sin.**)

Hiuen Tsiang (The name is spelt variously.) One of China's greatest scholars and her greatest pilgrim-traveller. Born in 602 in Loyang, he left China in 629 and returned in 645 with twenty horses laden with Sk. Bst. works from India. Spent remaining nineteen years of his life translating them into Chinese, thus in effect founding Chinese Bsm. In his epic journey (*see* Watters, *On Yuang Chwang's Travels in India,* 1904-5) he crossed the Gobi Desert, Hindu Kush and Pamirs and reached Bactria. Converted Emperor Harsha (q.v.) to M. Bsm., spent five years in the University of Nālanda (q.v.) and in China introduced the Dharma-lakshana School of Vasu-bandhu. *See* Beal's trans. of *The Life of Hiuen-Tsiang* by *Hwui-Li,* and Grousset, *In the Footsteps of the Buddha* (1932).

Hla, Kyaw Burmese Bst. living in Mandalay who acted as Burmese agent and local Secretary to the Bst. Society of Great Britain and Ireland (1907-23) and from 1924 as Burmese Secretary to the Buddhist Society. With U Kyaw Min raised £1,500 after the war for Bst. Society to publish Bst. books in London. Has since secured hundreds of members for the Society. The most valuable friend to Bsm. in England in the East.

Hō (Jap.) Japanese term for Dharma, the Buddha's teaching. Also used as a call by Zen monks as they file through the streets with a begging bowl. (*See* **Takuhatsu.**)

Hōben (Jap.) Means or device. (*See* **Upāya.**)

Holy Places of Buddhism The four sites visited by Buddhist pilgrims are the birth-place, Lumbinī Park (q.v.); Buddha

89

Gaya (q.v.), which is the site of the Enlightenment; Sarnath (q.v.), where the First Sermon was preached, and Kusinara (q.v.), the scene of the Great Decease.

Homelessness For the Going Forth, as the Buddha went forth to find salvation for mankind, *see* Pabbajjā, the symbolic leaving the world by the Sāmanera or Novice. A layman who leaves home in this sense is called an Anāgārika (q.v.).

Hondō (Jap.) The main hall, usually a separate building, in a Jap. monastery, used principally for lectures and meals. The image in it is usually that of the Founder. Cp. *Butsuden, Zen-dō.*

Hōnen Hōnen Shōnin (1133-1211) was the founder of the Jōdo-Shū or 'Pure Land' School in Japan. Standard life is: *Honen, His Life and Teaching,* Coates and Ishizuka. Kyoto (1925). (*See* **Jōdo, Pure Land, Shin.**)

Honolulu, Buddhism in *See* **Hunt, Dr Ernest.**

Horner, Miss I. B., M.A.(CANTAB.) English Pali scholar. Librarian, Newnham College, Cambridge, 1923-36. Pupil of Mrs Rhys Davids and succeeded her in 1942 as Hon. Secretary of the Pali Text Society (q.v.) Succeeded Dr. W. Stede (q.v.) as President in 1960. Vice-President of the Buddhist Society, London. Author of *Women under Primitive Buddhism* (1930), *The Early Buddhist Theory of Man Perfected* (1936), and co-author with Dr Ananda Coomaraswamy of *Gotama the Buddha* (1948).

Hōryūji (Jap.) Bst. monastery at Nara, Japan. Founded by Empress Suiko as college for Bst Philosophy. Opened by Prince Regent Shōtoku in 607. Contains some of oldest wooden buildings in the world. Treasure-house of Buddhist art, architectural and sculptural. The famous frescoes in Kondō destroyed by fire but superbly replaced. Architecture inspired by Chinese models of T'ang Dynasty through Korean copies.

Hossō (Jap.) Hossō School of Japanese Bsm. developed from the Mind-Only School of Vasubandhu brought to China from India by Hiuen Tsiang (q.v.). Brought to Japan by Dōshō (c. 653) and became one of the six Nara sects.

Hossu (Jap.) Short stick carried by Zen Masters. Originally a fly whisk, with a tuft of horse-tail at the end, it became a religious instrument used in ceremonies. Cp. *Keisaku, Shippei.*

Hōtei (Jap.) The well-known seated figure with the large paunch, usually laughing and hence called the Laughing Buddha. Historically derived from Maitreya (q.v.), the Buddha-to-be, through the Chinese form of Mi-lo-Fu, the figure has gradually lost religious significance and has become merely the God of Luck.

Hsin (Chin.) In Japanese Shin or Kokoro. A key term in Zen Bsm. Mind or heart, but not in Western sense of either term. The deepest aspects of both, inmost heart or deepest mind; soul but without that term's theological implications. That factor in each human being which is part of All-Mind. (*See* **Shin**.)

Hsin Hsin Ming (Chin.) In Japanese, Shin Jin Mei. A long and beautiful poem by Seng T'san, the Third Chinese Patriarch of Zen Bsm. Written c. 600 it contains a summary of Zen teaching. Translated as 'Believing in Mind' (Suzuki), 'On Trust in the Heart' (Waley), and as 'The Seal of Man Engraved' (A. F. Price). For commentary *see* Blyth, *Zen and Zen Classics*, Vol. I (1960), where the meaning of the title is explained.

Hsu Yün Chinese Ch'an master who died in Kiangsi, China, in 1959 at the age of 120. Recognized as the successor to all the 'Five Houses' (q.v.) of Ch'an Bsm. A few of his sermons appear in Chang Chen-chi, *The Practice of Zen* (1959) and more in Luk, *Ch'an and Zen Teaching* (1960). Autobiography

91

in preparation for publication. For portrait and account of traditional passing of Zen master, with final gāthā, *see, Middle Way,* Vol. 34, p. 172.

Hti (Burm.)   The umbrella-shaped top to a Stūpa, often hung with jewels. That on the Shwe Dagon (q.v.) is very large and of enormous value.

Huang-Po (Chin.)   In Jap. Ōbaku: d. 850. A pupil two generations removed from the Sixth Patriarch Hui-neng, Huang-Po was the Zen Master of Rinzai (q.v.) and so in some sense the founder of that School of Zen. The Ōbaku sub-School of Zen, however, was brought to Japan in 1654 by Ingen. Some of Huang-Po's teaching was recorded by P'ei Hsiu as *The Zen Teaching of Huang-Po on the Transmission of Mind,* for which see trans. by John Blofeld, 1958.

Hua Tou (Chin.)   Lit. a word's end. A shortened version of the Kōan (q.v.), in that a fragment only of the story or situation is used for this form of Zen meditation. Thus instead of the whole story of Jōshu's Mu (q.v.), the Chinese Hua Tou would be just Wu (Jap. Mu) meaning No!

Hui Hai (Chin.)   Chinese Zen Master (d. 788), a disciple of Matsu. Author of a work translated by John Blofeld as *The Path to Sudden Attainment* (1948). According to Suzuki, 'one of the most illuminating works on Zen Buddhism when it was about to attain its full development after Hui-neng'.

Hui-k'o (Chin.)   In Jap. Eka. The Second Chinese Zen Patriarch, who received his enlightenment from Bodhidharma (q.v.). A famous figure in Chinese art for his dramatic gesture in cutting off his arm as he stood outside in the snow, to impress Bodhidharma with his determination to be admitted and given Zen. (*See* **Patriarchs.**)

Hui-neng (Chin.) In Canton dialect, Wei-lang. In Jap., Enô (637-713). The famous Sixth Patriarch of Chinese Zen Bsm., the virtual founder of Ch'an (Zen) Bsm. as a School of its own. His was the 'Sudden' school as distinct from the 'Gradual' school of Shen-hsiu (q.v.), his fellow pupil of Hung-jen. The latter soon died out, but both the Rinzai and Sōtō branches of Hui-neng's School have flourished for a thousand years. Hui-neng was the last Zen Patriarch, though many famous Zen Masters followed him. For a trans. by Wong Mou-lam of the Tan Ching, the Platform Sutra of the Patriarch, *see* the *Sutra of Wei Lang (Hui-neng)* (1944) and subsequent editions.

Humphreys, Christmas, Q.C., M.A., LL.B.(CANTAB.), J.P. English Buddhist. Born 1901. Adopted Bsm. as way of life in 1918. Attended Bst. lectures by Francis Payne (q.v.) in 1923. On 19 November 1924 founded, with Miss Aileen Faulkner, later Mrs. Christmas Humphreys, Buddhist Lodge of the Theosophical Society, which in 1926 became the Buddhist Society. Elected founding President, with Miss Faulkner as Hon. Secretary. Principal author of *What is Buddhism?* (1928) and *Concentration and Meditation* (1935). Author of *Studies in the Middle Way* (1940), *Karma and Rebirth* (1943), *Walk On!* (1947), *Via Tokyo* (1948), *Zen Buddhism* (1949), *Buddhism* (Pelican Series, 1951). Edited *A Buddhist Students' Manual* (1956). Author of *The Way of Action* (1960), and *Zen Comes West* (1960). Editor of *The Wisdom of Buddhism* (1960), and of the present work. Most recent works include *A Western Approach to Zen* (1972) and *Exploring Buddhism* (1974). Vice-President of the World Fellowship of Buddhists. Agent in Europe for works of Dr D. T. Suzuki. A Trustee of the Mahatma Letters Trust for the book *The Mahatma Letters to A. P. Sinnett*.

Hung-jen (Chin.) In Jap. Gunin (605-675). The Fifth Chinese Zen Patriarch. He had, it is said, 500 disciples, the most famous being Shen-hsiu and Hui-neng (q.v.).

Hunt, Dr. Ernest Honolulu has a large Japanese Bst. population. After first World War, for want of Bst. Schools many Japanese forced to become Christians. Two English Buddhists, Dr. Ernest Hunt and his wife Dorothy, with help of Japanese of Shin-Shū, opened and obtained American recognition for Bst. Schools. Later Bst. temples of Shin-Shū and Sōtō Zen-Shū were opened, and Japanese now able to remain Bst. Founder Editor of *The Buddhist Annual of Hawaii*. [D. 1967.]

Hutukhtu Many spellings. The Mongol for Tulku (q.v.) which itself has many spellings in English.

Hyakujō (Jap.) (Chin., Pai-chang). Zen Master of China (720-814) who founded the Zen (Ch'an) monastic system. Before his time, Zen monks lived in the monasteries of the Vinaya School. Author of the phrase 'No work, no eating', he believed in the spiritual value of hard work, and made the whole work of the monastery and its grounds part of the monk's training.

Hyōshigi (Jap.) Two solid pieces of hard wood used as clappers in Rinzai Zen monasteries to mark periods in the meditation. The blocks may be six inchest to twelve inches long; the noise made is startling.

Ichinen (Jap.) A term of Zen Bsm. Lit. One thought, or mental event. When this first happens the mind is said to be 'disturbed', and there arises an awareness of duality, of true and untrue, good and evil. A mind which can revert to the state of No-Mind, before this 'disturbance' occurs, is free from the anxiety, fear and desire which all thought produces. Cp. *Ekacitta*.

I-ching (Chin.) The 'great spirit of inquiry', the 'perpetual knocking at a door' (Suzuki) which is necessary before the break-through to Satori is attained. The word 'doubt' is too negative, for the state of mind is also fiercely positive. Not to be confused with the Chinese classic, *I Ching* ('Book of Changes').

Iddhis (P.) (Sk., Riddhi). Attributes or powers of a state (of perfection). There are ten iddhis or supernormal powers developed on the path to arahatship, including clairvoyance, clairaudience, telepathy, recalling one's former lives and those of others. It is forbidden to use these psychic powers for one's personal benefit. The higher *iddhis* are the spiritual Modes of Insight attained by the practice of *Jhāna* (q.v.). Cp. *Siddhis* of Yoga teaching. (*See* **Abhijñā**.)

Ignorance *See* **Avidyā**.

Ikebana (Jap.) *See* **Flower Arrangement**.

India Bsm. founded in India by Gautama Buddha, sixth century B.C. Adopted by Asoka as state religion of his empire, c. 250 B.C. (*see* **Asoka**). Flourished under the kings Milinda (c. 100 B.C.), Kanishka (c. A.D. 80) and Harsha (A.D. 606-648), the two latter being converts to the Mahayana School. Declined after Moslem conquest of Sindh, A.D. 712, and finally suppressed by Moslem persecution A.D. 1200. *See* Pratt, *Pilgrimage of Buddhism*. (*See* **Maha Bodhi Society**.)

Indriya (P.) Faculty, a sense-organ. In the Abhidhamma (q.v.) twenty two are given. They include the six Sense organs, five kinds of Feeling, five Virtues, and three super-mundane faculties of the highest Knowledge. Paññindriya is reason, the faculty of Paññā (Prajñā), Wisdom.

Ingen (Jap.) Founder in 1654 of the Ōbaku (q.v.) School of Japanese Zen Bsm.

Inka (Jap.) *See* **Seal**.

Inkin (Jap.) A small sounding instrument of wood, carried in the hand and struck with a small stick attached to it with string. Used in a Rinzai Zendō to mark beginning and end of period of meditation. *See* Suzuk:, *The Training of the Zen Buddhist Monk*, p. 106 (1934).

Innen (Jap.) Zen term used to describe feeling of causal link or relationship of sympathetic affinity between speaker and some other person, as though coming from past Karma (q.v.).

Insight *See* **Vipassanā,** *but* cp. *Satori.*

Intoxicants The fifth of the Bst. Precepts (q.v.) is a vow to train oneself to avoid those intoxicants which tend to sloth, on the ground that as it is difficult enough at all times to remain 'mindful and self-possessed' it is foolish to make the task more difficult with alcohol. For those who meditate deeply, all alcohol is bad as it affects the finer sheathes of the tissues of the brain.

Intuition The faculty in the mind of im-mediate knowledge as distinct from the intellect which can never know more than 'about it and about'. It has been described as knowing without knowing how you know. The Bst. equivalent is Buddhi (q.v.) which, however, has a 'higher intellectual' content. Hence Dr Suzuki's insistence on a Zen intuition which is free from such taint.

Ippen (Jap.) Ippen Shōnin (1239-89), a wandering monk of the Pure Land School of Japanese Bsm., founded the Ji sect of it, or Ji-Shū, in 1276. As he left no writings the school has never become important.

Issā (P.) Envy.

Īs(h)vara (Sk.) 'He who wields sovereignty.' The Lord or Overlord in the Hindu pantheon, the Absolute personified. Esoterically, the Highest Self, as in Avalokitesvara, the Isvara, 'the Lord who is seen', looked up to, within.

I-Tsing Chinese scholar and pilgrim who, like Fa-Hsien and Hiuen-Tsiang before him, travelled through the Holy Places of Indian Bsm. and recorded what he found. In 671 he left on his travels by sea to Sumatra, thence to Bengal and Magadha (q.v.). He returned home in 695, having spent years in Sumatra translating his immense collection of Sk. MSS. into Chinese. His account of his travels (*The Buddhist Religion*, trans. Takakusu, 1896) shows a further decline of Bsm. in India on the earlier records of Fa-Hsien and Hiuen Tsiang (q.v.).

Jackson, R. J. First English Buddhist to declare himself as such, and to proclaim the Dhamma in public in England. Lectured from a box in Regent's Park in 1905. Original Member of the Buddhist Society of Great Britain and Ireland, 1907. Became a self-taught scholar on Theravāda and Indian philosophy, and wrote widely in Bst. journals. Author of *India's Quest for Reality* (1938). *See* 'Development of Buddhism in England' in B.S.M. [Died 1967.]

Jains A member of one of the many religions of India. So called after the first of its Tirthankaras, 'ford-makers', called Mahāvīra, the Jaina or Jina, Conqueror, a title also applied to the Buddha. The twenty-fourth in the line, Vardhamāna Mahāvīra (619-546 B.C.) was an elder contemporary of the Buddha. The Jains were known to the early Bsts. as Nirgranthas, 'without knots', and their variant teaching on the doctrine of Karma, Kiriyavāda, was freely discussed. See E. J. Thomas, *History of Buddhist Thought*, Chap. IX. They stress Ahimsā, harmlessness or non-violence, to an extreme degree.

Japan Bsm. entered Japan (c. A.D. 550) from Korea. The Empress Suiko became a convert, and the Prince Regent, known as Shōtoku Taishi (q.v.), did his best to encourage it. He drew up Japan's first 'Constitution', proclaiming the 'Triune Treasure' of Buddha, Dhamma and Sangha as the basis of the

97

national life. From that time on, Japan took over and made her own the fruits of Chinese culture. In the ninth century, Dengyō Daishi, the founder of the Tendai Sect, and Kōbō Daishi, the founder of the Shingon Sect, harmonized Buddhism with Shinto, producing the Ryōbu Shintō (q.v.), a fusion which lasted for a thousand years.

In the twelfth century Hōnen brought the Jōdo School to Japan, from which developed the Shin-Shū, founded by Shinran. About the same time Nichiren founded his School which is based on the Saddharma Pundarīka Sūtra, and the two branches of Zen Shū, Rinzai and Sōtō, were re-founded. In 1868, at the Meiji restoration, Bsm. was dis-established. The largest schools today are Shin and Zen.

Jarāmarana (Sk. and P.) Jarā, old age, and Marana, death. The twelfth of the Nidānas (q.v.). The word *marana* (cf. Latin *mors*) is related to *Māra* (q.v.).

Jātaka (P.) A birth story. A work of the Theravāda Canon (A.P.C. 277) containing a collection of 550 stories of the former lives of the Buddha Gotama. Of great value in folklore and Bst. mythology as the background of moral tales. For trans. *see* A.P.C.

Jāti (P.) Birth. The eleventh in the chain of the Nidānas (q.v.).

Javana (P.) Impulsion. Impulsive, kamma-producing moments, technical terms in the elaborate analysis of consciousness in the Abhidhamma (q.v.).

Jetavana The grove (*vana*) of Prince Jeta which Anathapindika of Sravasti bought from the Prince with as many pieces of gold as would cover the ground, and gave to the Buddha for the use by the Sangha as a Retreat (q.v.).

Jhāna (P.)   A state of serene contemplation attained by meditation. Eight states of Jhāna are recognized, but only in the highest is utter elimination of idea of 'self' attained, and the complete union with Reality (*Samādhi*) experienced. These mystic states are not an end in themselves but only means to attainment of *Jhānavimokkha*, i.e. emancipation through Jhāna. (*See* **Dhyāna, Samādhi, Tiloka.**)

Ji (Jap.)   (1) A suffix to a name, meaning temple-monastery. Thus Engaku-ji at Kamakura. The suffix -In has the same meaning, as in Chion-In, the mother temple of the Jōdo sect. The suffix -An means a smaller temple within a larger unit, as in Shōden-an, Dr Suzuki's house in Engaku-ji.

(2) (also pronounced Shi), teacher, as Hakuin Zen-ji, the Zen teacher.

(3) A fact, event, object, particular thing; the opposite to Ri (q.v.), which means principles, rather as spiritual principles. (*See* **Jijimuge.**)

Jijimuge (Jap.)   The unimpeded interdiffusion (*muge*) of all Ji meaning things, facts, objects. The summit of intellectual understanding of the non-duality of manifestation. The 'Thou art THAT' of Hindu philosophy still admits three things to be One; Jijimuge is beyond even Unity. The supreme teaching of the Kegon (q.v.) School of Japanese Bsm. *See* exposition by Suzuki, W. of Bsm. No. 106.

Jikijitsu (Jap.)   The leader of Zazen in the Zendō of a Rinzai Zen monastery. He is in charge of the meditation in the Zendō, keeps time with the clappers and gong, leads recitations and keeps discipline. The most important official after the Rōshi. Cp. *Jisha.*

Jina (Sk.)   A conqueror. One of the many terms used to describe the Buddha, though more usually applied to the Jains (q.v.) who have adopted it as a special title for their own leaders.

Jinarājadāsa, C., M.A.(CANTAB.) Distinguished Sinhalese Buddhist and Theosophist. When Vice-President of the Theosophical Society presented the Buddhist Society, London, then the Buddhist Lodge, with its Charter, 19/11/24. President of the Theosophical Society until death in 1953 at age of 78.

Jiriki (Jap.)   Salvation through one's own efforts, as opposed to *Tariki* (q.v.), salvation through the efforts of Another. All Japanese sects are attributable to one of these two divisions. Jōdo, for example, is a *Tariki* sect, and Zen, Jiriki. Here *Ji* means self.

Jisha (Jap.)   An important official in a Zen temple. With the Jikijitsu (q.v.) he handles all Zendō affairs. He keeps the Zendō clean, helps newcomers, serves tea, and reports regularly to the Rōshi. He is the administrative as distinct from the training official in the Zendō life.

Jīva (Sk. and P.)   Life, the life-principle. Life regarded as a principle; hence unit of life, the soul. Cp. *Ātman* and *see* **Self**.

Jizō (Jap.)   Sk. Kshitigarbha, Chin. Ti-Tsang. A Bodhisattva who in his travels from India through China to Japan has become the god of wayfarers and children, especially of children who died young. Stone statues to him are found in the fields all over Japan. In art he has always appeared with a crystal ball in the left hand and a staff in the right. Connexion with Bsm. obscure.

Jñāna (Sk.)   Wisdom, higher intellect. But the term is flexible and sometimes means no more than worldly knowledge. It appears in many compounds, as in Vi-jñāna, consciousness.

Jōdo (Jap.)The Pure Land School of China founded in the fourth century on the smaller and larger Sukhāvatī-vyūha Sutras and the Amitāyur-dhyāna Sutra. When transferred to Japan, Hōnen Shōnin and Shinran Shōnin (q.v.) turned this balanced doctrine of faith and works into an extremist practice of salvation by faith alone. (*See* **Hōnen, Pure Land School, Shin, Shinran Shōnin.**)

Jōriki (Jap.) The power derived from a concentrated mind, which enables such a mind to cope with all situations and thus to remain in control of circumstances. As taught in the Zen-shū it is this power which helps the seeker to achieve his first Kenshō (q.v.) or break-through into Non-Duality.

Josaphat (corruption of Bodhisat; other versions are Yosa-phat and Yudasaf) The account of the canonization of the Buddha by the Roman and Greek sects of Christianity is related in the story of Barlaam and Josaphat *See Buddhist Birth Stories* (Mrs Rh. Davids, pp. 239-242), *and Baralam and Yewasef*, Wallis Budge (1923). In the Greek Church 26 August is dedicated to St. Josaphat, and in the Roman Church, 27 November is dedicated to both Barlaam and Josaphat.

Jōshū (Ch. Chao-chou) One of the earliest and greatest Chinese Zen masters (778-897). Famous for his answer 'Mu' (q.v.) to the question, 'Has a dog Buddha-nature?' His methods were extremely 'direct', and his Goroku (sayings) pungent and penetrating.

Jūdō (Jap.) First known as Jū-jutsu, this Japanese form of wrestling applies the principles of Taoism and Zen to physical contest. Victory is gained by giving way, and the attacker's strength is used to his own undoing (cp. *Kendō*).

101

Jūshoku (Jap.) The head monk of a Zen temple, of which there may be many in a monastery. He may have the rank of Oshō (q.v.). He may hold both the office and the rank, as Professor Ogata (q.v.). Also used for the incumbent or 'parish priest' of a small temple.

Kahdam-pa (Tib.) A school of Tibetan Bsm. founded in the eleventh century by Atīsa (q.v.). Entirely reorganized and reformed by Tsongkha-pa in the fifteenth century as the Gelug-pa, the 'Yellow Hat' school of which the Dalai and Panchen Lamas are members.

Kakemono (Jap.) A Japanese scroll-picture. Painted with a brush and ink on silk or paper, and then mounted with rollers at top and bottom. One displayed at a time in the Tokonoma (q.v.), the rest of the collection being rolled up and stored. The subject may be religious or secular. Cp. *Makimono*.

Kālāmas (P.) A tribe in north-east India in the time of the Buddha known to history as the recipients of the Buddha's famous advice on the subject of authority in the search for Truth. The Buddhists' authority for refusing to recognize authority for Truth, and the basis of their tolerance. *See* W. of Bsm., No. 22.

Kali Yuga *See* **Yuga.**

Kalki Avatāra (Sk.) The White Horse Avatǎr. The Avatǎr (q.v.) of Vishnu yet to come, say the Hindus. According to the Buddhists he is the Buddha-to-be, Maitreya (q.v.).

Kalmuk The Kalmuk Tartars on the Volga are Bsts., but being nomad have never built temples. Recently dispersed, some 1,000 live in New Jersey, U.S.A. under the Dilowa Hutukhtu. A smaller group has settled down in Munich.

Kalpa (Sk.) The length of a Day and Night of Brahma, the 'Unrolling and rolling up' of the universe as described in the Pali Canon. It is given in Hindu chronology as 4,320,000,000 years. (*See* **Manvantara.**)

Kāma (Sk.) Desire of the senses, especially sexual desire. Kāma is one of the four *āsavas* (q.v.) or mental defilements, and is the first of the six factors of existence the elimination of which is essential for liberation from rebirth. The *kāmalokas* are the worlds of sense desire. (*Kāma* must not be confused with *kamma*, the Pali version of Karma.)

Kamakura (Jap.) Important period of Japanese history (1185-1335) when the rise of the Shōguns (q.v.) made Kamakura, a city on the sea to the south of Tokyo, a second capital, and drew teachers and artists from the seat of the Emperor, Kyoto. Here Bst. Schools from China, notably Rinzai Zen, found a new home. Here was the birthplace of Bushidō, and the rise in importance of Jūdō and Kendō. Engakuji (q.v.) was founded here in 1282, and the Daibutsu (q.v.) erected in 1252.

Kāma-loka (P.) *See* **Kāma** *and* **Tiloka.**

Kāmesu Micchācāra (P.) 'Wrong' (unwholesome) because sensual conduct; unlawful sexual intercourse. To undertake the training to abstain from this is the third Precept. (*See* **Pansil, Precepts.**)

Kami (Jap.) The nature forces or 'Gods' of Shintō (q.v.).

Kammanta (P.) Action. Sammā Kammanta, Right Action, is the fourth step on the Noble Eightfold Path (q.v.) and is there given as abstention from Killing, Stealing and unlawful Sexual Intercourse. In its expanded form, however, Right Action in Bsm. covers a very great deal more. *See* Humphreys, *The Way of Action* (1960).

Kammatthāna (P.) Subject of meditation. A term in the Abhidhamma philosophy.

Kammavipāka (P.) Maturing or ripening of past causes under the law of Karma (q.v.). Hence the results of deeds which have ripened. (*See* **Sin.**)

Kanchō (Jap.) The Abbot of a monastery. The administrative head, who may or may not act as Rōshi (q.v.).

Kandy Ancient capital of Ceylon, 1592 to 1815. Contains the Temple of the Tooth (Dalada Maligawa), inner shrine of which contains the famous Tooth relic in a series of magnificently jewelled gold caskets. Kandy is scene of the Perahera annual procession in August, when the Relic is carried round the city on elephant-back in a long torchlight procession.

Kanishka An Indo-Scythian king who was instrumental in spreading Mahāyāna Bsm. in India and Afghanistan (c. A.D. 80). He was a convert to Bsm. of M. School and convened the great Council at Purusapura (Peshawar) at which Asvaghosha is said to have confounded the adherents of the Theravāda doctrines. His powerful patronage spread Bsm. all over India. (*See* **Councils** *and* **Kashmir.**)

Kanjur (Tib.) 'The translation of the Word.' The first part of the Tibetan Bst. Canon, the other being the Tanjur (q.v.). The Kanjur contains 108 volumes. Some are concerned with the Vinaya, monastic discipline; some set forth the prajñā-pāramitā philosophy, some extol the virtues of the Bodhisattvas, and others expound the Trikāya and the Ālaya-Vijñāna doctrines. Most are translations from the Sk. and Chinese, of great value where the originals have been lost. (*See* **Bu-ston.**)

Kanna (Jap.) Form of Zen founded by Daie Sōkō in twelfth century. 'Patriarchal' as distinct from Mokushō Zen or

Tathāgata Zen. Rinzai as distinct from Sōtō Zen (q.v.) which favours still-sitting as compared with the more dynamic or sudden technique of the Rinzai School.

Kapilavastu (Sk.) **Kapilavatthu** (P.) The capital of the Sākya kingdom where dwelt King Suddhodana and his wife Māya. The child who became Buddha was born nearby at Lumbinī (q.v.).

Kara (Jap.) *See* **Kesa.**

Kargyut-pa (Tib.) One of the principal schools of Tibetan Bsm., founded in the eleventh century by Marpa, and his famous pupil Milarepa (q.v.). Known as the semi-reformed school as compared with the Reformed School of Tsong-kha-pa (fourteenth century), which he called the Gelug-pa, 'the Virtuous Ones', and the Nyingma-pa or unreformed school now largely found in Nepal, Sikkim and Kham, whose patron saint is Padma Sambhava. In the Kargyut-pa stress is laid on long periods of meditation. Lacking the strong monastic discipline and orthodox tradition of the Gelug-pas, it has produced great minds and great achievement while in its lower ranks descending to the level of the unreformed Nyingma-pas. Its members may marry. *See* Evans-Wentz, *Tibet's Great Yogi Milarepa* (1928). (*See* **Tibetan Buddhism, Schools of.**)

Kārli Buddhist Assembly Hall or Stūpa house cut out of rock face in the Western Ghats between Bombay and Poona. C. first century B.C. Main Hall is largest such in existence, being 124 feet by 25 feet by 40 feet in height, as large as nave of Norwich Cathedral. The Stūpa itself, and the Buddha Rūpa with feet down, is a magnificent specimen of early Bst. art.

Karma (Sk.) **Kamma** (P.) Root meaning 'Action'; derived meaning 'action and the appropriate result of action'; the law

105

of cause and effect. As applied to the moral sphere it is the Law of ethical Causation, through the operation of which a man 'reaps what he sows', builds his character, makes his destiny, and works out his salvation.

Karma is not limited by time or space, and is not strictly individual; there is group *karma*, family, national, etc.

The doctrine of re-birth is an essential corollary to that of *Karma*, the individual coming into physical life with a character and environment resulting from his actions in the past. His character, family, circumstance and destiny are all, therefore, his *Karma*, and according to his reaction to his present 'destiny' he modifies and builds his future. *Karma* does not, in itself, bind to the wheel of re-birth; the binding element is personal desire for the fruit of action. Liberation is therefore achieved by elimination of desire for self. *See* Humphreys, *Karma and Re-birth*. (*See* **Causation, Re-birth, Tanha.**)

Karuna (Sk.)   Active compassion. One of the 'two pillars' of Mahayana Bsm., the other being *Prajñā* (q.v.). One of the Four *Brahma Vihāras* or Divine States resulting from the elimination of selfish inclinations. (*See* **Bodhisattva, Compassion.**)

Kashmir, Buddhism in   Bsm. was early known in Kashmir, and Asoka (q.v.) added it to his empire. A later Bst. patron was the Kushan King Kanishka, who held a Bst. Council in the capital, Srinagar, which Asoka had founded. The Bst. art of the country, of high degree of workmanship, showed Greek influence.

Kasina (P.)   From Sk. Kritsna, complete, as a circle. Physical devices used as aids in early stages of meditation. In particular, coloured circles or discs. From the sight the meditator passes to the acquired image seen with closed eyes, thence to correlated images and so on until a condition is reached in which sense-reaction is suspended.

Kāsyapa (Sk.) **Kassapa** (P.) Or Mahā-Kāsyapa. A Brahmin of Magadha who became a close disciple of the Buddha, and was at the time of his death the senior member of his Sangha. He therefore presided over the first Council, held immediately after the passing. The Zen School regarded him as their First Patriarch from the story of the 'transmission' of the 'heart-seal' when the Buddha held up a golden flower and Mahā-kasyapa smiled.

Katmandu The present capital of Nepal. One of the three beautiful cities of the central plain. (*See* **Patan** *and* **Bhatgaon.**) Contains many Bst. temples and shrines. The fourth Congress of the World Fellowship of Buddhists was held there in November 1956.

Kats! Loud exclamation repeatedly used by Zen master Rinzai when assisting his pupils to achieve Satori. *See* Suzuki, *Essays in Zen Buddhism*, First Series, pp. 279-80.

Kāya (P.) Group, and hence body, as Dharma-kāya Cp. *Rūpa*.

Kegon (Jap.) In Chinese, Hua-yen. Bst. School founded in China in the seventh century and brought to Japan by Dōsen in 736. Mother temple is Tōdaiji at Nara, the largest wooden building in the world, which houses a vast figure of Vairocana (q.v.). The teaching centres round the Avatamsaka Sutra (q.v.), 'the culmination of Chinese Bst. thought' (Suzuki). (*See* **Jijimuge.**) Although one of the smallest Bst. schools its influence has been enormous.

Keisaku (Jap.) A light flat stick, representing the sword of Manjusri, used by a senior monk in the Zendō (q.v.) to rouse

107

monks falling asleep or, at invitation, to smack shoulder muscles grown stiff from sitting.

Kendō (Jap.) The Japanese form of fencing. A two-handed sword is used, of bamboo strips lightly bound in leather. Scoring points are limited to blows where an armoured man might be hit effectively, on the wrist, on the head or at the side. Light lacquered armour is worn, with gauntlets and an iron helmet. Much ceremony is observed in the formal contests. For the Zen spirit of the sword *see* Suzuki, *Zen and Japanese Culture*, Chaps. V and VI (1959).

Kenshō (Jap.) 'Seeing into one's own nature', the goal of Zen practice. The first experience of Satori (q.v.).

Kesa. (Jap.) Sk. Kāshāya. A brocade robe worn over the left shoulder by members of the Zen school. A much smaller version, a square apron hung from the neck, is known as the *rakusa*, and can also be worn by laymen. In daily conversation this smaller garment is often referred to as a *kesa*. All these garments are worn over the *koromo* (q.v.) which may vary with the Bst. school.

Khantaka (P.) The Buddha's horse. A favourite subject in Bst. art. His charioteer was Channa.

Khata (Tib.) The ceremonial white scarf, of humble or costly material according to the status of both parties, which is given to Tibetan dignitaries, ecclesiastical and lay, on formal occasions.

Khobilkhan Many variant spellings. The Mongolian term for the Tibetan Tulku (q.v.). Cp. *Hutukhtu*.

Kinhin (Jap.) 'Sutra-walking.' Formal marching round the

Zendō of a Zen monastery during periods of rest from Za-Zen meditation, to loosen stiff joints and exercise the body.

Kinkakuji (Jap.) The Golden Pavilion erected near Kyoto in 1383 by Ashikaga Yoshimitsu, one of the greatest of the Shōguns. One of the most beautiful buildings in Japan, in proportion, craftsmanship and setting. It was recently burnt down by a fanatic but rebuilt in replica. Cp. *Silver Pavilion*, erected by the Shōgun's grandson.

Kisāgotami The story of Kisāgotami and the Mustard Seed is charmingly related in the Fifth Book of the *Light of Asia* (Arnold) and reproduced in *The Wisdom of Bsm.* No. 39. It is the timeless story of the universality of sorrow.

Kiu-Te, The Book of An esoteric work of the Tibetan School of Bsm. referred to many times by the Masters who wrote *The Mahatma Letters to A. P. Sinnett* (q.v.) (1924). It contains thirty-five volumes of text and fourteen of Commentaries. *See* Section XLVII in the so-called third volume of *The Secret Doctrine*, being collected papers of H. P. Blavatsky.

Klesa (Sk.) **Kilesa** (P.) Defilement. Moral depravity; in particular the 'three fires' of hatred, lust and illusion which must be eliminated on the Path.

Kō-an (Jap.) From the Chin. Kung-an, a public document. A technical term in Rinzai Zen Bsm. A word or phrase of non-sensical language which cannot be 'solved' by the intellect but which holds its attention while a higher faculty takes over. Used as an exercise for breaking the limitations of thought and developing the intuition (q.v.), thereby attaining a flash of awareness beyond duality (Kenshō), and later Satori (q.v.). This exercise, and its companion the Mondō, is not used in Sōtō Zen. *See* Suzuki, *Essays in Zen Buddhism*, Second Series, Essay I (1933).

Kōbō Daishi (Kukai) The Founder of the Shingon (q.v.) School of Japanese Buddhism. A religious genius and social reformer, an engineer and artist. He was instrumental, with Dengyō Daishi (q.v.) in establishing the union of Shintō with Buddhism known as Ryōbu Shintō (q.v.). He died at the monastery founded by him on Mount Kōya (Kōyasan, q.v.), still the headquarters of Shingon. (*See* **Japan, Shingon.**)

Koicha (Jap.) Lit. thick tea. Tea used in the Tea-ceremony (Cha-no-yu) of Japan, to be distinguished from the 'thin' tea which usually follows.

Koji (Jap.) A Zen lay disciple.

Kokoro (Jap.) The Japanese reading of the ideograph of which the Sino-Japanese reading is Shin (q.v.), in the sense of the essence of man whether known as 'heart' or 'mind'.

Kokushi (Jap.) A title given to a great teacher in Japan by the Emperor of the day, meaning National Teacher, e.g. Daitō Kokushi, the posthumous title of Daitō, a great Zen Master of the fourteenth century, and founder of Daitokuji.

Korea Bsm. was introduced from China between A.D. 350-370, and by about A.D. 500 had become the state religion. Under its influence Korea attained a high state of prosperity and culture. Confucianism became state religion under new dynasty about A.D. 1500. Revival of Bsm. started about fifty years ago. The Bsm. of Korea is a blend of several M. Schools, but Rinzai Zen has long predominated. Korean art is largely Chinese, but a special Korean quality was added to the styles passed on to Japan. Thus, much of Nara Bst. art is Korean, perhaps wrought by Korean craftsmen. The Buddhist Association of Korea is hard at work rebuilding temples destroyed in the last war, and the Government of South Korea gives generous assistance. (*See* **Won.**)

Koromo (Jap.) The black or dark blue robe worn by a Japanese monk or priest over which he wears the *Kesa* (q.v.) or distinguishing garment of his Shū or Bst. school.

Körös, Alexander Csoma b. 1790. Hungarian scholar whose Tibetan-English Dictionary and Grammar of the Tibetan Language, published in Calcutta in 1834, paved the way for all later research into Tibetan Bsm.

Kosala The ruling clan in the Kingdom of Kosala at the time of the Buddha, in that part of N. India corresponding to modern Nepal. The capital city was Sravasti, where the Buddha spent much of his time. Benares was in the same kingdom, which was the paramount power in N. India from the seventh century B.C. until its absorption into that of Magadha, c. 300 B.C. (*See* **Magadha, Pali.**)

Kōyasan Mother temple of the Shingon School of Bsm. in Japan. Founded on a beautiful hill south of Kyoto by Kobo Daishi (q.v.) in 816. He is buried there and his tomb is the object of much devotion. One of the two most popular Bst. centres in Japan. (*See also* **Hiei.**)

Kriyā (Sk.) **Kiriya** (P.) Acting, Action. From the root Kri from which comes Karma (q.v.). In Pali a 'functional' action not producing Kamma. Cp. *Wu-wei.*

Ks(h)ānti (Sk.) One of the six Pāramitās (q.v.). Patient endurance, humility. Can also mean acceptance or recognition, as of Reality.

Kshatriya At the time of the Buddha the Aryan clans in India recognized four social grades called *varnas* (a colour), the highest being the Brahmin or priest. Next comes the Kshatriya, the Warrior-ruler; then the Vaishya, or merchant; and lastly

111

the Sudra or people of non-Aryan descent. The lines of demarcation between each *varna* were variable and undefined; the complexity and rigidity of the modern caste system was unknown. The Buddha belonged to the *kshatriya varna*.

Kshetra (Sk.) Field or land. Thus Buddha-Kshetra, the Buddha-land or Heaven.

Kufū (Jap.) Lit. a device, sometimes used as a synonym for Kōan (q.v.). The 'spiritual birth-pangs' (Suzuki) of seeking a way out of the blind alley created by thought. It is seeking to pass through a narrow gate by dropping the self which cannot get through the opening. *See* Suzuki, *Zen and Japanese Culture*, p. 178.

Kumārajīva (344-413) Famous Indian translator of Indian Bst. works into Chinese. During his stay in China for ten years, hundreds of scholars worked under his direction to produce some 300 works, including the Saddharmapundarīka Sutra, the Mahā Prajñāpāramitā Sutra and the Diamond Sutra. His outstanding genius as a linguist and scholar was largely responsible for the introduction of Bsm. into China.

Kum-Bum (Tib.) Enormous Bst. monastery in N.E. Tibet known as 'the Monastery of 100,000 Images' from the tree, still preserved in the grounds, each leaf of which shows a Tibetan sacred character. As the birthplace of Tsong-kha-pa (q.v.), founder of the Gelugpa or Reformed School, it is regarded with enormous veneration. Mme. David-Neel (q.v.) lived there for some years, and the eldest brother of the Dalai Lama, Thubten Norbu, was at one time Abbot. For his description of the life in Kum-Bum see his *Tibet is my Country* (1960).

Kundalini (Sk.) The fiery serpent-power which lies coiled in its *cakra* at the root of the spine. At a late stage in spiritual development it moves up through the other six *cakras* to open the '1,000-petalled Lotus' in the brain. A doctrine of esoteric Yoga and no part of Bst. teaching. Attempts to rouse this tremendous power before training in the hands of a master sufficiently advanced lead to complete insanity.

Kusala (P.) Wholesome. Akusala, unwholesome. Terms used to describe acts whose karmic effect will be to assist or retard progress in mind-development, or to produce pleasant or painful results.

Kushog (Tib.) A polite honorific, as Sir, but currently used for the Dalai Lama. Lit. the Presence.

Kusinagara (Kusinara) The modern Kasia. The 'little wattle-and-daub township in the midst of the jungle' where the Buddha passed into Parinirvāna. One of the four Holy Places of Bsm. (q.v.).

Kwan-yin (Ch.) **Kannon** (Jap.) The feminine aspect of the Bodhisattva Avalokitesvara (q.v.). In iconography there are early versions which are male, but these are more correctly images of Kwan-shai-yin. Later versions show a woman with child in arms, and as the 'Goddess of Mercy' the Mother and Child are revered throughout China and Japan. *See* Broughton's charming *Vision of Kwannon Sama* (1929).

Kyō (Jap.) A suffix to a name, meaning scripture. Thus Hoke-kyō, the Jap. for the Saddharma-pundarīka Sūtra. For euphony it may become 'gyō'.

Kyoto Original name, Heian-kyō. Capital of Japan from 794, when moved from Nara (q.v.) until Meiji Restoration in 1868, when capital moved to Yedo, renamed Tokyo. The religious centre of Japan. Laid out on grid principle with Palace in

113

centre in a plain with hills around of which chief is Mount Hiei (q.v.), the home of Tendai-Shū. The city contains a high proportion of Japan's greatest Bst. monasteries. These include Kiyomizu-dera of the Hossō-Shū; the East and West Hongwanji, of the Shin-Shū; Myōshin-ji (q.v.), Shōkoku-ji (q.v.), Daitoku-ji (q.v.) and Nanzen-ji of Rinzai Zen-Shū; Manpuku-ji of the Ōbaku sect of Zen-Shū; Chion-in of Jōdo-Shū, and Tō-ji of Shingon-Shū. The city, containing art treasures of inestimable value, was saved from destruction by American bombing in the war by the passionate plea of the late Langdon Warner, then Curator of the Fogg Museum of Harvard University.

Kyoung (Burm.)   The Burmese name for a *Vihāra* (q.v.).

Ladakh   A small country in the Western Himālayas between Tibet and Kashmir. The people are of Tibetan stock and therefore Buddhists. Bsm. was introduced in the reign of Asoka or earlier, and was, according to the Chinese pilgrim Fa Hsien, flourishing about 400. The present Bsm. is a low form of Tibetan Bsm., not having had the benefit of the periodic reform which purified the religion in Tibet. The capital is Leh. *See* Cunningham, *Ladak* (1854).

Lakshana (Sk.)   A mark or sign distinguishing one thing from another. Hence criterion or characteristic, as *anicca* of all phenomena. (*See* **Three Signs of Being**.)

Lalita Vistara (Sk.)   Lit. Account of the Sport, or Play (of the Bodhisattva). A Hīnayāna work of the Mahāsanghika School written in Sk. It is a biography of the Buddha which develops the legendary aspect of his life, and thus belongs to the M. School in its developed form. Krom's *Life of the Buddha* is drawn from the Lalita Vistara and Edwin Arnold's *Light of Asia* is based on it.

Lama (Tib.) A term which should be reserved for senior members of the Tibetan Order, who by rank or spiritual achievement deserve this title. A mere monk is a Gelong. Certain of the Lamas are recognized as Tulkus (q.v.) and as such are entitled to be called Rimpoche. The three senior Lamas are the Dalai Lama, the Panchen Lama and the Bog-do Lama of Urga, the head of Bsm. in Mongolia. (*See* **Tibetan Buddhist Order.**)

Lam Rim (Tib.) 'Stages in the Path.' Name of a class of Tibetan Bst. literature, but in particular the volume of Tsong-kha-pa (q.v.), which is the principal doctrinal book for the Gelugpa or Yellow Hat Order which he founded c. A.D. 1400. Only trans. to date is into Russian, save for extracts in H. P. Blavatsky's *Practical Occultism* (1923). This writer says it is in two parts, one exoteric and for ecclesiastical use, the other esoteric for Lanoos, disciples, only. (*See* **Golden Precepts, Kiu-te, Voice of the Silence.**)

Lanka Ancient name of Ceylon (q.v.).

Lankāvatāra Sūtra (Sk.) A scripture of the Yogācāra School of M. Bsm., written in Sanskrit in India (c. 350 A.D.). Contains an epitome of nearly all M. teaching. Teaches subjective idealism based on the Buddha's Enlightenment, and the doctrines of Sūnyatā and Mind-Only. Said to have been given by Bodhidharma to his disciple, the Second Patriarch, Hui-K'o, as containing the Buddha's teaching. For trans. *see* Suzuki, *The Lankavatara Sutra* (1932), and for commentary *see* his companion volume, *Studies in the Lankavatara Sutra* (1930).

Lepcha The indigenous inhabitants of Sikkim.

Lha (Tib.) A divinity comparable with the Devas of Indian mythology. Lha-sa, 'the land of the Lhas'.

115

'Light of Asia, The' Famous work by Sir Edwin Arnold, first published in 1879. The Life and Teaching of the Buddha in verse. Based on *Lalita Vistara* (q.v.).

Li Po (Chin.) Famous Chinese poet of the T'ang Dynasty in spite of being usually drunk. To the Bst. of interest as expressing perfectly the Chinese and Japanese love of nature. Of the mountains about which he loved to sing he wrote, 'We never get tired of each other, the mountain and I'.

Livelihood (*Sammā Ājīva*) Right Livelihood is the Fifth Stage of the Noble Eightfold Path (q.v.).

The ignoble trades—those which a Buddhist should avoid—include butchery, hunting and fishing, warfare and the making of weapons of war, and dealing in poisons, drugs and drinks which cause stupefaction and intoxication.

'Living Buddha' A misnomer for a class of Tibetan Lamas known as Tulkus (q.v.) who are given the high title of Rimpoche, 'Precious Ones'. They are not Buddhas, or necessarily of high spiritual attainment in their own right, but are used, or overshadowed by, and in some cases incarnations of some spiritual entity which in the same way used a previous holder of the office in question, such as the Abbot of a monastery. The Dalai Lama and the Panchen Lama are the best known examples of the practice, which is not confined to Tibetan Bsm. (*See* **Tulku**.)

Lobha (P.) Covetousness or greed. A synonym of *Tanhā* (q.v.) and *Rāga* (q.v.).

Lohan (Chin.) A Chinese word for Arhat (q.v.). One of sixteen chief Disciples of the Buddha. The famous Lohan in the British Museum is probably eighth century.

Loka (P.) World, e.g. Kāma-loka, the world of the five senses and their allure. For the Three Worlds *see* **Tiloka**.

Lokapāla (Sk.) The four Lokapālas, the Guardians of the Four Quarters (of the compass), and of the doors of temples, have many functions and ranks in Eastern mythology. As guardians of the temples of Japan these huge carved figures in full armour represent some of the finest Japanese sculpture. (*See* **Unkei**.)

Lokes(h)vara (Sk.) An aspect of the Buddha as Lord of the World. The form used in the carvings on Angkor Wat (q.v.) and in the Bst. art of Tibet and Nepal.

Lokottara (Sk.) **Lokuttara** (P.) The Transcendental, i.e. beyond the Three Worlds. (*See* **Tiloka**.)

London Buddhist League, The A short-lived Buddhist group collected from the audiences which gathered to hear the long series of public lectures on Bsm. given at the Essex Hall in London by Francis Payne (q.v.) in 1923, after the Buddhist Society of Great Britain and Ireland had ceased to function, and before the Buddhist Society was founded in 1924.

London Buddhist Vihara, The Bst. organization in London founded by Sinhalese to provide a residence for members of the Sangha of any country, and a centre for teaching of the Theravāda School. Opened by Ven. Nārada Mahāthera in May 1954. Two or more Bhikkhus from Ceylon usually in residence. Present address, 5 Heathfield Gardens, London, W.14. Present incumbent Ven. Saddhātissa Mahāthera.

Lotus A favourite Bst. symbol. Rooted in the mud, it rises through the water and opens in the air to receive the sun.

117

Padmāsana, the Lotus posture in meditation and art, is the Dhyanāsana, with both soles upward on the other thigh and the figure seated on an opening Lotus. *The Lotus of the Good Law* is a translation of the name, Saddharma-pundarīka (Sūtra). (*See* **Āsana, Mudrā, Om.**)

Lounsbery, Miss G. Constant American Buddhist resident in France who in 1929 founded Les Amis du Bouddhisme (q.v.) in Paris, and for many years financed its activities. Brought to Europe Bhikkhus from Ceylon and elsewhere. Procured publication in French of many works on Bsm. Ran yearly Bst. Summer School at home in La Tourballe, Brittany. Author of *Buddhist Meditation in the Southern School* (1935).

Lumbini (Sk. and P.) (Modern Rummindei). Birthplace of Siddhārtha Gautama, who became the Buddha. The site is now in the Nepal Therai, marked by a Pillar erected by the Emperor Asoka c. 250 B.C. One of the Holy Places of Bsm., the site was approved and roads built to it for the celebration of Buddha Jayantī (q.v.) in 1956.

Lung-Gom Pa (Tib.) Highly trained men in Tibet who acquire the ability to travel, by a kind of running leap, long distances at great speed and without rest. They move in profound concentration, as a sleep-walker, in some form of self-induced trance, and must not be disturbed as they run. Mme David-Neel describes the practice as she saw it in *With Mystics and Magicians in Tibet*, Ch. VI (1931).

Lung-men (Chin.) Series of Chinese caves carved into Bst. shrines c. 500 A.D. Grousset calls the style of many of the images Romanesque. The largest is a colossal image of the Buddha carved in 675 to the order of the reigning Empress.

Lust *See* **Kāma**, sensual desire; **Rāga**, passion, lust for emotional excitement; **Tanhā**, lust of life; all obstacles to liberation.

Madhya (Sk.)   Middle, as in the Mādhyamika School, 'pertaining to the Middle' (Way). Cp. Majjhima (P.) in the Majjhima Nikāya or Middle (length) Discourses in the Pali Canon.

Mādhyamika School (Sk.)   The Middle Doctrine School of M. Bsm. founded by Nāgārjuna (q.v.) in second century A.D. to harmonize rival doctrines on the nature of Reality. Recognizes two forms of Truth, a relative (Samvriti) and an absolute (Paramārtha), but the foundation of both is Sūnyatā, an absolute Voidness of all things or particulars, of which nothing can be said. Later teachers included Āryadeva (third century) and Sāntideva (seventh century). Cp. *Yogācāra School.*

Magadha   In the Buddha's day a province of India which, with the neighbouring Kosala (q.v.) covered the area of his Ministry. The capital in his day was Rajagriha, and the king was Dimbisara. Nālanda and Buddha Gāya lay within the kingdom.

Magga (P.) **Mārga** (Sk.)   A path or way. Generally used to describe the aryan or noble Middle Way (q.v.), or the Noble Eightfold Path (q.v.).

Magic   In the sense of using ritual or mantric formula for obtaining material benefits is deprecated in Bsm. Belief in the efficacy of rites and ceremonies (as means of attaining liberation) is one of the Ten Fetters to be cast off in following the Path. (*See* **Fetters**.)

Mahā (Sk.)   Great. As in Mahā-yāna, the great career or vehicle (of salvation).

119

Mahābhārata (Sk.)   The Great War. The Epic poem of India which includes the *Bhagavad Gītā*. The Ramāyāna is the source of most of the dramatic art in sculpture, mime and dancing in Thailand and Cambodia, and influenced all south-east Asia.

'Maha Bodhi Journal'   The monthly journal of the Maha Bodhi Society (q.v.). Published from Calcutta. Illustrated. Founded 1892 by the Anagarika Dharmapala (q.v.). Once edited by the Bhikshu Sangharakshita (q.v.).

Maha Bodhi Society   Founded in Calcutta in May 1891 by the Anagarika Dharmapala (q.v.) primarily to recover Buddha Gaya (q.v.) into Buddhist hands. The M.B.S. has formed branches in Ceylon and in many cities of India. It controls the site at Sarnath (q.v.). Its monthly Journal is the largest Buddhist periodical in print. (*See* **British Maha Bodhi Society.**)

Mahā Parinibbāna Sutta (P.)   The Sutta or Sermon of the Great Decease or passing into final Nirvāna. A.P.C. 16. A long Sutta containing a description of the Buddha's passing and much of his teaching. Cp. the Sk. *Mahā Parinirvāna Sūtra* of which there are two versions. One belongs to the Sarvāstivādin School and is a Sk. version of the above. For the other see below.

Mahā-Parinirvāna Sūtra (Sk.)   Important Mahāyāna Scripture written in Sk. and trans. into Chinese many times, first by Dharmaraksha in 423. Sometimes called the Paradise Sūtra. No complete translation in English. Treats of the Buddha nature and its relation to Nirvāna. To be distinguished from Pali Sutta of equivalent name, the Mahā-Parinibbāna Sutta (A.P.C. 16).

Mahāsanghika   The Mahāsanghikas, like the *Sarvāstivādins* (q.v.) were an early school of the *Hīnayāna* (q.v.). Some of its

120

Canon and other Scriptures survived the Moslem invasion of India, and famous works such as the *Mahāvastu* and the *Lalitavistara* belong to this school. The great poet Asvaghosha (q.v.) was a Mahāsanghika. To some extent this school is a bridge between the Hīnayāna and the Mahāyāna, having pantheistic leanings in its interpretation of the *Dhamma*.

Mahātma (Sk.) From mahā, great, and ātman, the highest principle in man. A name of honour which should be reserved for those of high spiritual attainment, such as the Rishis of India, or Masters of the Wisdom, but nowadays often used for a national saint like Mahātma Gandhi. *See, The Mahātma Letters to A. P. Sinnett* (1924).

Mahāvamsa (Sk.) The Great Chronicle. A record in verse of the early history of Ceylon, including its religious history. Compiled in fifth-sixth century. Much of our knowledge of the period derives from it. *See* Introduction to Thomas, *The History of Buddhist Thought* (1933).

Mahāvastu (Sk.) The Great Story or collection of stories. A Sk. Scripture of the Mahāsanghika (q.v.) School of the Hīnayāna, first produced in first century B.C. With its developed doctrine of the Bodhisattva it forms a bridge between the earlier schools and the M. In this work the ten steps (Dasabhūmika) of the Bodhisattva towards perfection are set out.

Mahāyāna The School of the Great Vehicle (of salvation), also called the Northern School as it embraces Tibet, Mongolia, China, Korea and Japan. Cp. *Theravāda*. The Mahāyāna gradually developed from the primitive teaching, and no sharp line of demarcation has ever existed; the doctrines of the Mahāsanghika School (q.v.) contain all the basic elements of the developed Mahāyāna. The teaching of the M. is more

121

distinctly religious, making its appeal to the heart and intuition rather than to the intellect. It seeks the spiritual interpretation of the verbal teaching, and endeavours to expound that teaching in a variety of forms calculated to appeal to every type of mind and every stage of spiritual development. That this method is but a concession to man's limitations, an accommodation of Truth to the intelligence of the hearer, must be borne in mind when considering certain M. teachings, especially of the 'Pure Land' School, which appear fundamentally opposed to the original teaching of the Buddha. Discountenances asceticism of any kind, its 'Sangha' being a body of teachers rather than monks. It is pantheistic rather than atheistic. The Theravāda, so far as it recognizes a transcendental Reality, conceives of it as obscured by the phenomenal: in M. the Real is being ever revealed by the phenomenal. The Goal of the Theravāda is the attainment of Arahatship, self-salvation; that of the M. is Bodhisattva-hood, renunciation of Nirvāna in order to help humanity in its pilgrimage thereto.

Mahinda Son of Emperor Asoka (q.v.) who, with his sister Sanghamitta entered Ceylon in 246 B.C. as members of the Order and converted the King to Bsm. Mahinda lived and died on Mihintale, a hill outside Anurādhapura (q.v.). Planted there a cutting of the Bo-tree (q.v.) from Buddha Gaya, which is thriving today, and is thus the oldest historical tree in the world.

Maithuna (Sk.) A term of Indian Tantric art to describe pairs of divinities in sexual embrace. For the symbolic meaning see **S(h)akti, Tantra, Yab-Yum.**

Maitreya (Sk.) **Metteya** (P.) Mi-lo-Fu (Chin.) Miroku (Jap.). The Buddha-to-come, the Bodhisattva who will be the next holder of the supreme office of Buddha. In the M. Maitreya ranks high as the highest of Bodhisattvas, and is most popular in Bst. art. He is well known in Japan as the fat, laughing figure of Hotei (q.v.).

Majjhima Nikāya The second of the five main divisions of the Sutta Pitaka. (*See* A.P.C.) Eng. trans. *Middle Length Sayings*, 3 vols. P.T.S.

Makimono (Jap.) Like a Kakemono (q.v.) but the picture is unrolled sideways instead of up and down. May be read like a book, from right to left, unrolling a brief portion as the story or the landscape literally unfolds. The art-form, like that of the Kakemono, came from China.

Malalasekera, Dr G. P., O.B.E., D.LITT.(LOND.), M.A., PH.D.(LOND.) Distinguished Sinhalese Buddhist. Born 1899. Dean of the Faculty of Oriental Studies, and Professor of Pali and Buddhist Civilization, University of Ceylon. 1950, Founding President of the World Fellowship of Buddhists (q.v.). Retired in favour of U Chan Htoon of Burma in 1958. 1957 appointed Ambassador for Ceylon in the U.S.S.R. General Editor of *The Encyclopaedia of Buddhism* (q.v.). Editor in Chief for many years of *The Buddhist* (q.v.). Author of *A Dictionary of Pali Proper Names*. [Died 1973.]

Mallas (P.) The Mallas of Kusinara were the tribe living about the site, Kusinara, where the Buddha died. Ananda presented them, family by family, to the dying Buddha and after his death they were made responsible for the cremation.

Māna (P.) Conceit. The eighth of the Ten Fetters, Samyojana (q.v.).

Manas (Sk.) **Mano** (P.) Mind. The rational faculty in man. That aspect of consciousness (*viññāna*) concerned with the relation of subject and object. Manas is essentially dual, its

123

lower aspect being concerned with and directed towards the worlds of sense, constituting the *Viññāna* of the perishable *Skandhas* (q.v.): and the higher, attracted to and illumined by *Buddhi* (q.v.) the faculty of intuition. (*See* Citta.)

Manasikāra (P.)   Deliberate attention to a subject of thought. Cp. *Ekāggatā*.

Mandala   A ritual or magic circle. In Tibet, a diagram used in invocations, meditation and temple services. Usually seen on *Than-kas* (q.v.) but also formed in sand and other media. Also found in the Shingon School of Japanese Buddhism. Dr Jung of Zurich has written on the production of the Mandala diagram in the unconscious mind of his patients.

Mani (Tib.)   Mani stones, engraved with the sacred invocation Om Mani Padme Hum (q.v.), are found wherever Tibetan Bsm. obtains, either piled up at key points such as a pass or at the foot of Chörtens (q.v.), or built into a Mani wall at the entrance to a village.

Manjus(h)rī (Sk.)   In Jap. Monju. The Buddha's Wisdom. Cp. Samantabhadra, the Buddha's Compassion in action. One of the Dhyāni-Bodhisattvas (q.v.). Negative aspect, Acala (q.v.). In art never appears with female counterpart. Shown with Sword of Wisdom in right hand and a volume of the Prajñāpāramitā literature in his left.

Mano-Vijñāna (Sk.)   The sixth sense-consciousness which unifies the other five, to relate those sense-impressions to Manas (q.v.), the seventh. *See* Ālaya-Vijñāna, the eighth.

Mantra(m) (Sk.)   A magical formula or invocation used in Tantric Bsm. in Tibet and in the Shingon School of Japan. The practice is based on a scientific knowledge of the occult power of sound. The most famous Mantra is Om Mani Padme Hūm (q.v.).

Manushi Also Manushya. Human embodiment. The human Buddha Gautama Siddhartha was the Manushi Buddha of the Dhyāni Bodhisattva Avalokiteshvara, who was an emanation of the Dhyāni Buddha Amitābha, who was in turn an emanation of Ādi-Buddha, the primordial Essence of Enlightenment. (*See* **Tantra**.)

Manvantara (Sk.) A great cycle of manifestation. The Hindus give its length as 432 millions of years. Each is made up of four Yugas, gold, silver, bronze and iron, of which we are now in the Iron Age. Two thousand Manvantaras or Mahāyugas make a Kalpa (q.v.). (*See* **Yuga**.)

Māra (Sk.) Lit. death. The tempter. The personification of evil in Bst. mythology. (*See* **Devil**.)

March, Arthur C. A Founding Member of the Buddhist Society in 1924. Founding Editor of 'Buddhism in England', later 'The Middle Way', the organ of the Society, in 1926, resigning in favour of Alan Watts in 1936. Compiled the *Analysis of the Pali Canon*, now incorporated in *A Buddhist Students' Manual*, and *A Brief Glossary of Buddhist Terms*, to which the same applies. In 1935 produced the *Buddhist Lodge Bibliography* (B.L.B.) with 2,000 entries, which had five annual supplements. Later retired to live in Guernsey. *See* also *Sixty Years of Buddhism in England*. [Died 1967.]

Marpa Founder of the Kargyut-pa School (q.v.) of Tibetan Bsm. in eleventh century. Milarepa (q.v.) was his famous pupil.

Marriage Bsm. is not concerned with the ceremony of marriage, but Bhikkhus, and monks of the M. Bst. Orders may be called in to recite Scriptures at a birth or funeral.

125

Mathurā Ancient Bst. centre in India 35 miles from Agra. Bst. stronghold from 500 B.C. to A.D. 500, where Bst. art during Gupta period (300-600), particularly Buddha Rūpas, never surpassed.

Maturing The experience of Satori does not in itself entitle a student of Zen Bsm. to teach others. Before he is accepted as a Rōshi, or Zen teacher, there is a long period of 'maturing' during which he must bring his new understanding into harmony with his thoughts, emotions and outward behaviour. This process may take place in the world. Only with still further training in actual teaching, with deep understanding of the particular pupil's needs, is the new master permitted to go forth as a Rōshi (q.v.).

Māyā (Sk.) Lit. illusion, and popularly used in this sense. Philosophically, whereas that alone which is changeless and eternal is real (*see* **Dharmakāya**), the phenomenal universe, subject to differentiation and impermanence, is *māyā*. (*See* **Moha**.) (2) The name of Buddha's mother.

Meat-eating Bsts. hold life to be one and therefore sacred. They do not, therefore, kill for sport or without excuse. But as life is taken even in the act of breathing each must apply for himself the first Precept (q.v.). Bhikkhus eat what is put into their begging-bowls; Japanese monks are mostly vegetarian. Lay Bsts. of any country apply the Precept as they think right, balancing the needs of compassion, personal health and their own view of priority of self-training and self-development. For M. viewpoint *see* Suzuki, *Studies in the Lankavatara Sutra*, pp. 368-371 (1930).

Meditation Meditation plays a very important part in Bsm., being the surest way to mind-control and purification. Right Mindfulness, the seventh step on the Eightfold Path, implies

126

constant control of the thoughts; the consequent Right Con-
centration, complete control of all the mental processes, results
in *Samādhi*, the attainment of spiritual insight and tranquillity.
These are the states of super-consciousness (*see* **Jhāna**.) Biblio:
Humphreys, *Concentration and Meditation* (1935). Also
Lounsbery, *Buddhist Meditation* (1935). (*See* **Bhāvanā,
Dhyāna, Samādhi.**)

Mediumship Mediumship may be positive or negative. The
former is rare, for it involves an advanced pupil, highly trained
for the purpose, who allows his Master to take possession of
his lower vehicles or personality while the pupil retains full
consciousness. Some light is thrown on this phenomenon in
The Mahatma Letters to A. P. Sinnett (1924). Negative
mediumship causes permanent damage to the medium, for as
control of the lower principles is loosened by the invasion of
some discarnate entity or elemental it becomes that much
easier for evil entities of any kind to take possession, and in
creasingly hard for the medium to resume responsibility. No
evolved being would so use a medium and in such practices
there is nothing whatsoever spiritual. (*See* **Bhūta**.)

Meraya (P.) A form of intoxicating drink mentioned in the
Fifth Precept (q.v.). *See* **Pansil** herein.

Merit The karmic result of unselfish action, mental or
physical. (*See* **Parivarta**.)

Mettā (P.) Love, active good will. The first of the four
Brahma-Vihāras (q.v.) in which the force of love is radiated
to all beings. Cp. *Karunā*, compassion.

Mettā Sutta The poem on True Fellowship: A.P.C.

Middle Way, The (1) The Majjhima Patipadā or Middle Way described by the Buddha in his First Sermon (q.v.). It is the Noble Eightfold Path (q.v.) between all extremes which leads to Enlightenment. *See* W. of Bsm. No. 13. (2) The name of the Journal of the Buddhist Society (q.v.) of London which was called, until 1943, *Buddhism in England*. (3) The Mādhyamika (q.v.) the Middle Way School founded by Nāgārjuna in the second century A.D.

Milarepa (Tib.) Lit. 'Mila, the cotton clad.' (1038-1122). Tibet's greatest saint, poet and magician. 'One of the most extraordinary personalities that Asia has produced' (Maraini). One of the Founders and the greatest figure in the Kargyut-pa School. Beginning as a great sinner, he became Tibet's most spectacular saint, and his Life, the Jetsün Kahbum, by his pupil Rechung, describes the entire process of conversion in detail. *See* Evans-Wentz, *Tibet's Great Yogi Milarepa* (1928). In iconography he has his right hand to his ear, listening to the hymns he set down in such abundance. (*See* **Marpa**.)

Milinda, Questions of the King *See* **Questions**.

Mindful and self-possessed A key term in all Schools of Bsm. A state of mind which in the monk or self-dedicated layman should be permanent, in which the Goal and the Way to it are constantly in view. This unremitting inward pressure of mind alone leads to enlightenment. (*See* **Sati**.)

Mind-Only A name used for the Yogācāra School (q.v.) of M. Bsm. Also known as the Vijñāna-vāda, or the 'doctrine of Consciousness'. In terms of philosophy pure, subjective idealism in which nothing exists save Mind.

Miracles In the sense of happenings resulting from the violation of natural law by an extra-cosmic being or beings, miracles are unknown in Bsm. Control of the physical world by physical methods is possible to a limited extent. Control of nature by super-physical methods through the development of the individual is possible to a much greater extent, but these methods are not supernatural and therefore not miraculous. (*See* **Iddhis**.)

Moggallāna (P.)   Also called Kolita, was one of the Buddha's chief disciples, being renowned for his supernormal powers (*iddhis*); also the name of a famous B. philosopher, the author of *Prajñaptishāstra*. (*See* **Relics, Sāriputta**.)

Moha (Sk. and P.)   Delusion, dullness, stupidity, infatuation. One of the 'Three Fires' which must be allowed to die out before Nirvāna is attained. *See also Rāga* and *Dosa*. Moha is the erroneous state of mind which arises from belief in 'self'. (*See* **Anattā, Avidyā, Māyā**.)

Moksha (Sk.)   Release. Hindu term for release from the round of birth and death, used in Bsm. as synonymous with Nirvāna.

Mokugyo (Jap.)   Lit. a wooden fish. The wooden drum hollowed from a block, used in Zen Bst. monasteries to call the monks to a service or to accompany Sutra chanting. Largest may be two to three feet high, on a large cushion; smallest may be held in hand. Large ones may be beautifully carved and lacquered to portray head of a dragon. *See* Appendices to Suzuki, *The Training of the Zen Buddhist Monk* (1934).

Mokushō (Jap.)   Form of Zen founded by Wanshi (q.v.) in the twelfth century which stressed still-sitting in silent medita-

129

tion to achieve awareness of already existing enlightenment. Much favoured in Sōtō Zen School (q.v.). Cp. Kanna Zen, the 'Patriarchal' as distinct from 'Tathāgata' Zen, which is the 'Sudden' or intense School of Rinzai Zen (q.v.).

Mondō (Jap.) 'Questions and answers.' The short, pithy dialogues between Zen masters and their disciples. The bulk of Zen literature consists of these *mondō* and commentaries upon them. Some of the answers may be used as a *Kōan* (q.v.).

Mongolia, Buddhism in The Chinese Emperor Kublai Khan (1259-1294), being converted to Bsm., encouraged its practice in all countries under his sway, including Mongolia, where he built many monasteries. Before long, however, this wave of interest died down until in the sixteenth century Tāranātha revived interest and founded the enormous Kuren monastery at Urga. His successors became Grand Lamas of Urga, a rank only junior in Tibetan Bsm. to the Dalai and Panchen Lamas. Under a treaty signed between the Grand Lama of Tibet (later the Dalai Lama) and the Emperor Alten Khan, Mongolia came under the jurisdiction of the Gelug-pa school. (*See* **Kalmuk.**)

'Monkey' Name of book by Wu Ch'eng-en (sixteenth century), trans. by Arthur Waley (1942). The hero, Tripitaka, is really the Chinese Bst. pilgrim Hiuen Tsiang (q.v.) but the story is a unique blend 'of beauty with absurdity, of profundity with nonsense' (Waley). Folk-lore, allegory, history, satire and poetry, all appear in it.

Motive No one Bst. term approximates to motive. Vāyāma and Hetu (q.v.) approximate. (*See also* **Merit.**) The lowest motive for action is that it pays, by producing at least the impression of happiness, by the law of Karma (q.v.). A higher motive is the will to reduce the suffering of all forms of life and to assist them towards Enlightenment. (*See* **Vows.**) Higher still is no motive, Purposelessness (q.v.).

Mu (Jap.) In Chinese, Wu. Not, or No, the Negative which is beyond mere positive and negative. (*See*, e.g. **No-Mind.**)

Muchi (Chin.) In Jap. Mokkei. Zen Bst. painter who flourished c. 1240. With Liang K'ai painted many Zen masters, but his name will live for his Six Persimmons and the Kannon in Daitokuji, Kyoto. Of all Zen painters perhaps nearest to expressing Zen with the brush.

Mudrā (Sk.) Ritual gestures of the hands used in symbolic magic, especially in the Tantric schools of Tibet. They are used in conjunction with Mantras (q.v.) and Yantras (q.v.) as aids to meditation. Buddha images (rūpas) are found in a variety of Mudrā positions. *See* A. Gordon, *Iconography of Tibetan Lamaism* (1939). (*See* **Buddha Rūpa.**)

Mui (Jap.) Purposelessness (q.v.).

Mūla (Sk. and P.) Root. As primordial, as in Mūla-Prakriti, cosmic substance, or causal, a technical term in the working out of Karma in relation to consciousness. (*See* **Hetu, Karma, Paccaya.**)

Mumonkan (Jap.) In Chinese Wu-men-kuan, 'Gateless Gate'. This collection of Kōans (q.v.) compiled in China in thirteenth century is only second to the Hekigan Roku (q.v.) in importance as such. Mumon (Wu-men) (1184-1260) collected 48 Kōans of famous Zen masters of the past and added his own comment in prose and verse. For trans. see Appendix to Ogata, *Zen for the West. See also* Dumoulin, *The Development of Chinese Zen after the Sixth Patriarch in the light of Mumonkan* (1953).

Muni (Sk.) A recluse. Name of the Buddha as Sākya Muni, the sage of the Sākyas, his tribe or clan.

Musā (P.) False. Musāvāda, lying speech, is the subject of the Fourth Precept in Pansil. (*See* **Precepts.**)

Mushin (Jap.) *See* **No-Mind.**

Myōshinji (Jap.) Mother temple in Kyoto of the Myōshinji teaching line of Rinzai Zen. Founded in 1337. Many stories are told of the Great Dragon painted in the roof of the Hondō.

Mysticism An awareness of the essential Oneness of the universe and all in it, achieved by a faculty beyond the intellect. There is mysticism in the Theravāda, but in the Mahāyāna it appears in many forms, and great mystical works are freely used in the monasteries. In a sense Zen Bsm. is itself a school of mysticism, for its first and final precept is: 'Look within; thou *art* Buddha'.

Nada (Sk.) Sound. Used in *The Voice of the Silence* (q.v.) as the soundless sound, or voice in the silence; hence voice of the silence.

Nāga (Sk.) A serpent. Snakes and dragons have been ambivalent symbols in all cultures. In India the Nāgas or Serpent Kings are symbols of initiates of the Wisdom. Cp. the dragon in China.

Nāgārjuna Buddhist philosopher and saint. Founder of the Mādhyamika School (M.) His date is doubtful, but is usually placed at beginning of second century A.D. Often called the 'Father of Mahāyāna', because he was first to teach the distinctively M. doctrine of S(*h*)ūnya (q.v.).

Nāgasena   *See* **Questions of King Milinda.**

Nālanda   The Buddhist University in N.E. India which flourished from the second to the eleventh century A.D. Site now being excavated with a view to re-foundation. At its height, 10,000 students from all parts of the East chose from a hundred lectures a day on every aspect of Buddhist thought. Its library was world-famous.

Naljor-pa (Tib.)   Lit. he who has attained serenity. Ascetic saints of Tibet who cut themselves off from society and practise a rigorous life of non-attachment. Many gain and use magical powers. The people hold them in great esteem. *See* Pallis, *Peaks and Lamas*, pp. 318-25 (1949).

Nāma (P.)   Lit. Name. Used as a collective term for the four *Skandhas* (q.v.) other than the first, Rūpa. As such called Nāma-kāya. *See* **Nāma-Rūpa**, the 4th link in the twelve Nidānas (q.v.).

Nāma-rūpa (Sk. and P.)   Name and Form, or Mind and Body. The 4th of the twelve Nidānas (q.v.) 'The psychophysical organism which uses its senses as instruments of craving' (Govinda).

Namaskāra (Sk.)   Homage. The Mudrā (q.v.) of folded hands raised in salutation. Hence a phrase of blessing.

Namo (P.)   Adoration. Blessing. A term of adoration best known in the taking of Pansil (q.v.).

Nanjio   Bunyiu Nanjio, Japanese scholar. Compiler of the 'Catalogue of the Chinese translations of the Buddhist Tripitaka: the sacred Canon of the Buddhists in China and Japan', pub. Oxford 1883, photographic reprint 1929. Works were quoted as 'Nanjiō No. . . .' His catalogue of Chinese texts has now been superseded by the Taishō Edition. (*See* **Taishō**.)

Nara Ancient capital of Japan (719-794) twenty miles from Kyoto. Contains many famous monasteries and temples, including Hōryūji (q.v.) erected in 607 by Regent Shōtoku (q.v.) who proclaimed Bsm. the state religion. (*See* **Tōdaiji**.)

Nārada, Mahā Thera Sinhalese Bst., born Ceylon 1898. Pali scholar and a leading exponent of Theravāda Bsm. Has travelled throughout the world, lecturing, broadcasting and founding Bst. organizations. Has stimulated Bst. study in Australia, China, Honolulu, Nepal, U.S.A. and London, where he opened the London Buddhist Vihāra in 1954. Has translated the Dhammapada and written many booklets on Theravāda Bsm.

Nat (Burm.) The nature spirits of Burma still worshipped in village shrines. Cp. the *devatās* of Ceylon.

Nature, love of The Chinese and Japanese love of nature is not irrelevant to the progress of Bsm. in those countries. Ch'an masters were great lovers of nature, and their mood was that of co-operation, not conquest. The landscape painting of China at its greatest was Zen inspired; the 'one corner' school (q.v.) was a Zen school, and in all Zen art the principles of Wabi and Sabi shine through as expressions of communion with nature. Still more does this apply in Japan, where much of the finest of Japanese culture, their gardens, flower-arrangement and spirit of poetry (*see* **Haiku**) are a combination of nature and Zen.

Nembutsu The invocation *Namu Amida Butsu* and the act of repeating it, by which rebirth into Amida's Paradise at death may be, according to the tenets of the Pure Land

School, assured. Esoterically, it implies concentration on the Buddha within for the purpose of attaining spiritual unity.

Nepal The Buddha was born at Lumbinī (q.v.) at the foot of the Nepal hills. His doctrines were re-introduced into Nepal by Asoka who included at least part of the country in his empire, and it was through Nepal that Bsm. first entered Tibet. The Bsm. of present Nepal is much corrupted by Indian Tantra. It has no Canon, but many valuable Sk. Bst. texts have been found in Nepal, and nine in particular, a curious assortment, are treated with special veneration. *See* Mitra, *Nepalese Buddhist Literature.* Of late the Ven. Amritānanda (q.v.) has founded a small centre for Theravāda study, and several Suttas are being made available in Newari. Katmandu was the scene of the 4th Congress of the World Fellowship of Buddhists in 1956. (*See* **Bodhināth, Swayambhū-nāth.**) *See* Snellgrove, *Buddhist Himālaya,* Ch. III.

Neti, Neti (Sk.) 'Not this, not this'—being all that can be said of the Absolute. The ultimate negation of all philosophy on those matters which transcend the intellect. The only possible description of the point where thought ends and No-thought, No-Mind, takes over. This Not-ness is in Bst. philosophy *S(h)ūnya* (q.v.).

Newari The indigenous inhabitants of Nepal. They are Bsts. The reigning family and nobility are Gurkhas, and Hindu.

Nichiren Japanese religious reformer, who founded (1253) the sect called after his name. Based his teachings on the *Saddharma Pundarīka* (q.v.) alone. Taught that the very name of the scripture had mantric power, and that by meditating on the formula *Namu myōhō-renge-kyō!* and repeating it as an invocation with the realization that you yourself are potentially Buddha, the barriers of the false self are removed and

135

enlightenment is attained. He still has a large following in Japan. *See* Anesaki, *Nichiren, the Buddhist Prophet.*

Nidānas (P.) The word *nidāna* means a link, and is used to describe the processes by which a being comes into existence, and which bind him to the Wheel of Life. Being a 'Wheel', there is no starting-point, but as Ignorance is the primary root of existence, and because its complete removal is essential for escape from rebirth, it is usually placed first.

The links are as follows:
On *Avijjā—Ignorance*—depend the *Sankhāras.*
On the *Sankhāras*—the karmic results of such illusion—depends *Viññāna.*
On *Viññāna* — individual consciousness — depends *Nāma-Rūpa.*
On *Nāma-Rūpa*—Mind, and its expression in Form — depends *Salāyatāna.*
On *Salāyatāna*—the six sense organs and their appropriate functions—depends *Phassa.*
On *Phassa*—touch: the sense, the object, and the sense impression—depends *Vedanā.*
On *Vedanā*—feeling, sensation—depends *Tanhā.*
On *Tanhā*—thirst, craving for personal experience—depends *Upādāna.*
On *Upādāna*—grasping, clinging to existence—depends *Bhava.*
On *Bhava*—becoming and re-becoming—depends *Jāti.*
On *Jāti*—birth—the final outcome of *kamma*—depends *Jarā-marana* (with *soka-parideva-dukkha-domanass'-upāyasa*) Old age and Death, with tribulation, grief, sorrow, distress, despair.

The technical term for the Nidāna Chain is Paticca-samuppāda (P., in Sk. Pratitya-samutpāda), arising from preceding condition, 'dependent origination'. But there is little authority for regarding the 'links' as fixed in number or connected by any rule of logical sequence. The relation between them is of mutual dependence rather than causal sequence. 'That arising, this becomes; this ceasing to be, that ceases to be'—this is the Bst. teaching, and the Nidānas are but one grouping of the factors involved in this tremendous process. (*See* **Wheel of Life.**)

Nihilism The philosophic doctrine that denies a substantial reality to the phenomenal universe. Bsm. takes the middle path between the realists (*astika*), who maintain the universe to be real, and the non-realists (*nāstika*), who deny all reality. The Buddha condemned both the *astika* and the *nāstika* concepts. (*See* **Mādhyamika.**)

Nikāya (P.) A chapter or section of a Scripture. (*See* **Sutta.**)

Nipāta (P.) Collection, as of some Suttas in the Sutta-nipāta (q.v.).

Niraya (P.) The downward path, to hell. One of the hell states (*see* **Apāya**) none of which is in Bst. doctrine permanent.

Nirmānakāya (Sk.) The 'body of transformation', by which the Buddha remains in contact with phenomenal existence for the helping of humanity on its pilgrimage. The condition of the *Dharmakāya* (q.v.) in manifestation (*Samsāra*), as distinct from its condition in the sight of the Bodhisattvas, *Sambhogakāya* (q.v.). (*See* **Trikāya, Tulku.**)

Nirodha (P.) Extinction (q.v.). Also Cessation, in sense of stopping of undesirable conditions. As the cessation or annihilation of all the attributes of finite existence, equates with Nirvāna (q.v.). Cp. *Nirvritti*. (*See* **Four Noble Truths.**)

Nirvāna (Sk.) **Nibbāna** (P.)   The supreme Goal of Buddhist endeavour; release from the limitations of existence. The word is derived from a root meaning extinguished through lack of fuel, and since rebirth is the result of desire (*tanhā*), freedom from rebirth is attained by the extinguishing of all such desire. Nirvāna is, therefore, a state attainable in this life by right aspiration, purity of life, and the elimination of egoism. This is cessation of existence, as we know existence; the attainment of Being (as distinct from becoming); union with Ultimate Reality. The Buddha speaks of it as 'unborn, unoriginated, uncreated, unformed', contrasting it with the born, originated, created and formed phenomenal world.

The Theravāda School tends to view Nirvāna as escape from life by overcoming its attractions; the Mahāyāna views it as the fruition of life, the unfolding of the infinite possibilities of the innate Buddha-nature, and exalts the Bodhisattva (q.v.) who remains in touch with life rather than the saint who relinquishes all connection with it. (*See* **Parinirvāna**.)

Nirvritti (Sk.)   Completion. A 'flowing back'. Involution as the opposite of Pravritti, evolution.

Nīvarana (P.)   Hindrances. The five factors which blind our vision from the truth. They are lust, ill-will, torpor, worry and sceptical doubt.

Nō (Jap.)   Lit. Performance. The Nō plays of Japan date from seventh century. Many have a Bst. theme. The action and manner of dancing and of speech became highly stylized, and today the art is a cult of the few learned enough to understand the symbolic meaning. Women's parts are taken by men. Many of the principal actors wear masks. The costumes are gorgeous and very valuable. *See* Beatrice Lane Suzuki, *Nōgaku, Japanese Nō Plays* (1932). A. Waley, *The Nō Plays of Japan* (1921).

138

Noble Eightfold Path The Bst. scheme of moral and spiritual self-development leading to Enlightenment. The eight constituent parts are: (1) *Sammā Ditthi*, Right View; (2) *Sammā Sankappa*, Right Mental Attitude or Motive; (3) *Sammā Vācā*, Right Speech; (4) *Sammā Kammanta*, Right Action; (5) *Sammā Ājīva*, Right Pursuits, including means of Livelihood; (6) *Sammā Vāyāma*, Right Effort; (7) *Sammā Sati*, Right Mindfulness; (8) *Sammā Samādhi*, Right Contemplation. (*See* **Sammā**.)

No-Mind Phrase used to translate various terms in Ch'an and Zen Bsm. It describes a state of consciousness before the division into duality created by thought takes place. Wu-hsin (in Jap. Mu-shin) means no-mindness, or no-thoughtness, as the Unconscious behind all conscious activity. Yet this Unconscious is at the same time conscious, a mind unconscious of itself. This is a paradox without meaning save as achieved in direct spiritual experience. It is the purpose of Zen training to achieve and maintain this state of mind. *See* Suzuki, *Zen and Japanese Culture* (1959), pp. 111-117.

Nuns, Nunneries Women were admitted as Bhikkhunīs into the Sangha in the Buddha's lifetime, though according to tradition, with some misgiving. The female branch of the Order has died out, but in Tibet and Japan there are many nuns and nunneries, many of which in the course of centuries have produced a number of outstanding minds. (*See* **Women**.)

Nyanatiloka, Mahā Thera Famous German Bst. born 1878 as Anton Gueth, who became a Bhikkhu in Rangoon in 1904. Spent most of his life in Ceylon where founded the Island Hermitage at Dodonduwa in 1911. Great Pali scholar, translated many Bst. Scriptures with commentary. Best known original work *A Buddhist Dictionary* (1950), and *The Word of the Buddha*, the first and still most popular compendium

139

of Theravāda Bsm. for the layman. Of many disciples best known is Nyanaponika Thera. Died 1957.

Nyingma-pa (Tib.)   The Red Hat or Unreformed school of Tibetan Bsm. Padma Sambhava (q.v.) is credited with founding it in the eighth century though there is little evidence of the school's existence as such before the twelfth. The Nyingma-pa is found largely in Nepal, Sikkim and in Kham, to the north-east of Tibet. It is the oldest of the Tibetan schools of Bsm., but one of the lowest in spiritual worth. *The Tibetan Book of the Dead* was produced in it. *See* Evans-Wentz, *Tibetan Yoga and Secret Doctrines*, Book V (1935).

Nyorai (Jap.)   In Sk. Tathāgata. There are five Nyorai in Jap. iconography, Dainichi (Vairocana, q.v.), Akshobya (q.v.), Ratnasambhava, Amoghasiddhi (q.v.) and Amitāyus. Cp. the five Myōō of which the most famous is Acala (q.v.). (*See* **Dhyāni Buddhas.**)

Ōbaku (Jap.)   (1) Japanese name for Huang-Po (q.v.). (2) The Ōbaku-Shū, no connection with above, is a third and later sect of the Zen-Shū in Japan, introduced by Ingen (q.v.) 1654. Main temple, Manpukuji, built in Chinese style, 1659. The sect has 503 temples. Cp. *Rinzai* and *Soto* Zen schools.

Ogata, Sōhaku   Japanese Bst., born 1901. Chief Monk of Chōtoku-In, a sub-temple of Shōkokuji (q.v.), a Rinzai Zen monastery in Kyoto. Has for thirty years assisted Western students of Zen in their studies in Japan, as host, interpreter, teacher and friend. Has studied and taught in Chicago University. Visited England in 1957 as guest of the Buddhist Society, London. Author of *A Guide to Zen Practice* (1923) and *Zen for the West* (1959). [Died 1973.]

Olcott, H. S.   Founder with H. P. Blavatsky of Theosophical

Society, 1875. Organizer of the last Buddhist revival in Ceylon (*see* **Ceylon**). Author of *Buddhist Catechism,* and compiler of the Fourteen Fundamental Buddhist Beliefs (q.v.). Died 1906.

Om A *mantra* (q.v.) used in Tibetan Buddhism. The invocation 'Om Mani Padme Hūm' is found throughout Tibet and is usually translated, 'Hail to the Jewel in the Lotus'. The symbolic meanings are manifold. *See* Govinda, *Foundations of Tibetan Mysticism* (1960.) (*See* **Aum.**)

One and Many In Bsm. there is no final distinction between the One and the Many, both being relative aspects of the Absolute behind all duality. One in All and All in One is a statement of spiritual experience, not to be intellectually analysed. Bsm. is not pantheism, for Samsara, the world of particulars, IS Nirvāna, the Absolute, and about their relationship nothing more can be usefully said.

One-Corner Style of Painting Originated with Bayen (Ma Yuan circa 1200), a great Zen painter of the Sung Dynasty of China. Bayen's Fishing Boat is the supreme example of this style of painting only a corner of the picture yet somehow leaving the vacant space alive. Here is S(h)ūnya (q.v.) in art, a nothingness more powerful than any thing.

Order, the Buddhist *See* **Sangha.**

Ordination *See* **Upasampadā.**

Oshō (Jap.) A rank as distinct from an office in a Zen monastery. A title accorded by the governing body of the monastery. A Jūshoku (q.v.), the head monk of a temple within the monastery, would probably be accorded such rank. Cp. Kanchō, the Abbot of the monastery and Rōshi, the Zen teacher in it.

Oxherding Pictures The ten Oxherding Pictures, first made known to the West by D. T. Suzuki in his *Manual of Zen Buddhism* (1935), are the work of Kakuan, a Zen master of China of the Sung Dynasty. There are various versions of this symbolic epitome of Zen training, but the point of Kakuan's ten, as distinct from early shorter versions is that the empty circle of Sūnyatā is not the goal. The rider on the now tamed Ox of self returns to the city 'with bliss-bestowing hands'.

Pabbajjā (P.) Lit. Going forth, to the homeless life. Thus the formal admission of a novice or Sāmanera to the Sangha (q.v.). (*See also* **Bhikkhu.**)

Paccaya (P.) Condition. Important but difficult term in the Abhidhamma in the analysis of causation. 'Something on which something else, the conditioned thing, is dependent, and without which the latter cannot be' (Nyanatiloka). *See* **Nidānas** and '*Paccaya*' in Nyanatiloka, *A Buddhist Dictionary* (1950). (*See* **Pratyaya.**)

Padmapāni Lit. the Lotus Born. A name for Avalokiteshvara, the Mind-born son or Bodhisattva of Amitābha, of whom Gautama the Buddha was the Manushi or human form.

Padma Sambhava Indian Bst. of the eighth century who visited Tibet at the invitation of the reigning king, and taught a variety of Bst. principles. He is credited with founding the Nyingma-pa School, but there is at present no evidence of its existence prior to the twelfth century. He initiated a period of translation, and the Bardo Thödol (q.v.) is associated with his name. Still venerated in the Nyingma-pa School as a saint only second to the Buddha. For Life *see* Evans-Wentz, *The Tibetan Book of the Great Liberation* (1954).

Pagan Deserted Bst. city in Upper Burma. Filled with thousands of temples and shrines, many of very high workman-

142

ship. Founded in 847, reached zenith in eleventh century. Abandoned about 1300. Most beautiful building is Temple of Ānanda (eleventh century).

Pagoda The Pagoda form developed from Bst. Stūpa (q.v.) in India. Appeared in present form in Nepal in sixth century. Further developed in China and then Japan.

Pāla (Sk.) Under the Pāla Dynasty of Magadha (740-1197) some of the finest Indian Bst. art was produced. From Nālanda came figures in its famous black slate; from elsewhere the bronze for Rūpas of great elegance of form and beauty of spiritual expression. Under this Dynasty the scholars of Nālanda University achieved the final synthesis of M. philosophy. Hence the term 'Pāla Buddhism'.

Pāli One of the basic languages in which the Bst tradition is preserved. A form of Prākrit later adopted by the Theravādins for the preservation of the Dhamma when it was first reduced to writing in Ceylon in the first century B.C.

Pāli Canon The Scriptures of the Theravāda School (q.v.). Part at least written down in Pali in Ceylon in the first century B.C. In three divisions or 'baskets' (Pitaka, q.v.), the Vinaya, Rules for the Order, the Suttas or Sermons, and the Abhidhamma, 'beyond Dhamma', a collection of material on mind-development. The whole, with commentaries, made available in English by the Pali Text Society (q.v.). For analysis and bibliog., *see* A.P.C. (*See* **Scriptures**.)

Pali Text Society Founded in London in 1881 by Professor and Mrs Rhys Davids (q.v.) to publish Pali texts and commentaries in Roman script, and to publish English translations. The whole work is now almost complete. The Canon of

143

the Theravāda was in fact available to the English-speaking world in its entirety before the peoples of Theravāda countries could read it in their own language. Miss I. B. Horner (q.v.) succeeded Mrs Rhys Davids (q.v.) as Hon. Secretary in 1942 and became President, on the death of Dr Stede (q.v.) in 1960.

Pamāda (P.) Heedlessness, mental sloth as the opposite of right Mindfulness (q.v.). See fifth of the Precepts in which intoxicating drinks are proscribed as tending to lead to Pamāda.

Panchen Lama (Tib.) The Panchen Lama ranks only second to the Dalai Lama (q.v.) among the Grand Lamas of the Gelugpa School of Tibetan Bsm. His seat is in the Tashilhumpo monastery at Shigatse; hence the common but inaccurate description of him as the Tashi Lama. In 1640 the 5th Dalai Lama, having with the aid of the Mongols acquired temporal as well as spiritual control of the whole country, honoured his own tutor with the title of Panchen (from Pandita, learned) Lama, and built for him the Tashilhumpo Monastery. On the death of the title-holder the new Lama is found in the body of a small child, as in the case of the Dalai Lama, and no new Lama is recognized as such by the people until examined and approved by a Tibetan commission appointed for the purpose. As the present user of the title has not been so examined he is not yet accepted by the people as the 9th Panchen Lama. When so accepted he is regarded as a manifestation of Amitābha (Tib. O Pamé) the Dhyāni-Buddha of Infinite Light. (*See* **Tulku**.)

Paññindriya (P.) Paññā, wisdom, indriya, faculty. Pure reason, the faculty of Paññā (Prajñā in Sk.), Wisdom.

Pansil (P.) An abbreviation of Pancha Sila, Five Precepts (q.v.). Primary meaning, the five moral rules which all Bsts.

of the Theravāda School undertake to observe. Second meaning, the whole of the invocation recited in Pali on Bst. occasions which includes the triple invocation to the Buddha, the three Refuges (q.v.) and Pansil proper. For trans. of the entire formula *see* Saddhatissa, *Buddhist Ethics* (1970).

Pantheism Bsm. is not a form of pantheism, for it lacks the duality of thought implied in the God-concept and that which the God creates. In Bsm. the One and the All are not different but exist in absolute self-identity (q.v.).

Parabrahman (Sk.) *See* **Absolute**.

Paradox Bsm. regards Truth as in Non-duality, and thus beyond the condition of the opposites. Any statement, therefore, is only partially true, its opposite being also partially true. Only in paradox, therefore, taken to its limits, can Truth be, however inadequately, expressed. In Zen teaching it is taught that A is A *because* A is not A. (*See* **Zen Logic**.) Or, in the words of a Zen master, 'If you have a staff I will give you one; if you have not, I will take it away'.

Paramānu (Sk.) The smallest conceivable thing. Comparison with modern discoveries on the atom are unavoidable in the light of descriptions of Paramānu.

Paramārtha Satya (Sk.) Absolute as distinct from relative Truth. Cp. Samvriti. Several Bst. Schools admit this distinction.

Pāramitā (Sk.) Perfection. The six (or ten) stages of spiritual perfection followed by the Bodhisattva in his progress to Buddhahood. They consist of the practice and highest possible development of *dāna*, charity, *sīla*, morality, *kshānti*, patience, *vīrya*, vigour, *dhyāna*, meditation, and *prajñā*, wisdom. The

145

following four are sometimes added: skilful means of teaching, power over obstacles, spiritual aspiration, and knowledge, these last four being, however, regarded as amplifications of *Prajñā*, wisdom.

Parāvritti (Sk.) The 'turning about' or sudden 'revulsion at the deepest seat of consciousness' which is the Buddhist moment of conversion. Collates with *Ālayavijñāna* (q.v.). (*See* Suzuki, *Studies in the Lankavatara Sutra*.)

Parikalpita (Sk.) 'Falsely imagined.' Refers in particular to the Yogācāra teaching (q.v.) to the effect that all phenomena have no reality.

Parināmanā (Sk.) *See* **Parivarta.**

Parinirvāna (Sk.) The state of Nirvāna achieved by one who has completed the incarnation in which he achieved Nirvāna and will not be reborn on earth.

Parivarta (Sk.) The 'turning over' of merit acquired by good deeds of an individual to the benefit of another being, or of all beings. The doctrine appears in the Theravāda but is more fully developed in the Mahāyāna. (Cp. *Parināmana*, which has the same meaning.)

Patan One of three beautiful cities of the plain of Nepal near Katmandu (q.v.). It was once the royal city, and Asoka (q.v.) built five Stūpas there, all of which exist today. Contains a wealth of carved wooden buildings, including many Bst. temples and shrines.

Path of Purification *See* **Visuddhi Magga.**

Paticcasamuppāda *See* **Nidānas.**

146

Patigha (P.) Lit. reaction, as distinct from indifference to stimulus. Dislike, almost coterminous with Dosa, hatred (q.v.). One of the Three Fires of hatred, lust and illusion.

Pātimokkha (P.) **Prātimoksha** (Sk.) The 227 disciplinary rules binding on the Bhikkhu (q.v.), and recited on *Uposatha* days (q.v.) for purposes of confession. These are enumerated in the *Suttavibhanga,* the first part of the *Vinaya Pitaka* (q.v.). *See* S.B.E. xiii, pp. 1-69.

Patipadā (P.) Progress, which may be painful or pleasant. *Majjhima Patipadā,* the Middle Way (q.v.).

Pātra (Sk.) *See* **Begging Bowl**.

Patriarchs The Zen School of China and Japan claims a line of twenty-eight Patriarchs beginning with the Buddha himself and passing through many famous names, such as Asvaghosha, Nāgārjuna and Vasubandhu to Bodhidharma of India, who was the twenty-eighth Indian and first Chinese Zen Patriarch. The six Chinese Patriarchs were (1) Bodhidharma (Ch. Tamo, Jap. Daruma) who reached China in 520, (2) Hui-k'o (Jap. Eka) 486-593, (3) Seng-t'san (Jap. Sosan) died 606, (4) Tao-hsin (Jap. Dōshin) 579-651, (5) Hung-jen (Jap. Gunin) 601-675, and (6) Hui-neng (Jap. Enō or Yenō) 637-713, who left no successor as Patriarch. *See* these Chinese names and also Shen-Hsiu (Jap. Shinshū) and Shen-hui (Jap. Jinne).

Payne, Francis One of the great figures in the early history of Bsm. in England. A declared Buddhist in 1905. A founding Member of the Buddhist Society of Great Britain and Ireland (q.v.). In 1923, when this Society ceased to operate, gave a series of thirty-six lectures at the Essex Hall, and from those who attended founded the London Buddhist League (q.v.). Active member of the British Maha Bodhi Society (q.v.) and of all joint Committees of the Bst. organizations in London. Planned to rewrite Scriptures of Theravāda in Elizabethan English. Died 1954, aged 84.

Perahera Sinhalese term for the torchlight procession held every August at Kandy when the Tooth Relic is brought from the Temple of the Tooth (Dalada Maligawa) and carried round the city on elephant-back with a great following.

Personality For the folly of believing in the personality as permanent, *see* **Sakkāya-ditthi** *and* **Atta-vāda,** the false belief in the permanence of any aspect of the total self as different from the rest. This is one of fundamental Bst. doctrines on which all Schools are agreed. (*See* **Anattā, Ātman, Soul.**)

Pessimism The philosophic doctrine that the Universe is fundamentally evil. Bsm. is not pessimistic but asserts that sorrow or evil is due to ignorance of the true nature of Reality and false conceptions of 'self'. The Noble Eightfold Path (q.v.) teaches the way out of sorrow into the enlightenment and peace of Nirvāna. (*See* Holmes, *Creed of Buddha,* pp. 207-211.)

Phala (Sk. & P.) Fruits or fruition, and thus results. Technical term for state of consciousness following the attainment of Vipassanā, Insight (q.v.).

Phassa (P.) **Spars(h)a** (Sk.) Contact. The mental impression from contact with sense-objects. One of the twelve *Nidānas* (q.v.).

Pilgrims Famous Buddhist pilgrims were Fa-Hsien (q.v.) (399-413), Hiuen Tsiang (q.v.) (629-645), I-Tsing (q.v.) (671-695), who were Chinese Bhikkhus from China to India, and Sung Yun, a layman, sent from China to study Indian Bsm. (c. A.D. 518).

Buddhist Pilgrim's Progress: a famous Chinese work of religious fiction based on the pilgrimage of Hiuen Tsiang. Abridged translations by T. Richard, *A Mission to Heaven*, and Helen M. Hayes, *The Buddhist Pilgrim's Progress*. *See also* Arthur Waley's *Monkey*. (*See* **Holy Places of Bsm.**)

Piprawa In 1898 a Stūpa was unearthed at Piprawa, in Nepal, which contained a steatite vase containing pieces of charred bone. An inscription is translated by some scholars as asserting that the remains were relics of the Buddha. The Stūpa is therefore assumed to be that erected by the Sākyas of Kapilavatthu over their share of the ashes of the Buddha. (*See* **Relics.**)

Pirit Sinhalese term derived from *Paritta* (P.), *Paritra* (Sk.). Protection. A ceremony of protection from evil practised in Ceylon. Comparable with the ward-rune of Western folk-lore.

Pirivena (Sinhalese) A meeting or school of and for Bhikkhus. An assembly of Bhikkhus and Theras forming an educational unit. Thus the Vidyodaya Pirivena at Colombo was the nucleus of the new Vidyodaya University of Ceylon.

Pitaka A basket. The Buddhist Pali Canon contains the *Tipitaka* (three baskets). These are called Vinaya P., Sutta P., and Abhidhamma P. Applied in the sense of 'handing on', as baskets are used to hand on earth in excavation work. For details of Pitakas *see* **Pāli Canon.**

Pīti (P.) Rapture, as a high degree of enthusiasm. A joyful state of consciousness. A mental factor in the Abhidhamma analysis of mind.

Polonnaruwa One of the 'lost' cities of Ceylon, now partly uncovered. Capital of Ceylon 729 to 1314. King Parakrama-

149

bahu I built most of finest religious buildings (twelfth century). Sights include the Gal Vihāra with statue of Ānanda, and the Reclining Buddha. *See* Mitton, *The Lost Cities of Ceylon* (1916).

Pongyi (Burm.)   The Burmese word for a Thera (q.v.).

Potala (Tib.)   The enormous fortress-palace built on a high natural hill in the centre of Lhasa in the seventeenth century by the Regent of the 5th Dalai Lama. It is the residence of the Dalai Lama, and contains a complete monastery with its own Temple, the mausolea of previous Dalai Lamas, and enormous treasure, in works of art and specie. Built on the site of an earlier fortress, it is 900 feet long, and the stone walls are painted in various symbolic colours. The most magnificent palace in the world, in size, site and contents, it dominates the city. (*See* **Dalai Lama.**)

Pradaksinā (Sk.)   Keeping to the right. Ritual circumambulation of a Stūpa or holy object, keeping the object or person to the right. The same was observed in European pilgrimage at a shrine. In the same way visitors to the Buddha kept him to their right as they approached and sat down on his left.

Prajñā (Sk.) **Paññā** (P.)   Transcendental wisdom, divine intuition. One of the six *Pāramitās* (q.v.). One of the two pillars of the M., the other being *Karunā* (q.v.). For comparison with *Dhyāna, see* Suzuki, *Living by Zen,* Ch. V, *and* Suzuki, *The Zen Doctrine of No-Mind,* pp. 95-97.

Prajñānanda, The Lama Dorje   English Bst. born 1879 as Frederic Fletcher. Oxford University and Royal Engineers. In 1922 to Tibet with Knight, Ellam and McGovern, only McGovern reaching *To Lhasa in Disguise* (1924). P. remained at Shigatze, where he took the Robe and became in time a

Lama. Later in Ceylon he became a Bhikkhu and lived in Rangoon until his death in 1950. A keen student of H. P. Blavatsky, he was an exemplar rather than a writer, and had considerable influence in Rangoon.

Prajñā-pāramitā (Sk.)   The literature known generally as the Prajñā-pāramitā (the 'Wisdom which has gone beyond') was compiled in India over many centuries, beginning in the first century B.C. The leading authority, Dr E. Conze, distinguishes four phases. *See* his *Selected Sayings from the Perfection of Wisdom (Buddhist Society,* 1955). During the third phase the great mass was condensed and summarized. The two most famous epitomes are the *Diamond Sutra* (q.v.) and the *Heart Sutra* (q.v.), both of the fourth century A.D. *See* Conze, *Two Buddhist Wisdom Books* (1958). The most famous summary is the Abhisamayālankāra (trans. Conze, Rome 1954). Of the subject matter Conze says that it is 'a state of intoxication with the Unconditioned', being an attempt to analyse the ultimate theme of Sūnyatā, the Voidness of all things which is the ground of all Wisdom. This is the heart of many of the greatest M. writing, and meditation on Sūnyatā, or its more positive aspect Tathatā (Suchness), may lead the expanding mind to the direct awareness of that 'wisdom which has gone beyond'. (*See* **Pāramitā, Prajñā**.)

Prakriti (Sk.)   Primordial matter, as one of the 'pairs of opposites' into which the Oneness of the universe divides on manifestation, the other being Purusha (q.v.). Spirit. According to Bst. philosophy even this duality is 'falsely imagined', for this Matter is the crystallization of Spirit, and Spirit the ultimate sublimation of Matter. Behind them both is Nonduality.

Prānava (Sk.)   The name for the syllable A U M or Om (q.v.). Often pronounced Pranām.

151

Prānayāma (Sk.)   Breath-control.

Pranidhāna (Sk.)   A vow, an earnest wish. A vow to oneself, as self-dedication. Hence the Bodhisattva's vow to save mankind before benefiting from his own enlightenment. (*See* **Vows**.)

Pratisandhi (Sk.) **Patisandhi** (P.) Lit. 'Combination on return'. Hence birth and rebirth as reunion of parts. The first moment of consciousness on rebirth.

Pratyaya (Sk.)   Causation. Pratītyasamutpāda, the theory of Causation better known as Paticcasamuppāda (P.), for which see Nidānas. (*See* **Paccaya**.)

Pratyeka (Sk.) **Pacceka** (P.)   A Pratyeka Buddha is the solitary sage of Indian life whose ideal was incompatible with that of the Bodhisattva (q.v.), in that he 'walked alone', and having attained his Enlightenment, passed into Nirvāna, indifferent to the woes of men. The Mahāyānists grouped together Srāvaka (Disciples) and Pratyeka Buddhas as followers of an inferior way to theirs.

Pravritti (Sk.)   Lit. flowing forth, unfolding; hence evolution as the opposite of Nirvritti (q.v.), involution. Also used as the rising up or appearance of consciousness as reaction to sense stimulus.

Prayer   In the sense of intercession, petition to an external Deity for personal benefits, is unknown in Bsm. Meditation (q.v.) takes its place.

Prayer-Flags   The long coloured flags attached longitudinally to tall bamboo poles and placed outside the Gompas or monasteries of Tibet, Nepal and wherever Tibetan religious buildings are found. The gay colours are symbolic.

Prayer Wheels The 'Prayer-Wheel' used in Tibet and in other places where Tibetan Bsm. is found consists of a revolving metal cylinder containing a mantram (q.v.) or passages from the Scriptures, the whole being mounted on a short handle. Materials vary from wood and copper to beautifully wrought ivory and silver. The purpose is not for prayer, but to hold the attention of the senses while the mind, in uninterrupted 'mindfulness', concentrates on the subject of meditation in hand. Cp. *Rosary*.

Precepts There are ten moral 'precepts' in Bsm., which pledge those who take them not to: (1) take life, (2) steal, (3) indulge in sensuality, (4) lie, (5) become intoxicated by drink or drugs, (6) eat at unseasonable times, (7) attend worldly amusements, (8) use perfumes or wear ornaments, (9) sleep on a luxurious bed, (10) possess gold or silver.

The first Five Precepts (*see* **Pansil**) were originally binding on all who entered the Sangha; later, other five were added, the ten being binding on all *Bhikkhus*. Later, it became the custom for the pious layman to take the first five, and these are now considered as the minimum moral code to be followed by all who call themselves Buddhists. Public recital of the 'Three Refuges' (q.v.) and the 'Five Precepts' is in Theravāda countries the outward form of 'becoming a Buddhist'. On Uposatha Days and at Wesak, the lay disciple often keeps the first eight of the Ten Precepts.

Note that the Precepts are not commandments. They are aspirations or vows (to one's higher self). (*See* **Bhikkhu.**)

Preta (Sk.) Peta (P.) The 'hungry ghosts', shown in the lower segments of the Tibetan 'Wheel of Life' (q.v.). This is the Bst. purgatory where men in between lives are for a while tortured by their own unsatisfied desires. But no Bst. hell lasts longer than the causes which created it. (*See* **Hell.**)

Pudgala (Sk.) Puggala (P.) Nearest approach in Bsm. to Western theory of a soul. The Pudgalavāda was a 'heresy' of the Vātsīputrīya or Sammitīya (q.v.) School of the eighteen sects of the Hīnayāna (q.v.). It held that the Self is the Skandhas (q.v.) but also something more, though this 'more' need not be changeless, as the Ātman (q.v.). This is a 'quasi-soul', between the doctrine of no-self and of a permanent Self, between Ātman and Anattā. The doctrine could accept that of S(h)ūnya (q.v.) while postulating a relative, changing, reincarnating Self, the product of Karmic causes, which ultimately merges in the Void, its source. (*See* **Anattā, Ātman, Sammitīya, Self.**)

Pūjā (Sk.) A gesture of worship or respect, usually that of raising the hands, palms together, the height of the hands indicating the degree of reverence.

Pure Land School Founded as White Lotus Sect in China by Hui-yuan (circa A.D. 400); introduced into Japan by Hōnen (1133-1211). The Pure Land (Jap. *Jōdo*) doctrine personifies the Higher Self or Buddha-nature as Bodhisattva Amitābha (Amida), teaching that faith in Amida will ensure rebirth in his Western Paradise (*Sukhāvatī*), the 'Pure Land', where the attainment of Nirvāna is easy and certain. The Shin-shū, founded by Hōnen's disciple Shinran, teaches salvation by mere repetition of name of Amida (Nembutsu), the mantram being '*Namu Amida Butsu*'. Scriptures are: Asvaghosa's *Awakening of Faith in the Mahāyāna*, the short and long *Sukhāvatī Sūtras*, and *Amitāyurdhyāna Sūtra*, with the *Kyogyo-shin-sho* by Shinran for the Shin Sect. (*See* **Amitābha, Faith, Hōnen, Jōdo, Shinran Shōnin.**)

Purposelessness In Bsm. motive must be steadily purified and purged of self-interest. Finally, as taught in the Zen

154

School, the goal is seen as purposelessness, no goal. The spiritual as distinct from the social-moral life is sufficient unto itself and needs no goal or purpose by which to shape the means of the present moment. For this moment of now-doing is No-moment, and the doing is in No-mind (q.v.) (*See* **Mui.**)

Purus(h)a (Sk.)   Spirit, as one of the basic 'pairs of opposites' into which the Oneness of the universe divides on manifestation, the other being Prakriti (q.v.). Yet these remain One, a Non-duality in dual aspect.

Pusa (Chin.)   The Chinese name for a Bodhisattva.

Questions of King Milinda   (*Milinda Pañha*). Records of discussions on the principles of Bsm. between the Greek king Menander (Milinda) and the Buddhist Thera, Nāgasena. Written in Pali circa 100 B.C. Although non-canonical, Q.K.M. was acknowledged as authoritative by Buddhaghosa, this being the only work outside the Pali Canon thus recognized. *See, Questions of King Milinda*, S.B.E., xxxv, xxxvi. For a critical study of the work, *see* Mrs Rh. Davids, *The Milinda Questions* (1930).

Radong (Tib.)   The trumpets, of beaten copper bound in brass, sometimes 10 feet long, used in Tibetan monasteries to summon the monks for services, and for other religious purposes.

Rāga (P.)   Greed; passion; uncontrolled lust of every kind: with Dosa (q.v.) and Moha (q.v.) forming the three cardinal blemishes of character.

Rāhula   A fetter. The name of the Buddha's son, born shortly before he left his home on his quest for enlightenment. Rāhula entered the Sangha at about the age of 15 and became

155

one of the 12 'Elders'. Thera-Gāthā 296 records his attainment of Arhatship.

Rainy Season *See* **Was,** a corruption of Vassa.

Rājagriha (Sk.) **Rājagaha** (P.)   King Bimbisara's capital of Magadha (q.v.). The University of Nālanda is nearby, as is the Saptaparna Cave (q.v.) the site of the first Council. Rājagriha (now Rajgir in the Patna district of Bihar) was the site of many incidents in the life of the Buddha.

Rakusa (Jap.)   *See* **Kesa.**

Ratna (Sk.) **Ratana** (P.)   Jewel. Three Jewels of Buddha, Dhamma, Sangha. (*See* **Tiratana**.) Cp. Mani, the Jewel in the Lotus.

Ratnasambhava (Sk.)   The Jewel born. One of the five Dhyāni-Buddhas (q.v.) of Tibetan Bsm., known as the Compassionate Giver.

Reality   *See* **Absolute, Nirvāna, S(h)ūnya, Tathatā.**

Rebirth   An Indian doctrine which the Buddha embodied in his own teaching in a modified form. To be distinguished from transmigration, for the latter implies the return to earth in a new body of a distinct entity which may be called a soul. In Bsm. Rebirth is the corollary of *Karma* (q.v.); i.e., no immortal entity passes from life to life, but each life must be considered the karmic effect of the previous life and the cause of the following life. The *karma* which causes man to return to this world in a cycle of rebirths is the result of desire (q.v.). (*See* **Anattā, Karma, Nirvāna, Wheel of Life.**)

Red Hats   A term used especially of members of the Nyingma-pa School of Tibetan Bsm. In fact the senior members of all Tibetan schools wear red hats on ceremonial occasions, save the Gelugpa Order, who wear yellow hats.

Refuge A translation of the P. term Saranam, which occurs e.g. in Pansil (q.v.). 'I take refuge in the Buddha . . . Dhamma . . . Sangha'. But 'taking refuge' does not save the lost one. He must still gain the refuge by his own efforts, and use it well.

Relics The veneration of relics began immediately after the *Parinibbāna* of the Buddha, religious pilgrimages being made to the ten Stūpas erected over his ashes, and to the Four Holy Places (q.v.). Stūpas were also erected over the ashes of *Arhats*, and these became objects of veneration.

The famous 'Tooth Relic' is preserved at the Dalada Maligawa Temple, near Kandy, where its vicissitudes have been bound up with Sinhalese history for over 2,000 years.

In 1947 the relics of *Sāriputta* (q.v.) and *Mogallāna* (q.v.), which had been found at Sanchi by Sir William Cunningham in the nineteenth century, and transferred to the Victoria and Albert Museum in London, were formally handed back to the Buddhists of Ceylon for transmission to a new shrine at Sanchi specially built to house them. The ceremony of re-interment took place in 1953. *See* Law and Stede, *Dathavamsa* (History of the Tooth Relic). (*See* **Moggallāna, Piprawa, Sāriputta.**)

Renunciation Sacrifice of self-interest, the only kind of sacrifice recognized as of any value in treading the Path. The two great Renunciations in the life of Buddha were: (1) The renunciation of home, family and kingdom, and (2) the renunciation of Nirvāna at the 'Enlightenment' in favour of teaching the Good Law. The esoteric schools of Mahāyāna add a third, the renunciation of *Parinirvāna* and the taking of the Nirmānakāya vesture. (*See* **Bodhisattva, Trikāya.**)

157

Retreat In the course of his Ministry the Buddha was given various places of retreat, Vihāras, where members of the Sangha could spend the rainy period of Was and use as a permanent residence. Such were the Jetavana Park, the Bamboo Grove, the Vulture's Peak and the Deer Park near Benares, now Sarnath (q.v.). (*See* **Vihāra**.)

Revelation Bsm. recognizes no revelation in the sense of a disclosure of Truth to mankind by favour of a deity. Revelation of Truth is attained by each individual for and by himself by the removal of error from the mind and its consequent illumination or 'Enlightenment'.

Ri (Jap.) General principle, law, wholeness as compared with particularity. 'Innerliness' (Suzuki). Cp. the other of the 'pair of opposites' Ji (3). (*See* **Jijimuge**.)

Rimpoche (Tib.) Lit. Precious One. A title of great honour given to Tulkus (q.v.) and a few others of high rank and attainment.

Rinzai (Jap.) In Chin., Lin-chi. d. 867. The famous Zen Master, a pupil of Huang-Po (q.v.) who founded the Sudden School of Zen Bsm. which bears his name. His Sayings quoted in the Rinzai Roku (q.v.) are regarded as a supreme example of Zen literature.

Rinzai Roku (Jap.) **Lin-chi Lu** (Chin.) The recorded sayings of Rinzai (q.v.), founder of the Rinzai School of Zen Bsm. in ninth century. Considered by some as the supreme specimen of Zen literature. For complete translation into English, *see* Schloegl, *The Record of Rinzai* (1975).

Rinzai School of Zen Buddhism Founded by Rinzai (q.v.) c. 850, a pupil of Huang-Po and a follower of the Sudden

School of Hui-neng (q.v.). It was taken to Japan by Eisai in 1190. This School of Zen Bsm. became known to the West through the work of Dr D. T. Suzuki (cp. Sōtō Zen). The Kōan and Mondō are used in Rinzai Zen, but very little in Sōtō Zen.

Rishi (Sk.)   Indian term for holy sage of advanced spiritual attainment. Cp. *Mahātma*.

Ritsu (Jap.)   Jap. term for the Vinaya division of the Pali Canon, the Disciplinary Rules for the Sangha. The Lu-tsung School of Bsm. in China, taken in 735 to Japan by Dōsen, a Chinese pupil of Hiuen Tsiang (q.v.). The School is now small, but has had strong influence on the development of Japanese Bsm.

Ritual   Early Bsm. deprecated ritual, and the Southern School still makes little use of ceremony. The Tantric Schools of Tibet and the Shingon of Japan use elaborate rituals. (*See* **Fetters, Magic, Pansil.**)

Rosary   Bsts. were using the rosary long before it can be suggested the cult came from Christianity. The Tibetan and Chinese form is of 108 beads; the Japanese use a smaller type, held over the hand. The purpose is the same, to help concentration on the subject for meditation, and to retain 'mindfulness' (q.v.).

Rōshi (Jap.)   Lit. The old teacher. Rōshi is the name given to the Zen Master of a monastery who takes the pupil-monks and laymen in *San-Zen* (q.v.) and gives them Zen instruction. He may be at the same time the Abbot, but in large monasteries the two offices are frequently distinct, the Abbot concentrating on administration while the Rōshi confines himself to practical instruction in Zen. Cp. *Kanchō*.

159

Rūpa (P. and Sk.)   Form. Arūpa, formless. Form implies limitation, and form as cognized by the lower mind persists into the lower heaven worlds. The higher heaven worlds are called formless because the mind is free from the limitations of particular forms. Desire for life in the worlds of form (rūparāga) is the sixth Fetter to be cast off, and arūparāga the seventh. (*See* **Four Paths.**) Rūpa, an image, especially of the Buddha. Thus Buddha rūpa (q.v.). For Rūpa as the physical body *see* **Skandha.**

Rūpa Loka (P.)   The world of fine form as distinct from Arūpa Loka, the formless world. The middle of the three worlds (Tiloka, q.v.) which embrace all manifestation.

Ryōanji   Supreme example of a Japanese 'Flat Garden' in Kyoto (fifteenth century). Probably work of Sōami. Consists of fifteen stones set in five groups in an oblong 'lawn' of combed white sand surrounded by a low wall. No bushes or flowers at all. Symbolic meaning of the grouping now unknown.

Ryōbu Shintō (Jap.)   The fusion of Bsm. with Shintō effected by Dengyō Daishi and Kōbō Daishi in the ninth century A.D. in Japan. By this Shintō and Bsm. were shown as two sides of the same basic truths; the ancestral Sun Goddess Amaterasu was made identical with the Buddha Vairocana (*Dainichi*) and the lesser Shintō deities were declared to be manifestations of attributes of the Eternal Ādi-Buddha. This union lasted until the 'Restoration' in 1868, when Shintō was restored as the State religion and efforts were made to suppress Bsm. In 1872, however, complete religious liberty was established, and Buddhist and Shintō priests were equally recognized as 'Kyō-dōshoku' (official moral instructors).

Ryōsen-an   A sub-temple of Daitokuji (q.v.) at Kyoto, Japan, re-founded by Mrs Ruth Sasaki (q.v.) as a training centre for

Western Zen students. At the formal opening in 1958 Mrs Sasaki was given the title of Jūshoku or head-priest, an honour never before accorded a Westerner or a woman.

Sabi (Jap.)   A term used in Japanese art. A special attitude to things which is the objective counterpart to *Wabi* (q.v.). Things are valued for qualities irrespective of age, beauty or rarity.

Sacred   In Bsm. there is no division of life into the dualism of sacred and profane, or of good and evil. (*See* **Evil**.) Veneration is shown for holiness of life, especially for the basic virtue of altruism.

Sacred Books of the Buddhists   A series of publications comprising the Jātakamāla, and the Dialogues of the Buddha. Founded by Max Müller, and continued after his death by Mrs Rhys Davids. Published by Oxford University Press, and Luzac.

Sacred Books of the East   Series (ed. Max Müller) published by Oxford University Press. Buddhist volumes are Nos. 10, 11, 13, 17, 19, 20, 21, 35, 36 and 49.

Saddharma Pundarīka (Sk.)   Jap., Hokekyō. Scripture written in India probably in the second century A.D. *See, The Lotus of the Wonderful Law*, abridged version by Soothill from the Chinese (Oxford, 1930). Teaches the identification of the historical Buddha with the transcendental Buddha existing from the beginning of this age, his appearance in the phenomenal world being only a skilful device (*upāya*) adopted to preach the Dharma to mankind. Salvation is attained by the grace of the Bodhisattvas, the Theravāda method of salvation being regarded as inadequate.

161

Sakadāgāmin (P.) 'A once-returner.' (*See* **Four Paths.**)

Sakkāya (P.) Derivation disputed but used in Pali Canon as collective name for five *Skandhas* (q.v.). Sakkāya-ditthi is the false view that this Sakkāya or group of components is permanent and unchanging, an 'immortal soul'. (*See* **Anattā**.) The first of the Ten Fetters (*see* **Four Paths**), cp. *Attavāda*.

Sākya The name of the tribe or clan to which Gautama the Buddha belonged. Hence Sākya Muni, the Sage of the Sākyas. The tribe was at the time subject to the Kosalas (q.v.) whose capital was Srāvasti (P. Sāvatthi).

S(h)ākya Muni The Sage of the Sākyas. A title applied to the Buddha by those outside the Sākyan clan.

Sākya-pa (Tib.) A school of Tibetan Bsm. contemporary with the Kargyut-pa School (q.v.). The Sākya monastery was founded in 1071, and the sect was at one time of importance. Tsong-kha-pa was a member.

Salāyatana (P.) Six of the Āyatana (q.v.) or sense-bases—eye, ear, nose, tongue, body (touch) and mind. (*See* **Nidānas.**)

Samādhi (Sk. and P.) Contemplation on Reality, the state of even-mindedness when the dualism caused by thought has ceased to ruffle the surface of the ocean of Truth. In it the distinction between the mind, the object and their relationship is transcended. Sammā Samādhi is the last step on the Noble Eightfold Path (q.v.) and a prelude to Nirvāna. But the final step is a large one, from duality to Non-duality. (*See* **Dhyāna, Prajñā, Satori**.)

Samāgama (P.) Assembly or Association, as the Buddha Sāsana Samāgama of Rangoon.

162

Sāmanera (P.) A novice who keeps the Precepts but who has not yet achieved full ordination to the rank of *Bhikkhu* (q.v.) by the ceremony of *Upasampadā* (q.v.).

Samantabhadra (Sk.) In Japanese, Fugen. One of the five Dhyāni-Bodhisattvas (q.v.) of Tibetan Bsm. The All-Compassionate One of perfect Activity. Cp. Mañjusrī, for perfect Wisdom, the pair representing Wisdom and its application in Compassion. The aspect in which the Nyingma-pa School (q.v.) view Ādi-Buddha, the primordial Reality. Often personified in Vairocana (q.v.). In art appears seated on a white elephant.

Samāpatti (Sk. and P.) Attainments. There are many lists of such set out according to context.

Samatā (Sk.) Sameness. As sameness of mind, cp. Upekkhā.

Samatha (Sk. and P.) Tranquillity of mind, rather in the negative sense of withdrawal. Cp. Vipassanā, the more positive achievement.

Sambhogakāya (Sk.) The 'Bliss Body' of the triune Buddha. The Buddha considered as communicating the Dharma to the Bodhisattvas, as distinct from Nirmānakāya, his manifestation in the ordinary world of *samsāra.* (*See* Trikāya.).

Sambodhi (P.) The insight, wisdom, and assimilation of Truth essential to the attainment of the three higher stages of Arhatship. The seven successive factors which lead to Sambodhi are: mindfulness, investigation of the Dhamma, zeal, joy, tranquillity of mind, concentration, equanimity. Sammā sambodhi is the supreme spiritual insight of a Buddha. *See, Dial,* 1, 190-192. (*See* Bojjhanga.)

Sāmkhya (Sk.) One of the philosophical schools of India said to have influenced the development of Bsm. Its doctrines included the three Gunas, the evolution of this threefold Nature from Prakriti, and the Ātman or Purusha, the Life of nature's Form.

Sammā (P.) Samyak (Sk.) Supreme; the highest point or summit. In its relative meaning it is used to describe each step of the Noble Eightfold Path, being usually translated 'Right'. Here it means the highest state possible for any given individual to attain, according to his mental and moral development and his environment. In its absolute sense it means 'supreme', as in the invocation: *Namo tassa Bhagavato Arahato Sammā Sambuddhassa!* Homage to him, Blessed One, Worthy One, Supreme in Highest Wisdom (Supremely Enlightened).

Sammitīya The Sammitīyas formed one of the sects of the Hīnayāna School (q.v.), and Hiuen Tsiang, who studied them in the seventh century, estimated their numbers then as about 43,000 *Bhikkhus*. Their views are interesting on the subject of Anattā (q.v.), on which they were regarded as most unorthodox. Accepting the non-existence of any permanent 'self' in the five *Skandhas* (q.v.), they argued the existence of some carrier of karmic impulses from life to life, else rebirth was a doctrine without meaning. The Buddha, they pointed out, nowhere denied the existence of such a Self, which was that which entered, when finally purged of imperfection, into Nirvāna. (*See* **Pudgalas**.) The Vātsīputrīyas, who held the same view, were another sub-sect which later merged with the Sammitīyas.

Sampadā (P.) Attainment as desirable attainment. Five are given as Faith, Morality, Learning, Liberality, Wisdom, but other lists exist.

Samsāra (Sk. and P.) Also spelt Sangsāra. Lit. Faring on, a stream (of becoming). The world of flux, change and ceaseless becoming in which we live. Daily life. In Bsm. the field of deliverance from its bondage of limitation; there is none other. In the very world in which the 'three fires' of hatred, lust and illusion are kept burning by man's desire for self is to be worked out deliverance from this Wheel of Becoming on which, self-bound, we turn, life after life. The purpose of the Noble Eightfold Path (q.v.) is to enable one to step off the Wheel, into the state of Nirvāna (q.v.). But in the M. School it is taught that no such escape is truly possible, for Samsāra and Nirvāna are two aspects of one Reality; they are an inseverable, two-fold aspect of the ultimate Non-duality. (*See* **Wheel of Life**.)

Samskāra (Sk.) **Sankhāra** (P.) (1) The second link in the chain of Nidānas (q.v.) and one of the five *Skandhas* (q.v.). In the Nidānas this arises becáuse of Avidyā, ignorance, and in turn gives rise to consciousness. In this context the group consists of 'Karma-formations' (Nyanatiloka). In that these formations give rise to consciousness they are called Impulses (Conze). In the five *Skandhas*, or analysis of the personality, the Samskāras are placed below consciousness. In either case the collection of mental contents contains complexes, conditioned reflexes and mental habits of all kinds, including subconscious habits and memories. Indeed the term seems to include all contents of the mind at any one moment which will condition the functioning of consciousness and be influenced in turn by that functioning. (2) 'Compounded thing', as in formula, *Sabbe sankhāra anicca*, 'all compounded things are impermanent'. (*See* **Three Signs of Being**.)

Samskrita (Sk.) A somewhat vague term in Mahāyāna philosophy which Suzuki defines as 'anything that does something and is productive of some effect' that comes under the law of causation and of mutual dependence. (*See* **Causation, Karma, Nidānas**.) In the sense of 'made up', hence not grown naturally, it is used for the language called Sanskrit.

165

Samudaya (P.) Lit. Origin. The second Noble Truth, that the origin of suffering (*dukkha*) is Tanhā, craving, selfish desire (q.v.).

Samurai (Jap.) The Japanese warrior who, imbued with the spirit of Bushidō (q.v.), the 'Way to Knightly Virtue', was trained mentally and physically to apply, in the service of his Lord or Emperor, the highest principles of bravery, chivalry, honour and contempt for death.

Samvriti (Sk.) Relative as distinct from Absolute Truth, which is Paramārtha Satya (Truth). The distinction is basic in the Mādhyamika School (q.v.).

Samyojana (P.) Fetters. There are Ten Fetters binding beings to the Wheel of Becoming. (1) Belief in a permanent self (Sakkāya-ditthi), (2) Sceptical Doubt (Vicikicchā), (3) Clinging to Rules and Ritual, a special form of Upādāna, (4) Sensuous Craving (Kāma-rāga), (5) Ill-will, (6) and (7) Craving for the worlds of form or the formless world, (8) Conceit (Māna), (9) Restlessness (Uddhacca), and (10) Ignorance (Avidyā, P. Avijjā). There are other versions of the ten. For the Four Stages and the Fetters *see* Item 21 in W. of Bsm. (*See* **Four Paths, Rūpa.**)

Samyutta (P.) Joined, grouped or connected. Used in particular for sections of the Pali Canon. *See* A.P.C.

Samyutta Nikāya The third of the five main divisions of the *Sutta Pitaka. See* A.P.C. Translated into English as the *Book of the Kindred Sayings.*

Sanchi Site in Bhopal, India, of a famous group of Bst. buildings. The Great Stūpa was built in reign of Asoka (q.v.) and recased with addition of famous gates in the Andhra

166

Period (first century B.C.). In a second Stūpa were found relics of Moggallāna and Sāriputta, famous disciples of the Buddha, which have now been re-interred in a Shrine specially built for the purpose. (*See* **Relics.**)

'Sangha' The title of the monthly periodical of the English Sangha Association (q.v.). Founded 1957.

Sangha An Assembly. The monastic order founded by the Buddha, the members of which are called *Bhikkhus* (m) or *Bhikkhunīs* (f). It is the oldest monastic order in the world. The act of admission to the order is called *pabbajjā* (renouncing the world). The hair of the head and beard is shaved, the yellow Robe (consisting of three garments) is donned, and the *Tisarana* (q.v.) is recited. The candidate is then a novice. The ordination ceremony (*upasampadā*) takes place before a chapter of senior *Bhikkhus* and *Theras*. No oaths are taken, and the *Bhikkhu* is free to leave the Order at any time if he desires to do so. The *Bhikkhu* possesses only his robes, alms-bowl, razor, needle and water-strainer. He eats only one meal a day, no food being taken after mid-day. *See* Dutt, *Early Buddhist Monachism*. (*See* **Bhikkhu, Pātimokkha, Upasampadā.**)

In the Mahāyāna, monasteries are training colleges rather than retreats. The monks keep a strict discipline. Ordained temple priests may now marry. *See* Suzuki, *The Training of the Zen Buddhist Monk* (1934).

Sanghakamma (P.) The collective voice of the Sangha (q.v.). A kind of democratic council to preserve discipline and regulate the Sangha's collective affairs. *See* article by S. Dutt in the volume of Specimen Articles for *The Encyclopaedia of Buddhism*, Colombo, 1957.

Sangharakshita, The Sthavira Born Denis Lingwood, found himself in India in the war and spent spare time studying all

167

forms of Eastern philosophy. Travelled widely as an Anāgā-rika (q.v.) and took Robe as Sangharakshita Bhikshu of M. School in 1950. Founded branch of Y.M.B.A. (Young Men's Buddhist Association) in Kalimpong and later founded there the Triyāna Vardhana Vihāra. Editor of Journal of the Maha Bodhi Society (q.v.). Toured India, lecturing on Bsm. and stimulating the work founded by the late Dr Ambedkar (q.v.). Author of *A Survey of Buddhism* (1957). Now Leader of Friends of the Western Buddhist Order. Headquarters in London.

Sangyas (Tib.) A Tibetan name for the Buddha.

Sankappa (P.) Mindedness free from sensuous desire, ill-will and other such taints. The second step on the Noble Eightfold Path (q.v.). May be extended to right intent or Motive (q.v.), not only the state of mind but the purpose for which the Path is trodden.

Sankhāra (P.) *See* **Samskāra.**

Saññā (P.) Perception; awareness of and assimilation of sensation. (*See* **Skandha.**)

Sanron (Jap.) Japanese name for Chinese San-lun Bst. sect, based on the Yogācāra School of India (q.v.). Name means three treatises, being two of Nāgārjuna and one of Āryadeva. Arrived in Japan from Korea in 625. Its scholars also studied the Theravāda teachings. No longer extant as separate organization.

Santāna (P.) Continuity. The individual 'stream of consciousness'.

San-Zen (Jap.) Tense interview between a Rōshi, or Rinzai Zen Master, and a monk or layman under Zen training. Sub-

168

ject is usually the Kōan, on which the student is then engaged. Interview may take seconds or minutes. May take place daily or several times a day. (*See* **Dokusan, Sesshin, Za-Zen.**) San-Zen is the heart of the Rinzai Zen training.

Saptaparna (Sk.)   Lit. seven-leaved. The cave near Rājagriha (q.v.) where the Buddha taught and in which the first Council (q.v.) was held after his death. The sixth Council (q.v.) was held at Rangoon in 1954-56 in a new building designed to imitate this cave.

Sarana(m) (P.)   *See* **Refuge.** The Refuge or Island of Refuge in the taking of Pansil (q.v.).

Sāriputta (P.) **S(h)āriputra** (Sk.)   One of the two chief disciples of the Buddha, also called Upatissa. Regarded as second only to the Buddha in 'turning the Wheel of the Law'. His ashes were found with those of Moggallana (q.v.) in one of the Stūpas at Sanchi (q.v.). *See* **Relics** for their later move to London and back.

Sarnath   The site near Benares where the Buddha preached his First Sermon. The 'Deer Park at Isipatana' of the Pali Canon. Now a Buddhist monastery and temple run by the Maha Bodhi Society (q.v.). One of the four Holy Places of Buddhism.

Sarvāstivādin (Sk.)   The Sarvāstivādins formed one of the eighteen sects into which the Hīnayāna School (q.v.) had divided by the third century B.C. Its Canon, though not as complete as that of the Theravāda (q.v.), has largely survived in Chinese translation, where the four Nikāyas of the *Sutta Pitaka* are known as Āgamas (q.v.). It was from this sect, and even more from a third of the Hīnayāna sects, the Mahāsanghikas (q.v.) that the doctrines of the Mahāyāna developed.

169

Sasaki, Sōkei-an The first Zen Rōshi to make his home in the West. Born 1882 in Japan. To New York in 1906. The group he instructed formed the society, now called the First Zen Institute of America (q.v.) in 1930. Married Mrs Ruth Fuller Sasaki (q.v.) during the war. Died in 1945. Wrote most of *The Cat's Yawn* (q.v.) His numerous sermons are to be published by the Institute.

Sasaki, Mrs Ruth Fuller American Zen Buddhist, widow of Sōkei-an Sasaki (q.v.). Now 'chief monk' of Ryōsen-an, a sub-temple of Daitokuji, Kyoto, rebuilt in its grounds under her auspices for Western students of Zen. The first Western Bst. to be given this or any rank in Zen Bsm. An early member of the First Zen Institute of New York, later renamed the First Zen Institute of America, which was formed round the lectures of the late Sōkei-an Sasaki, and the Institute was for long housed in her New York home. Mrs. Sasaki now divides her time between New York and Ryōsen-an. Editor of *The Development of Chinese Zen*, being her translation from the German of Heinrich Dumoulin, with Notes. A further range of Zen Classics is to be published by the Japanese branch of the Institute. [Died 1967.]

Sāsana (P.) Doctrine. The Dhamma as taught by Buddha.

Sat (Sk.) Being, or more correctly Be-ness, for, although in one sense its opposite is Asat, no-being, it is also a term for that which lies beyond all duality. Non-Duality.

Sati (P.) **Smriti** (Sk.) Attentiveness. The seventh step on the Noble Eightfold Path (q.v.). The system of Mindfulness built about the concept is mainly analytical, in contemplating the divers factors in the body, the sensations, the thought-processes and phenomena, but goes further in a higher synthesis of consciousness in Samādhi (q.v.). (*See* **Sati-patthāna**.)

170

Sati-patthāna (P.) 'Awareness of Attentiveness.' A system of mind development by the analysis of consciousness based on the Satipatthāna Sutta of the Pali Canon. The most important aspect of the Abhidhamma (q.v.), the third section of the Canon. Contemplation on Body, Feelings, Mind and Mind-objects is taken to the minutest detail, with the interrelation of states of consciousness arising from such contemplation. Thereafter the mind is re-integrated towards the experience of Samādhi. *See* Nyanaponika, *The Heart of Buddhist Meditation* (1956). (*See* **Āsāpāna Sati.**)

Satori (Jap.) In Chin., Wu. A technical term used in Zen Bsm. to describe a state of consciousness beyond the plane of discrimination and differentiation. It may vary in quality and duration from a flash of intuitive awareness to Nirvāna. It is the beginning and not the end of true Zen training. After this 'break-through' to No-Thought, or No-Mind (q.v.), there is a period of maturing (q.v.) and then the rebuilding of the whole man in the light of this direct experience of Non-Duality. In Rinzai Zen the Kōan and Mondō (q.v.) are used to achieve Satori; in Sōtō Zen (q.v.) they are used very rarely. In either event the experience itself is unmistakable and incommunicable. (*See* **Enlightenment, Kenshō.**)

Sattva (Sk.) **Satta** (P.) Being or essence. (*See* **Bodhisattva** *and* **Guna.**)

Satya (Sk.) **Sacca** (P.) Truth, which may be Absolute, Paramārtha, or Relative, Samvriti. The Ariya Sacca (P.) are the Four Noble Truths (q.v.).

Sautrantikas (Sk.) An early School of Bsm. which in doctrine formed a bridge between the earlier sects of the Hīnayāna (q.v.) and the Mādhyamika School from which the Mahāyāna School developed. Described as critical realists, they produced

171

the doctrine of Conceptual Construction, *Vikalpa* (q.v.) in reaction to the doctrine of the Abhidharmika system of the Sarvāstivādins (q.v.). *See* Murti, *The Central Philosophy of Buddhism* (1955).

Sayadaw (Burm.) Lit. Teacher. Burmese Buddhist title of rank and respect. In theory reserved for heads of monasteries, but sometimes used as an honorary title for a very distinguished *Thera* (q.v.) such as the Sayadaw U Thittila (q.v.).

Scriptures, The Buddhist Those of the Theravāda are to be found in the Tipitaka (q.v.) or three 'baskets' of the Pali Canon. For trans. into English *see* Pali Text Society. For an Analysis *see* A.P.C. new edn. The S. of the Māhāyana are in Sk., Chinese, Japanese and Tibetan. For Analysis *see* B.S.M. Chap. 5. No Scripture is to a Bst. a sufficient authority for the truth of its contents. (*See* **Kālāma**.) The Suttas of the Theravāda are presented as actual sermons of the Buddha; those of the M. are frankly later compilations put into his mouth. Shāstras (q.v.) are Commentaries by later writers. Many of most famous M. Sūtras only survive in trans. into some other Eastern language. Many exist in different forms in different languages. Only a portion of the M. Scriptures so far translated into English. For anthologies in English *see* Conze (Ed.), *Buddhist Texts*, and Humphreys (Ed.), *The Wisdom of Buddhism*. (*See* **Kanjur, Sūtra, Tanjur**.)

Seal The Seal of Transmission, the Heart-Seal of the Buddha, are terms used to describe what each of the Patriarchs of Chinese Zen handed to his successor. This is the wordless transmission from Guru to Chela, from Master to pupil, of that which nevertheless cannot be transmitted, for it is the *Bodhi-dharma*, the Wisdom that has gone beyond, that dwells for ever, waiting to be revealed, in each aspect of All-Mind. (*See* **Heart-Doctrine, Transmission**.)

'Secret Doctrine, The' A work in two volumes by H. P. Blavatsky (q.v.) published in London in 1888. It is an elaborate commentary on the Stanzas of Dzyan (q.v.) divided into Cosmogenesis and Anthropogenesis, from material taught her in Tibet and later by two Masters of the esoteric Wisdom who in writing used the initials M. and K. H. *See, The Mahatma Letters to A. P. Sinnett* (1923). The doctrines will be found to underlie the inner teachings of all religions, and are gradually being verified by modern science and philosophy.

Seeing A technical term in Zen Bsm. To see is to see all things in their state of Tathatā, 'Suchness' (q.v.), just as they are. This is not a matter of physiology or psychology but of personal spiritual experience. To see that all is well as it is, in its 'isness', is liberation from the bonds of self and separateness and illusion. In philosophy this is seeing the suchness of things as 'good'; in psychology, 'to see the absolute ego as reflected in the relative ego and acting through it' (Suzuki); in Zen, seeing into one's own nature.

Sei (Jap.) Purity.

Self The doctrine of 'no-soul', anattā (q.v.) is basic to all schools of Buddhism. The illusion that the separated 'self' is permanent and has interests of its own is the cause of suffering and the barrier to enlightenment. (*See* **Anattā, Ātman, Ego, Soul.**)

Self-Identity The ultimate foundation of the Mahāyāna. To be distinguished from mere identity, in which there are still two objects. 'In self-identity there is just one object or subject, one only, and this identifies itself by going out of itself. Self-identity is the mind going out of itself in order to see itself reflected in itself. Self-identity is the logic of pure experience, or of "Emptiness". In self-identity there are no contradictions

173

whatever. Buddhists call this "Suchness" ' (q.v.), from Suzuki. (*See* **Zen Logic**.)

Sengai (Jap.) (1750-1837) Abbot of Shōfukuji in Kyushu, Japan, for many years, Sengai was one of the greatest painters of his time. His paintings show his Zen training, as do his poems, full of humour and direct vision.

Seng-t'san (Chin.) In Jap., Sosan. d. 606. The Third Chinese Zen Patriarch, famous for his long poem 'On Trust in the Heart'. *See* W. of Bsm., No. 111.

Senzaki, The Ven. Nyogen Japanese Rinzai Zen teacher, contemporary with D. T. Suzuki in 1895-96 at Engakuji (q.v.). To California in 1906 where spent rest of his life. Died 1958. Author, with Ruth McCandless, of *Buddhism and Zen* (1953).

Senzar The secret sacerdotal language, the direct progenitor of Vedic Sanskrit, in which the Masters of the Wisdom of Asia, by whatever name known, preserve the Wisdom of the ages. The Stanzas of Dzyan on which H. P. Blavatsky based her *Secret Doctrine* are written in Senzar, the key to which is exoterically lost.

Sera (Tib.) Large monastic college in Lhasa. One of the three most powerful in Tibet. (*See* **Depung** *and* **Ganden**.)

Sesshin (Jap.) Period of intensive meditation in a Rinzai Zen monastery, sometimes lasting a week, during which the monks sit in meditation for a large proportion of the day and night with frequent visits to the Rōshi (q.v.) for San-Zen (q.v.).

Sesshū (Jap.) One of the most famous Bst. artists of Japan (1421-1506). His range of technique varied from trees and birds to landscapes of Zen 'violence' never surpassed. Has been called the Wu-tao-Tsu (q.v.) of Japan.

Setchō (Jap.) **Hsueh-tou** (Chin.) One of the great Chinese Zen Masters (980-1052). He collected one hundred cases or stories of the earlier Chinese Masters and wrote on each a commentary in verse. These were later used by Engo (q.v.) in his own sermons. His own comments and Introductory Words were collected by his pupils and in 1125 published as the Hekigan Roku (q.v.).

Shaberon (Tib.) A superior adept in Tibetan Bsm.

S(h)akti (Sk.) Lit. Power or energy. A practice of Hindu Tantra (q.v.), used very differently in the Bst. Tantra of Tibet. The power of the Hindu deities is shown in art as a female companion or 'power' in sexual union. In the Bst. Tantra the sexual polarity is reversed, and the female represents Wisdom (Prajñā), while the male is its expression in action. The figures symbolize to the meditating mind the closest possible union of the Yab-Yum or basic duality of the manifested universe, and are to the Tibetan mind pure symbol. It is the Western mind which has added the erotic connotation. (*See* **Tantra**.) *See* Woodroffe, *Shakti* and *Shakta* (1920).

Shamanism The cult, found in many parts of Buddhist Asia and elsewhere, which centres round an intermediary whose psychic powers are so developed that he can link the ordinary daily world with the world of spirits. It has affinities with Bön (q.v.).

S(h)āntideva One of the most important writers of the Mahāyāna School. He lived in the seventh century A.D. and compiled two important works entitled *Siksha-Samuccaya* and *Bodhicaryāvatāra*. The former is a compendium of the doctrine of the M. School, and is compiled from over a hundred earlier M. works, many of them no longer extant. The latter deals with the rules of discipline for those following the Bodhisattva Path

175

of the M. School. *See* Bendall, *Siksha-Samuccaya* (Ldn.), 1922, *and* Barnett, *Path of Light* (1909).

S(h)arira (Sk.) An indestructible substance in pellet form said to be found in ashes of great saints on cremation.

S(h)ástra (Sk.) A discourse or philosophical analysis of the contents of a Sūtra, which thus becomes a commentary.

Shen-hsiu (Chin.) In Jap., Jinshu (605-706). One of the two most famous disciples of Hung-jen, the Fifth Patriarch, Chinese Bsm., the other being Hui-neng, the Sixth. The rival Schools founded by the two men, the North and South, became known as the Gradual and the Sudden respectively. Shen-hsiu's school, although patronized by the reigning Emperor, did not last very long, but from the Sudden School of Hui-neng sprang the present Rinzai and Sōtō Schools of Zen. For the two Gāthās, or poems, about the mirror and dust upon it, which epitomized their teachings, *see, The Sutra of Wei-Lang* (Hui-neng) trans. by Wong Mou-lam (1944).

Shen-hui (Chin.) In Jap., Jinne. One of the principal disciples of Hui-neng (q.v.), the Sixth Patriarch of Chin. Zen Bsm. (686-760). 'One of the most noteworthy characters in the early history of Zen thought' (Suzuki). From Dr Suzuki's occasional translations of some of Shen-hui's 'Sayings' it is clear that this is so.

Sherpa The Sherpas are Tibetan-Nepalese living in Nepal. Famous as natural mountaineers and the inseparable companions of all who climb in the Eastern Himalayas. They are Buddhists. The Sherpa Tensing was, with Sir Edmund Hillary, the first to climb Everest.

Shigatse Town in Tibet in which is the Tashilhumpo monastery, the seat of the Panchen Lama (q.v.).

Shikan Taza (Jap.) 'Sitting in awareness', a Sōtō Zen practice of quiet meditation, to be compared with the Rinzai Zen use of Kōans (q.v.). (*See* **Sōtō**.)

Shin (Jap.) The Shin-Shū, or Jōdo Shin-Shū is the School of Japanese Bsm. in which the teaching of Hōnen Shōnin (q.v.), of the Pure Land of Amida, was carried to its culmination by Shinran Shōnin (q.v.). Whereas in Hōnen's Jōdo-Shū faith and works went hand in hand, in Shinran's Shin-Shū faith in Amida will alone suffice. The Shin-Shū and Zen-Shū are the two largest schools of Bsm. in Japan today. (*See* **Jōdo, Pure Land**.) *See* Suzuki, *A Miscellany on the Shin Teaching of Buddhism,* Kyoto (1949) and *Shin Buddhism* (1970).

Shingon (Jap.) Japanese Buddhist School of the True Word. Established in Japan by Kōbō Daishi, c. A.D. 806. He was a great harmonizer, seeing every religion as an expression of definite stages in the pilgrimage of humanity to the self-realization of Buddhahood. He divided these stages into ten, from the lowest state of the man absorbed in material things, in whom the Buddha-nature had hardly begun to function, to the highest state of Shingon mysticism. The 'Hīnayāna' stage comes fourth in his scheme. The Shingon doctrine, derived from the Hindu Tantras (q.v.), is a pantheistic mysticism which sees the universe as an expression of ultimate reality, its goal the fruition of the Buddha-nature in the heart of man. It relies largely on ritual, such as the use of invocations (*mantras*) and hand poses (*mudrās*) (q.v.). The Supreme Reality is personified in Vairocana Buddha, the Buddha Sakyamuni being viewed as a partial manifestation of Vairocana (q.v.). The chief scriptures are *Mahāvairocana Sūtra* and *Vajrasekhara Sūtra*. (*See* **Japan, Kōbō Daishi, Kōyasan**.)

Shinran Shōnin 1173-1262. Founder of the Jōdo-Shin sect of Japan. A disciple of Hōnen (Jōdo sect), he carried the doctrine of salvation by faith in Amida to the extreme of one 'calling', of the name of Amida, being sufficient if done with a pure heart. He advocated marriage of priests, and was himself married. He popularized congregational worship, and wrote about four hundred hymns (*gāthās*) for use at the temple services. He also wrote the *Kyōgyōshinshū Monrui*, which deals exhaustively with the cardinal doctrines of Jōdo-shin Buddhism. (*See* **Jōdo, Shin.**) *See* G. Sasaki, *A Study of Shin Buddhism*, Tokyo (1925).

Shin-Shū (Jap.) *See* **Pure Land School.**

Shintō In Japan known as Kami-no-Michi, the Way of the Gods. Form of ancestor and nature worship which is indigenous religion of Japan. Has its own style of architecture for numerous temples and shrines. The Torii arch is Shintō. The Kami are primarily personifications of the feeling of holiness which some things, as trees and waterfalls, give to the beholder; hence forces of nature.

Shippei (Jap.) A stick on which a Zen Master supports himself and which he uses to deliver blows. Cp. *Hossu, Keisaku, Thirty Blows*.

Shōbōgenzō (Jap.) 'The Eye of the True Law.' One of the most famous works of Dōgen (q.v.) the Founder of Sōtō Zen in Japan. *See* Masunaga, *The Soto Approach to Zen*, for partial translation. (*See* **Sōtō.**)

Shōdōka (Jap.) The Song of Enlightenment of Yōka Daishi (Chin., Yung-chia), a pupil of Hui-neng, who died in 713. The poem is immensely popular in China and Japan. For trans. *see* Suzuki, *Manual of Zen Buddhism* (1935) and for trans. with commentary, Senzaki and McCandless, *Buddhism and Zen* (1953).

178

Shōgun (Jap.) Lit. Military commander. The title assumed by a line of military dictators who ruled Japan in dual control with the Emperor from 1192 to 1868, when the reigning Emperor reassumed control. The most famous family of Shōguns was that of the Tokugawa.

Shōji (Jap.) The sliding screens, still made of one thickness of white, semi-opaque paper, which form the outer walls of the rooms of a Japanese monastic building or house. Wooden shutters may be closed over them at night. *Shōji* carry no decoration. Cp. *Fusuma*, the inner screens or room walls, of double thickness of paper, on which some of the greatest art of Japan has been painted.

Shōkokuji (Jap.) Rinzai Zen monastery in Kyoto founded in 1383 by the most famous of the Ashikaga Shōguns, Yoshimitsu. It was he who built the Golden Pavilion (q.v.). Professor Sōhaku Ogata (q.v.), long the patron of Western Zen students visiting Japan, lived in Chōtoku-in, one of the sub-temples.

Shōnin (Jap.) 'A superior man.' Title of honour used from early times for a Bst. monk of superior attainment, e.g. Hōnen Shōnin and Shinran Shōnin.

Shōtoku, Prince (Jap.) 574-622. One of the greatest men in Japanese history. Suzuki calls him the father of Japanese Bsm. As Prince Regent to his aunt, the Empress Suiko, he used his patronage and genius to see that Bsm. struck root in Japanese soil. He built many monasteries, the most famous being Hōryūji (q.v.) near Nara, and wrote commentaries on three famous Sutras, the Saddharma Pundarīka (Hokekyō), the Srīmālā (Shōmangyō) and the Vimalakīrti (Yuimakyō).

Shōyō Roku (Jap.) Collection of stories of Chinese Zen masters made by Wanshi (q.v.) (1090-1157) of the Sōtō School.

179

To these stories Bashō (1165-1246) added his comment to make the Shōyō Roku, even as Engo's comments on Setchō's stories made the Hekigan Roku.

Shū (Jap.) A school or sub-division of a larger School of Japanese Bsm. Thus, the Shin-Shū or Zen-Shū.

S(h)ūnya (Sk.) Void. S(h)ūnyatā, Voidness. A doctrine fundamental to all M. philosophy; the dominant theme of the Prajñā-pāramitā literature (q.v.), of the Mādhyamika School of Nāgārjuna (q.v.), and behind the psychological terms of the Yogācāra School (q.v.). Yet Sūnyatā is not empty, being empty also of the concept of emptiness. To the extent that it is negative, its positive aspect is Tathatā (q.v.), the suchness or 'isness' of each thing. In the state of Prajñā, Wisdom, both emptiness and form are non-existent (*see Heart Sutra*). Behind all dualism, however subtly conceived, is Non-duality.

Shwe Dagon Most famous Bst. temple in Burma. Date of origin unknown, but very early. Approached by flight of steps to large platform from which rises enormous bell-shaped Stūpa to height of 370 feet. Lower part of Stūpa covered with gold plates and upper with gold leaf, constantly added to by devotees. The Hti (q.v.) or umbrella at top is studded with precious stones. Main Stūpa surrounded with great number of smaller shrines of differing artistic merit.

Siam (Thailand) The only Buddhist kingdom. Bsm. was introduced into Siam via Cambodia about A.D. 422. The doctrine is that of the Theravāda School. The King exercises authority over the monasteries and himself nominates the *Sangharāja* or head of the Sangha. King Mongkut reformed the Sangha, and encouraged the study of Pali. His son, King Chulalongkorn, had the whole of the Tipitaka printed at Bangkok in 1893, and distributed copies amongst the scholars and libraries of Europe and America. *See* Alabaster, *Wheel of the Law*; Young, *Kingdom of the Yellow Robe. (See* **Wat.**)

Siamese Sect The Siyama Samāgama was founded in Ceylon in the eighteenth century by Theras brought from Siam when the condition of the Sinhalese Sangha was at a low ebb. It is now an influential sect of high standing.

Siddhārtha (Sk.) Siddhattha (P.) The personal name of Gautama (P. Gotama), who became the Buddha. It means 'he whose aim is accomplished'.

Siddhas (Sk.) A list of eighty-four Perfected Ones (*siddha*) common to the Bst. and Shaivite tradition found in the Bsm. of Tibet. Their biographies are told in the Tibetan Canon, covering the seventh to the eleventh century. They have in common a dedication to the life of helping others, as taught by their various masters.

Siddhi (Sk.) From *sidh*, to attain. Spiritual powers, of two kinds, the lower and merely psychic, and the higher, the fruits of long periods of spiritual training. The former are involved in self; the latter are only available to those in whom self is dead. (*See* **Iddhis.**)

Sigiriya On the Lion Rock of Sigiriya, a natural fortress of rock rising from the jungle of Ceylon, King Kassapa built himself a palace, and there immured himself from his enemies from A.D. 479 to 497. Some of the exquisite frescoes then painted on the rock, preserved from the climate by an overhang, have survived to this day as fresh as when painted. They are of Apsarās (q.v.).

Sikkhā (P.) Training. The training of the would-be Bst. in the higher realms of Sīla (Morality), Samādhi (q.v.) and Paññā (q.v.), a threefold division of the Noble Eightfold Path (q.v.).

181

Sikkhāpada (P.) Steps of training; moral rules. For the five rules of self-training taken by all Bsts. *see* **Pansil**; for the eight rules taken for special periods *see* Attha-sīla and for the ten binding on all entrants to the **Sangha** (Order) *see* **Dasa-Sīla** *and* **Precepts**.)

Sikkim A small Bst. country in the Eastern Himalayas. The people are Lepchas, but in the seventeenth century a group of Tibetan families gained control, and the present royal family is of Tibetan descent. The Bsm. is that of the Nyingma-pa and Dug-pa sects of the unreformed Bsm. of Tibet.

Sīla (Sk. and P.) (1) Habit, behaviour, nature, character, e.g. *adānasīla*, not-giving-nature—stingy; *pāpasīla*, evil-nature —wicked. (2) Moral precepts, code of morality, Buddhist ethics. *Panca-sīla*, the Five Precepts; *Dasa-Sīla*, the Ten Precepts. (*See* **Precepts**.)

One of the moral trinity of *Dāna*, benevolence, *Sīla*, right deeds, *Bhāvanā*, purification and discipline of the mind, from which *Paññā*, wisdom, follows. (*See* **Pansil**.)

Dasa-Sīla, the ten points of good character, are: (1) To avoid taking life; (2) to avoid stealing; (3) to avoid indulgence in sensuality; (4) to avoid lying; (5) to avoid intoxication; (6) to avoid slandering and reviling others; (7) to avoid self-praise and frivolous talk; (8) to avoid avarice and covetousness; (9) to avoid enmity and malevolence; (10) to avoid heretical views, and deriding the Buddha, the Dhamma, the Sangha.

Sīlacāra, The Bikkhu Born J. F. M'Kechnie. On reading a copy of *Buddhism* (q.v.) published in Rangoon by the Bhikkhu Ananda Metteyya (q.v.), he sailed for Rangoon and there helped A. M. organize his Mission to London. Entered Order as Bhikkhu Silacara. Returned to England, actively helped with new Bst. Society of Great Britain and Ireland.

Trans. works of Paul Dahlke (q.v.) into English, and other works from Pali and German. But best known for own booklets, *Lotus Blossoms, A Young People's Life of the Buddha* and others on the basic principles of Theravāda. Retired to Sussex and died in 1951.

Silver Pavilion In Japanese Ginkakuji. Beautifully proportioned building near Kyoto erected by the Shōgun Yoshimasa in 1473. Less perfect than the Golden Pavilion (q.v.) it nevertheless has the original Tearoom. (*See* Cha-no-yu.)

Sin Bsm. recognizes no original sin in man, save those results of his own past causes which have not yet 'ripened'. The effects of any new act which is *akusala*, unwholesome, will be borne by the causer under the law of Karma. Hence the Bst. saying, 'we are punished by our sins, not for them'. (*See* Avidyā, Kammavipāka.)

Sinha (Sk. and P.) A lion. The inhabitants of Ceylon call themselves Sinhalese, the people of the Lion. Cp. Singha, the last name of all Sikhs.

Skandha (Sk.) **Khandha** (P.) The five causally conditioned elements of existence forming a being or entity. In the personal sense, the *Skandhas* are the elements which make up the personality in the sphere of *Samsāra* (q.v.). The five *Skandhas* are inherent in every form of life, either in an active or a potential state. In man, all five elements are active; (1) *Rūpa*, (2) *Vedanā*, (3) *Saññā*, (4) *Sankhāra*, (5) *Viññāna* (q.v.). Nowhere in these is there a permanent Self.

All are subject to the characteristics of existence, *Anicca, Dukkha, Anattā*. They form the temporal or phenomenal nature of man, and the belief that this collection constitutes a separate self or ego is the heresy of *sakkāyaditthi*, the first of the 'Ten Fetters' which bind men to the Wheel of Life.

Rūpa: Form, body, shape. Rūpa is not physical alone; there is a psychical rūpa, a mental rūpa, etc., but in considering the five *skandhas* it is usual to consider Rūpa as the material body composed of physical and etheric matter.

Vedanā: (q.v.) Feeling or sensation.

Saññā: (q.v.) Perception; awareness of, and assimilation of sensation.

Sankhāra: (q.v.) Impressions resulting from *vedanā* and *saññā*. The elements of consciousness. Emotional reactions.

Viññāna: (q.v.) Consciousness, the relation between subject and object.

The *Skandhas* dissolve after death so that the memory of personal experiences is not brought over to the next physical life. The result of that experience is, however, built into the character, so that the man is truly the result of his past thinking and doing. (*See* **Anattā, Ego, Sammitīya**.)

Smriti (Sk.) Mindfulness. *See* **Sati** (P.).

Sōdō (Jap.) The training school for monks in a Zen monastery. It has its Zendō (q.v.) where the monks meditate by day and sleep by night, and quarters for the Rōshi, the Zen teacher. It has its terms like any other school.

Sono Mama (Jap.) Colloquial meaning, 'just as it is'. As a Zen term, equivalent to the Sk. Tathatā, the Suchness or Isness of all things which ever is before 'things' are born.

Sotāpanna (P.) 'He who has entered the stream'. The first of the Four Paths (q.v.) to liberation. *Sotāpatti*, the state of a *sotāpanna*. One who has had vision of Nirvāna.

Sōtō (Jap.) The Sōtō Zen School of Japanese Bsm. was founded by Dōgen (q.v.), who brought the Chinese Tsao-tung

184

School to Japan in 1127. Teaching descended from Hui-neng through Tōsan and Wanshi (q.v.), as did Rinzai Zen through Huang Po (Ōbaku) and Rinzai (Lin-chi) and Eisai, who brought it to Japan in the same period. The West knows little of Sōtō Zen, most writers drawing their knowledge from D. T. Suzuki who is Rinzai. Sōtō relies on Shikan Taza (q.v.), deep meditation, rather than the 'sudden' methods with Kōan and Mondō of Rinzai, which concentrates on prajñā, Wisdom, and its direct attainment. Sōtō aims at repentance, then moral training, then meditation in the light of the Enlightenment which already exists within. The three, meditation, moral training and Enlightenment are facets of one process. We should live 'as if' we were what we are, enlightened Buddhas. 'Life is the active expression of Buddha at work', and we should act accordingly. The mother temples of the two branches are Eiheiji, near Fukui, and Sōjiji at the back of Yokohama. See Masunaga, The Sōtō Approach to Zen. (See Dōgen for Scriptures.) Cp. Rinzai.

Soul A term usually avoided by Buddhists to avoid misconception. Bsm. does not admit an immortal, unchanging entity created by a Deity, the destiny of which may be eternal happiness or eternal misery according to the deeds of the personality it ensouls. The 'soul' is the character created by experience in the phenomenal worlds, becoming more and more enlightened by following the Path, or more degraded by departing from it. (See Anattā, Ātman, Ego.)

Spars(h)a (Sk.) See Phassa (P.).

S(h)rāvaka (Sk.) Lit. a hearer, hence a pupil or beginner. When he undertakes the practice he becomes a Srāmanera, or Sāmanera (P.) (q.v.). Many M. scriptures refer to non-Mahāyānist schools as those of Srāvakas or Pratyeka-Buddhas (q.v.), by the former meaning the remaining schools of the Hīnayāna.

S(h)rāvasti (Sk.) In P. Sāvatthi. The capital of the kingdom of Kosala (q.v.) which, with the kingdom of Magadha (q.v.) covered most of the country in which the Buddha served his Ministry. Here Anāthapindika, the merchant, erected the Vihāra in the Jetavana Grove which he bought by covering it with pieces of gold.

S(h)rīmālā (Sk.) Queen Srīmālā of Ayodhya, recognized as a Bodhisattva, wrote a Sūtra bearing her name on which the great Regent Prince Shotoku (574-622) of Nara wrote a commentary, together with commentaries on the Saddharma-pundarīka and Vimalakīrti Nirdesa, and thus made Bsm. the national religion in Japan.

Srong Tsan Gampo (Tib.) A great king of Tibet (630-698) and its first patron of learning. Introduced the Indian alphabet, and built a fort on the site of the present Potala. His two wives, being princesses of China and Nepal, were Bsts. They converted the king to Bsm. and he in turn made Bsm. the religion of Tibet. (*See* **Tārā, Tibet.**)

States of Consciousness The Abhidhamma (q.v.) section of the Pali Canon analyses consciousness into 89 or 121 states, variously called Dhammā or Cittāni. See also the four Bhūmi or four worlds of Kāma-, Rūpa-, Arūpa-loka and Lokuttara (q.v.). For table *see* Nyanatiloka, *Buddhist Dictionary* (1950).

Stede, Dr William Born 1882. German Pali scholar who spent his life in England. Bst. and Theosophist. Lecturer in School of Oriental Studies 1926-49. Compiled with Professor Rhys Davids the *Pali-English Dictionary* pub. by P.T.S. President of P.T.S. 1950 to death in 1958.

Sthavira (Sk.) The Sk. and less known form of the Pali *Thera*, a senior monk of the Theravāda School (q.v.). Theras
186

and Bhikkhus deriving their ordination from Theravāda sources but working in M. countries, where the Sk. form is better known, use Sthavira and Bhikshu for their rank instead of Thera and Bhikkhu.

Stopping In Bst. philosophy the mind must for ever flow and never be 'stopped' or 'blocked' in a thought. 'Let the mind abide nowhere.' The ideal is to 'walk on' through all problems and situations. To pause is to be locked in a concept; to stop is spiritually to die.

Stūpa (Sk.) **Thupa** (P.) Burial mound. At first a mound of earth, later cased in brick, containing the ashes or relics of an important person. Some very small, some very large as at Piprawa (q.v.), said to have been the height of St Paul's Cathedral. All built on same symbolic pattern. In Ceylon called Dagoba (q.v.). In Nepal they appeared early as Pagodas (q.v.) and thus passed to China and Japan. In Tibet called Chörten (q.v.). Cp. *Caitya.*

Subha (Sk. and P.) Beauty, the beautiful. (*See* **Beauty.**)

Suchness *See* **Tathatā**.

Sudden School of Zen Bsm. Cp. Gradual. Much has been written of the difference between the Sudden School of Hui-neng, the 6th Patriarch of Zen Bsm., and the Gradual School of Shen-hsiu, his fellow pupil of the 5th Patriarch, Hung-jen. Perhaps the two methods reflect two types of mind. For some, spiritual understanding is of slow growth, achieved step by step to the end. As against this systematic type is the intuitive mind which, however short or long the preparation, in the end leaps suddenly and absolutely to an awareness beyond thought. For the 'moment' of Satori (q.v.) in Rinzai Zen is a touch of the Absolute; as such, incomparable with any awareness achieved up to that moment. There is Enlightenment and not-yet-Enlightenment; there is no bridge between. Yet long preparation is necessary for all, in one life or another, and Enlightenment itself may be graded in quality and completeness. Only the Buddha achieved the level of Sambuddha, the All-Enlightened One.

Suddhodana The father of Gautama Siddhārtha, the Buddha. Rāja of the Sākya clan, whose capital was Kapilavastu.

Suffering *See* **Dukkha.**

Suicide According to Bst. doctrine a man cannot avoid suffering by taking his life, nor does he escape from the 'Wheel of Life' by so doing. The destruction of the physical body merely transfers the entity to other spheres of existence, and rebirth into the physical follows. Physical life is considered of great importance, as it is only here that the Way of Liberation can be followed, and Enlightenment attained. Taking one's life is, therefore, waste of opportunity. Voluntary sacrifice of one's life for the welfare of others is considered meritorious, the motive being altruistic.

Sukha (P.) Happiness. The opposite of Dukkha (q.v.) suffering.

Sukhāvati (Sk.) The Paradise or Pure Land of the Jōdo and Shin Schools of Japan. The 'Western Paradise' of Amida. Its glories are described in Oriental metaphor in the two *Sukhāvati Vyūha Sūtras.* For English translations see vol. 49 S.B.E. (*See* **Pure Land, Shin.**)

Sukhodaya (or Sukhotai) (Siam.) Site of a city now in ruins in N. Central Thailand which in thirteenth century became first Thai capital. The S. School of sculpture, a fusion of many cultures, is unique and famous for style of Buddha Rūpas. *See* Le May, *The Buddhist Art of Siam* (1938).

Sumeru (or Meru) The mythological mountain at the centre of the Universe. Shared by Hindu and Bst., the name of the god at the top varies accordingly.

Sumi-e (Jap.) The Chinese-Japanese method of writing and painting with a brush on absorbent paper or silk. No re-touching is possible, and all that is to be written or painted must be clear in the mind before the brush touches the paper. A wide range of brushes is used, but the 'colour' is confined to shades of dark brown to black. The technique required is a perfect instrument for the lightness of touch and spontaneity of the Zen mind.

Sūrangama Sūtra (Sk.) A large and somewhat shapeless Sūtra probably compiled in China. Known in Japan as the Ryōgonkyō. In it the Buddha reveals the causes of the illusion which leads to existence and how to escape from it. For analysis *see* Suzuki, *Manual of Zen Buddhism* (1935), chap. VI. For trans. extract *see* W. of Bsm., Nos. 72-3.

Sutta (P.) **Sūtra** (Sk.) Lit. a thread on which jewels are strung. Applied to that part of the Canon containing the dialogues or discourses of the Buddha. The *Sutta Pitaka* consists of the five Nikāyas, i.e. Dīgha, Majjhima, Samyutta, Anguttara, Khuddaka. For further details see A.P.C.

In the M. School no serious claim is made that its Sūtras are the words of the Buddha, and the authors are unknown. All save one, however, are put into the mouth of the Buddha, the exception being the Platform Sūtra of Hui-neng (q.v.).

Sutta Nipāta (P.) One of the oldest collections of Suttas (Sermons) in the Pali Canon, and one of the most popular.

A.P.C. 267. Written in a mixture of prose and verse. The two most famous are the Mettā (Goodwill) Sutta and the Mahā-Mangala (Greatest Blessing) Sutta. Cp. Dhammapada which has some material in common. *See, Woven Cadences of Early Buddhists,* trans. Hare (1945).

Suzuki, Daisetz Teitaro, LITT.D.(OTANI UNIV.) Japanese philosopher and writer, born 18 October 1870 of a Rinzai Zen family. While at Imperial Univ. Tokyo studied Zen at Kamakura under the Rōshi Imagita Kosen. On the death of the Rōshi studied under his successor, Sōyen Shaku (author of *Sermons of a Buddhist Abbot* (1906), and under him gained his enlightenment. To Chicago in 1897 to help Paul Carus in his Open Court Publishing Co. In 1900 published trans. of *The Awakening of Faith,* his first major work. In 1908 to Europe, and again in 1910 when he studied in London and Paris. In 1911, married Beatrice Lane Suzuki, d. 1939. In 1920 founded *The Eastern Buddhist* (1921-39) (q.v.). In 1927-34 produced three vols. of *Essays in Zen Buddhism.* 1936, to London for World Congress of Faiths. Spent war years at Kamakura in Engakuji (q.v.), writing. 1949, made Member of the Japanese Academy and decorated by Emperor with Cultural Medal. 1950-58, travelled widely in the West; to Honolulu, California, London for three visits, and some years in New York, lecturing. In 1958 retired to Japan to organize the Matsugaoka Library, which he had founded with the library of his wife on her death in 1939; 90th birthday celebrated in 1960 at Kyoto with presentation to him of *Buddhism and Culture,* Ed. Prof. S. Yamaguchi. Author of a score of major works in English, more in Japanese, and innumerable articles, nearly all on Zen Buddhism, attempting to explain its nature and importance to the Western world. [Died 1966.]

Svabhāva (Sk.) As applied cosmically, the 'own-nature' basic substance of the universal Mūlaprakriti or root essence,

thus equating with Tathatā (q.v.). At human level it equates
with Ātman. Svabhāvakāya, 'Own nature body' equates with
Dharmakāya (q.v.).

Swastika (Sk.) The revolving cross. It symbolizes the ceaseless activity of the universal life principle evolving the cosmos.
Its form as 卐 symbolizes *Pravritti* (q.v.), the outgoing flow of
the universe. The reverse form symbolizes the return flow,
Nirvritti (q.v.). Hence 'two forms of Brahma'.

The Swastika is used in China and Japan as the symbol of
prosperity and long life.

Swayambhūnāth Large temple-monastery on a hill outside
Katmandu. Used by Buddhists and Hindus alike, and thus
unique in Asia. The site was already old in the time of Asoka
(third century B.C.). The golden top of the central Stūpa or
garbha can be seen from far over the plain. At one side is the
modern Theravāda Vihāra founded by the Ven. Amritānanda,
the leading Buddhist in Nepal (q.v.).

Tai Hsü Famous modern Chinese Bst. Organized revival of
Bsm. in China between the wars, for which founded Chinese
Bst. Association and the journal Hai Cha'o Yin, the Voice of
the Tide. Travelled in Europe 1928-9 when founded Les
Amis du Bouddhisme (q.v.) in Paris. Worked hard to improve
relations between Bsts. of East and West. Sole work in
English is trans. of *Lectures in Buddhism*, a booklet published
in Paris, 1928.

Taishō The Taishō Issaikyō is the name of an edition in
55 vols. of all Bst. Scriptures extant in Chinese compiled by
J. Takakusu in 1924-32. Generally adopted as superseding the
compilation by Nanjio (q.v.). The Index to titles of the Taishō
edition exists in two versions: (1) the *Catalogue Annexe du
Taisho Issaikyo*, Tokyo, 1929, and (2) *Fascicule Annexe* to
the Hōbōgirin (Encyclopaedic-dictionary of Bsm. from

Chinese and Japanese sources), Tokyo, 1931. The Taishō edition is usually quoted as T.

Takuhatsu (Jap.) Periodic tour through the streets near a Zen monastery by monks wearing special dress, to beg for food or money for the upkeep of the monastery. (*See* **Hō.**)

Tan (Jap.) The raised platform round the sides of the Zen-dō (q.v.) of a Zen monastery covered with tatami, straw mats, on which the monks meditate by day and sleep by night.

Tan-ching (Chin.) The shortened version of the Chinese name for the work translated into English as 'The Sūtra spoken by the Sixth Patriarch on the High Seat of the Vehicle of the Law', usually known as the Sūtra of Hui-neng (q.v.).

Tanhā (P.) **Trishnā** (Sk.) Thirst for sentient existence. (*See* **Desire.**)

Tanjur (Tib.) 'Translation of Treatises.' The second part of the Tibetan Bst. Canon, the first being the Kanjur (q.v.). The collection contains 225 volumes of works by Indian masters, being partly commentaries on the Sūtras and partly on the Tantras. These translations from the Sk. are all the more valuable where the original has been lost. Little has yet been translated into any European language. (*See* **Bu-ston.**)

Tanka (1) (Tib.) Painted religious wall-hanging on foundation of linen. For more usual spelling *see* **Than-ka.** (2) (Jap.) The verse form of 31 syllables arranged in five lines of 5, 7, 5, 7, 7. Cp. better known *Haiku* of three lines arranged 5, 7, 5.

Tantra (Sk.) The Tantras are writings dating from the sixth century A.D. in India. There are now two types, Hindu and Bst. Both are systems of meditation with the use of ritual,

192

highly cryptic in form, the meaning being handed down from Guru to Chela. Both symbolize the basic duality of manifestation in figures, in sculpture or in pictures, composed of some deity or aspect of Reality with a female partner locked in sexual embrace. In the Hindu Tantras these Saktis (q.v.) represent the female 'power' of the god, whereas in the Vajrayāna or Bst. Tantras of Tibet the female represents Wisdom (Prajñā), and the male is the active 'use' or compassionate 'skill in means' of that Wisdom. The ritual to aid meditation involves the use of Mantras (q.v.), Mudrās (q.v.) and Yantras (q.v.). To the Vajrayāna belongs the conception of five Dhyāni-Buddhas with their corresponding Dhyāni-Bodhisattvas, aspects which appear in meditation (Dhyāna) of the one primordial Adi-Buddha (q.v.). Tantric doctrines spread from India to Peking as the Mantra School, and thence to Japan as the Shingon School (q.v.). For Indian Tantra *see* Woodroffe, *Shakti and Shakta* (1920). For Bst. Tantra *see* Govinda, *Foundations of Tibetan Mysticism* (1959). For both, *see* Snellgrove, *Buddhist Himalaya* (1957).

Tantrayāna (Sk.) Alternative name for Vajrayāna (q.v.) the Tantric school of Tibet.

Tao (Chin.) A term having three separate meanings. In the sense of a Way, it implies the Way of Heaven; in the sense of leader-follower or one who follows a leader, it implies a pilgrim of the Way, and in its third sense, that of to tell or proclaim, it echoes the Buddha's injunction to his Bhikkhus to 'proclaim the Doctrine glorious . . .', i.e. his Middle Way to liberation. Tao is the central concept of the *Tao Tê Ching*, the classic of Taoism, the teaching of Lao-tzu in the sixth century B.C. With its gentle mysticism it has been called the mother of Zen Buddhism, the fierce and masculine father being *Bodhidharma* (q.v.). *See, Tao Tê Ching*. Trans. Ch'u Ta-kao, Buddhist Society (1937). (*See* **Chuang Tzu**.)

193

Tao-hsin (Chin.) In Jap. Dōshin. The Fourth Chinese Zen Patriarch (580-651). He asked his master, Seng-t'san, the Third Patriarch, to show him the way to deliverance. 'Who puts you under restraint?' asked the master. 'No one,' admitted the pupil. 'Then why do you ask for deliverance?', asked the master, and Tao-hsin had his enlightenment.

Taoism One of the 'tripod' or three religions of China, founded by Lao Tzu circa 600 B.C. Its principles are derived mainly from the *Tao Tê Ching* and from the writings of Chuang Tzu who lived some 200 years later. Has had great influence on Chinese Bsm. and especially on Zen. Often called 'the Mother of Zen'. (*See* **Tao.**)

Tapas (Sk.) **Tapa** (P.) Austerities, renounced by the Buddha in the course of his search for Enlightenment as being useless.

Tārā (Sk.) In Tibetan Dōlma. The Tibetan Goddess of Mercy. The Wisdom of Avalokiteshvara (Tib. Chenresi) who manifests in the Dalai Lama. When King Sron-tsan-Gampo married two Bst. wives from China and Nepal in the seventh century they converted him to Bsm., and Tibet became a Bst. country. The two Queens were thenceforth regarded as the White Tara and the Green Tara respectively. The White Tara is depicted in art as having eyes in her forehead, hands and feet in order to see and thus to help all suffering; the Green Tara is seated with one foot down. Other Taras were added to the pantheon later.

Tariki (Jap.) Salvation by 'other Power', usually the personification of the Absolute in *Amida* (q.v.). To be distinguished from *Jiriki* (q.v.), salvation by one's own efforts as advocated in the Theravāda. (*See* **Pure Land School.**)

Tashi Lama (Tib.) The Panchen Lama or Panchen Rimpoche, because his seat is at the Tashilhumpo monastery at

Shigatse, became known in European literature as the Tashi Lama. Tibetans would not know him by this designation. (*See* **Panchen Lama.**)

Tashilhumpo A large monastery near Shigatse, Tibet, founded in 1445. The official residence of the Panchen Lama (q.v.). It is from this word that the incorrect title Tashi Lama (q.v.) was taken.

Tatami (Jap.) The thick straw mats which cover the floor of a Japanese room. Of standard size, 6 feet by 3 feet, they are used for the measurement of a room. A Tea-room e.g. may be described as a 4½ mat room, thus 9 feet square. As the users of such a room sit on cushions on the floor, shoes are removed on entering.

Tathāgata (Sk.) A title of the Buddha, used by his followers, and also by himself when speaking of himself. Derivation doubtful, but usually derived from *tathā-āgata* (thus come), or *tathā-gata* (thus gone), and given the meaning 'He who has come and gone as former Buddhas': i.e. teaching the same truths, and following the same Path to the same Goal.
The M. School prefer: One who has attained full realization of Suchness (*Tatha-tā*); i.e., become one with the Absolute (*Dharmakāya*), so that he 'neither comes from anywhere (*na āgamana*), nor goes to anywhere (*na gamana*)'.

Tathatā (Sk.) Lit. 'Thusness' or 'Suchness'. Term used in Mahāyāna for the ultimate and unconditioned nature of all things. In one sense it is *S(h)ūnya* (q.v.) expressed positively. It is that which is expressed in all separate things, which is not different from them and which is not divided by them. It cannot be called the One as distinct from the Many, for it is not distinct from anything. Nothing can be denied or affirmed

195

concerning it, for these are modes of expression which exclude and thereby create opposition. It can only be understood by realizing that one can neither find it by searching nor lose it by trying to separate oneself from it. Yet it has to be found. Cp. *Dharmakāya, S(h)ūnya, Yathābhūtam.*

Teishō (Jap.) A sermon, with commentary, on a text from a Scripture, given by the Rōshi during a period of Sesshin (q.v.) in a Rinzai Zen temple.

Tejas (Sk.) **Tejasa** (P.) Shining, radiant.

Tendai (Jap.) Japanese Bst. School founded by Dengyō Daishi (767-822) on Mt. Hiei near Kyoto in 805. It derives from the T'ien-t'ai of China which in turn derives from the Yogācāra of India. Dengyō aimed at a synthesis of existing Bst. teaching, and his School was the source and inspiration of much later development. It remained, however, largely intellectual, and left the way clear for the ritual of Shingon, the dynamic immediacy of intuitive Zen and the religious simplicity of Shin (q.v.).

Terma (Tib.) Revelations. Scriptures said to be from time to time discovered in caves and other hidden places by members of the Nyingma-pa School (q.v.) of Tibetan Bsm. They are alleged to be the esoteric teachings of Padma Sambhava (q.v.).

Thailand *See* **Siam.**

Than-ka (Tib.) Tibetan paintings, usually in tempera, of divinities. Hieratic in form, and produced on a rigid formula, they are often of very high craftsmanship and beauty of colour. Many are Mandalas (q.v.). They are used on the walls of temples and shrines as subjects for meditation, and as banners. *See* A. Gordon, *The Iconography of Tibetan Lamaism* (1939).

Thera (P.)   An 'Elder' in the Sangha (q.v.). A senior member of the Order who, by length of years as a respected Bhikkhu or by exceptional qualities of character, is generally accorded this honorary title. (Cp. *Lama, Sayadaw.*)

Thera-gāthā and **Theri-gāthā**   The names of two works of the Pali Canon (A.P.C. 275, 276). An important collection of poems or hymns relating to the experiences of arhatship. Eng. trans. *Psalms of the Brethren,* and *Psalms of the Sisters* (P.T.S.).

Theravāda   The 'Doctrine of the Elders' who formed the 1st Buddhist Council (q.v.). The sole survivor of the 18 sects into which by the third century B.C. the original Hīnayāna School of Bsm. was divided. Until recently this school was known in the West by its generic name of Hīnayāna, which means small or lesser vehicle (of salvation), but this term of reproach, coined by the Mahāyānists, has now been dropped in favour of the more accurate and less discourteous name of *Theravāda,* the Way of the Elders. (*See* **Hīnayāna, Mahā-yāna.**) As the Theravāda school covers Ceylon, Burma, Siam and Cambodia it is sometimes called the Southern School, to distinguish it from the Northern or Mahāyāna School which covers Tibet, Mongolia, China, Korea and Japan. (*See* **Pitaka.**)

Theosophy   Wisdom Religion, or Wisdom of the Gods. Sometimes incorrectly rendered as the 'Wisdom of God'. The substratum of Truth on which all religions are based; the source from which they derive whatever Truth they contain. The esoteric interpretation of all religious doctrines and dogmas. The various cults and practices now grafted on to certain Theosophical Societies have little in common with the original teaching, for which see *Key to Theosophy* and other works by H. P. Blavatsky (q.v.). (*See* **Blavatsky, Olcott.**)

'Thirty Blows' This phrase, a favourite of the Zen Master Tokusan, who sometimes threatened his monks with 'thirty blows' whatever they said in answer to his questions, has become a symbol of so-called violent methods of Zen masters for helping pupils to break through the fetters of thought and attain Satori. The violence, amounting to an occasional buffet, is merely one means of bringing long-built-up tension to the breaking point of this supreme experience. Where words are useless other means must be used, a joke, a gesture, silence— or a blow.

Thittila, The Ven. U Thittila, Mahā Thera Born 1896. Distinguished Burmese Bst. A brilliant scholar, he studied at the Theosophical Society at Adyar before coming to England, where he spent the war years. While employed on a Burmese dictionary he was invited to become a Bst. worker in England and lectured widely for the Buddhist Society, of which he became Librarian. On return to Burma became Lecturer in Abhidhamma in Rangoon University, with frequent visits to Europe and U.S.A.

Three Signs of Being This famous trilogy, a fundamental doctrine in the Theravāda, points out that all manifested things without exception are inseparable from Anicca, change, Dukkha, suffering or imperfection, and Anattā, which negatively means possessing no separate and immortal soul or spiritual entity, and positively implies the oneness and inseverability of life, the life-force of the universe, however different and fleeting its forms.

'Thus Have I Heard' 'Evam me Sutam' (P.). A phrase with

which Bhikkhus open their recitation of a Scripture to show
that they are repeating the Scriptures as handed down.

Tibet Bsm. was introduced into Tibet about 640 A.D. but
made little progress until visit by Padma Sambhava (q.v.) in
eighth century when it seems that he introduced the Vinaya
Rules, some Yogācāra doctrines and something of the Tantras
of Bengal. A period of translation followed, but the newly
established religion degenerated until in the eleventh century
Atīsa (q.v.) reformed the existing Bsm. and founded the Kahdam-pa Order. About the same time Marpa and Milarepa
founded the Kargyut-pa School, and the Nyingma-pa appears
as an organized School. In the fifteenth century Tsong-kha-pa
carried out sweeping reforms and founded his own Gelug-pa
Order, the Yellow Hats, to which the Dalai and Panchen
Lama of the day belong. Tantric ritual plays a large part in
all the Orders or Schools, and all levels of spiritual development are to be found, from the indigenous Bön (q.v.) to the
greatest heights of spirituality achieved by man. For ranks
within the Order, *see* **Tibetan Buddhist Order**. (*See also*
Tantra, Tibetan Buddhism, Schools of, *and* **Tulku**.)

'Tibetan Book of the Dead, The' A book published in 1927
as an English rendering of the Tibetan Bardo Thödöl by the
Lama Kazi Dawa-Samdup, edited by Dr W. Y. Evans-Wentz.
The Bardo Thödöl is a work of the Nyingma-pa School (q.v.).
It is a Tantric work based on Indian Hatha Yoga, and means
'Liberation by hearing on the After-death Plane'. It purports
to describe methods of enabling a dying man to pass through
death and rebirth without losing consciousness.

Tibetan Buddhism, Schools of In approximate chronological
order the main schools are: The Nyingma-pa, usually credited
to Padma Sambhava in the eighth century and certainly
flourishing in the twelfth. The Kahdam-pa, founded by Atīsa

199

in 1038. The Kargyut-pa founded by Marpa and Milarepa in the eleventh century with its off-shoot, the Dug-pa. The Sakya-pa, of about the same date, and the Gelug-pa, founded by Tsong-kha-pa in the late fourteenth century as the Reformed School. Compared with the considerable reforms carried out by Tsong-kha-pa, the Kargyut-pa and Sakya-pa are but semi-reformed, while the Dug-pa and the Nyingma-pa were unaffected.

Tibetan Buddhist Order The ranks in the Order, itself called Gendun are, first, a Trapa, which means a monk, of any rank. The novice, equivalent to the Theravāda Sāmanera, is a Getsul. The fully ordained monk is a Gelong. A Lama is of senior standing, in years or prestige, and is at least of the rank of a Thera. A Geshe is literally a spiritual teacher, but has the rank equivalent to a doctor of divinity, a man learned in ecclesiastical law and practice. A Tulku (q.v.) will be called Lama, but also bear the title Rimpoche (q.v.).

Tiloka (P.) **Triloka** (Sk.) The Three Worlds, a phrase meant to embrace all manifestations. The worlds are (i) Kāma-loka, the field of the five senses, (ii) Rūpa-loka, the plane of invisible yet existing form corresponding to certain of the *Jhānas* (q.v.) or planes of meditation, and (iii) Arūpa-loka, the 'formless' world corresponding to the higher levels of the *Jhānas. See* **States of Consciousness.**

Tipitaka (P.) The three Baskets of the Law, being divisions of the Pali Canon. (*See* **Pitaka.**)

Ti-ratana (P.) The 'Three Jewels' or Gems of Bsm. The Buddha, the Dhamma, and the Sangha.

Tirthakara (Sk.) A philosopher not belonging to Bsm. or who at least is not on the Bodhisattva path. Usually classed with

200

Srāvakas, mere hearers and Pratyeka Buddhas, who are not dedicated to the service of mankind.

Tīrthika (Sk.) Lit. a lord-user. A term used in Buddhism to apply to members of the other schools, with the implication of unbelievers.

Ti-sarana (P.) The Threefold Refuge in *Buddha, Dhamma* and *Sangha*, which follows the invocation to the Buddha in *Pansil* (q.v.) and precedes the five-fold vow of *Pansil* or *Pancha-Sīla*.

Tōdaiji (Jap.) Bst. Temple at Nara, Japan. Mother temple of Kegon School. The Hondō is largest wooden building in the world. Rebuilt in twelfth century but houses enormous figure of Vairocana Buddha 53 feet high, finished in 749. Before the Hondō is famous bronze lantern whose panels portray celestial figures.

Tokonoma (Jap.) The alcove in the principal room of a Japanese house, once a shrine for some deity and still a shrine for beauty. Only a single picture and a single vase with one or two blooms will be found therein, but these will be as perfect as the owner's purse and taste allow.

Torana (Sk.) Ornamental gateway. From this word may be derived the Shintō Torii arch of Japan. Also used of the doors or gates of a Mandala (q.v.).

Tōsan Ryōkai (Jap.) The real Founder of the Sōtō Zen School (q.v.). Tung-shang Liang-chich (Chin.). He lived 807-69 and was therefore a contemporary of Rinzai, the Founder of Rinzai Zen. He developed the doctrine of Five Ranks (q.v.) which, however, later fell into disrepute and was not used by Dōgen, the founder of the Sōtō School in Japan.

Transference of Merit   In Pali, Patti-dāna. (*See* **Merit, Parivarta.**)

Transmission of the Heart-Seal of the Buddha   Hui-neng, the Sixth Patriarch of Zen Bsm., was given the Seal of the true Dharma by his master Hung-jen, the Fifth Patriarch, as described in the former's Platform Sutra. He did not pass it on to a successor. Here is a paradox, for there were many great Masters after him. Yet there is no Truth to transmit, seeing that all minds are inseverably Mind-Only, and as such already enlightened. But a master can and does 'seal' his pupil's achievement of the same Enlightenment, by testing and approving it as true. (*See* **Inka, Seal.**)

Transmission of the Lamp   In Chinese, Ch'uan Teng Lu. In Japanese Dentō Roku. Collection, compiled about 1004 by Tao-yuan, of stories and sayings of Zen masters. It is the earliest collection extant. Never yet translated in full, it is the source of large numbers of stories quoted by writers on Zen in English, including Dr Suzuki.

Trapa (Tib.)   A monk of the Tibetan Bst. Order. A generic term, for the Trapa may be a Gelong, of full ordination, a Lama of much senior standing, a Geshe, or 'doctor of divinity' or a Tulku, entitled to the name of Rimpoche. (*See* **Tibetan Buddhist Order.**)

Trikāya (Sk.)   The M. doctrine of the Three Bodies. Originally the doctrine of the basic unity of the Reality underlying manifestation, the phenomenal or Nirmānakāya (q.v.), and the noumenal or Sambhogakāya (q.v.), being aspects of the One Ultimate Reality, the Dharmakāya (q.v.), one in essence with Tathatā (q.v.).
   As applied to the development of Buddhahood and Bodhisattvahood, the doctrine teaches that each aspirant for

Buddhahood may, on attaining the Goal, renounce final Nirvāna and keep in touch with humanity by dwelling in the Nirmānakāya, through which he may function at will on any of the phenomenal planes of existence, the Sambhogakāya being the vehicle of the Divine Power of the Dharmakāya. (*See* **Tulku.**)

Trishnā (Sk.) **Tanhā** (P.) Thirst for sentient existence. (*See* **Desire.**)

Tsong-kha-pa (Tib.) 'The man from the land of Onions' (1355-1417). One of the greatest names in Tibetan history, he was born on the site of the present Kum-bum monastery (q.v.), and at an early age dedicated his life to the complete reform of Tibetan Bsm. He founded the Ganden (q.v.) monastery 26 miles from Lhasa and called his new Order the Gelug-pa, 'the virtuous ones'. To this day the senior members wear on important occasions a yellow headdress, all others still wearing the red hat which, however, is usually associated with the Red Hat or Nyingma-pa School (q.v.). In the new Order, which replaced the Kahdam-pa founded by Atisa (q.v.), he made no great innovations, but tightened the discipline, abolished alcohol, enforced celibacy, cut down magic and the proliferation of divinities, and for his students wrote a special Lam-rim (q.v.) or set of precepts which is still the Order's basic text-book. Both the Dalai and the Panchen Lama are members of this Order. Other Schools adopted the reforms at least in part, being now referred to as semi-reformed. Others, e.g. the Nyingma-pa, remained unaffected. Tsong-kha-pa died at Ganden, and is enshrined there in a magnificent casket of gold.

Tucci, Guiseppe b. 1901. Italian authority on Tibetan Bsm. Professor of Sanskrit in the University of Rome. Founder and Head of IsMEO (Istituto Italjano per il Medio ed Extremo

Oriente). Author of many works in Italian. In English, *Tibetan Painted Scrolls*, 3 vols. (1949), *To Lhasa and Beyond* (1956).

Tulku (Tib.) Or Trulku. Spelt Sprul-sku. Mongol. equivalent Hutukhtu, also Khobilkhan. Lit. Emanation, a form created and thus a phantom. A difficult subject as many doctrines blend in it; hence divergent descriptions all partially true. (1) The Nirmānakāya (q.v.), itself a doctrine of great complexity. The appearance-on-earth body of a Buddha, who has to this extent refused Nirvāna to be available to help mankind. (2) The Bodhisattva's power to produce emanations at will as 'skilful means', to help humanity towards Enlightenment. (3) The overshadowing and partial using by a spiritual power of a human body chosen for the purpose. In this sense Jesus was a Tulku of the Christ-Principle. (4) The actual reincarnation of a holy man, whether a great teacher or merely a previous Abbot of the monastery. In all cases the recognition of the status of Tulku (q.v.), who is given the title Rimpoche, 'Precious One' (q.v.), in the body of a child, is a matter of diligent inquiry and strict rules of proof. *See* Norbu, *Tibet is my Country*, chap. 9 (1960). Rimpoche are not necessarily great men in the human sense, in intellectual strength or holiness, nor do they wield power as such, save as the vehicles of a Power beyond them. The outstanding examples of the doctrine are the Dalai and Panchen Lamas, whose Power is that of Avalokitesvara and Amitābha respectively.

Tum-mo (Tib.) Vital heat, the driving force of inner self-training. In its highest manifestation cognate with Kundalinī (q.v.) and at its lowest a method of inducing physical warmth which enables the trainee to meditate naked in the snow at 10,000-15,000 feet. Mme David-Neel (q.v.) acquired this power while living in Tibet. *See* her *With Mystics and Magicians in Tibet* (1931), pp. 216-229.

Tun-huang (Chin.) Site of a famous series of caves in China re-discovered in 1900 after being sealed since circa A.D. 1000. Contained magnificent collection of pictures, sculpture and MS. which have affected modern views on T'ang Dynasty art and learning. Contents date from A.D. 600 to 1000. Indian influence strong in Cave of a Thousand Buddhas, and in some painting. *See* Gray and Vincent, *Buddhist Cave Paintings at Tun-huang* (1959).

Tushita (Sk.) The Heaven world in which the Buddha-to-be, Maitreya (q.v.), waits for his coming.

Twelve Principles of Buddhism In 1945 the Buddhist Society drafted Twelve principles of Buddhism in the hope that they might be widely accepted as common to all Schools of Bsm. In 1946 they were accepted at Kyoto at a meeting of a Committee of all Bst. Schools in Japan convened by Christmas Humphreys, and later accepted by the Sangharāja or supreme Patriarch of Thailand and the Thai Sangha's supreme Council. They were later approved by senior members of the Sangha of Burma and Ceylon. They have been translated into sixteen languages. They appear in Humphreys' *Buddhism*, and are published separately by the Buddhist Society (q.v.). (*See also* **Olcott.**)

Uccheda (P.) Annihilation.

Udāna Lit. a 'breathing out', an 'exultant cry'. The title of one of the oldest works in the Pali Pitakas. *See* A.P.C. 265. Trans. into English: D. M. Strong, *The Udana, or the Solemn Utterances of the Buddha* (Luzac, 1902).

Udgīta (Sk.) The invocation OM (q.v.), 'the highest and most concentrated mantric expression into which the essence of the universe, as realized within the human consciousness, is compressed' (Govinda). (*See also* **Pranava.**)

Umpan (Jap.) Lit. 'Cloud-plate'. A hanging gong of bronze used in Zen monasteries to announce that a meal is ready. *See* Appendices to Suzuki, *The Training of the Zen Buddhist Monk* (1934).

Unconscious A term used by D. T. Suzuki to translate the Chinese *wu-hsin*, lit. 'no mind' or 'no thought'. This does not mean mere vacuity, but rather freedom from attachment to thoughts. This should be distinguished from the Unconscious of modern psychology. (*See* **Bhavanga, Viññāna.**)

Unkei (Jap.) Famous Jap. sculptor (1150-1220). His realism suited the Kamakura period (q.v.) with its rising cult of Bushidō and Zen Bsm. Some of Unkei's temple guardians (*see* **Lokapāla**) are as fine as any sculpture achieved in China. Langdon Warner compares him with Michelangelo.

Upādāna (P.) Clingi.＿ to existence; the 'will to live'. That which supports existence. The ninth link in the Chain of Causation. (*See* **Nidānas.**)

Upādhi (Sk. and P.) Nyanatiloka calls it 'substratum of existence'. Many meanings in Hindu philosophy. Base, ground, as canvas on which picture yet to be painted. Vehicle, as body is *upādhi* of its mind.

Upanishads The concluding portion of the Vedas, the early religious writings of the Hindus; hence called the Vedānta, the end of the Vedas. The foundation of most later Indian thought, 108 in number, they are intuitive rather than logical in form, but exhibit throughout 'a vivid sense of spiritual reality' (Radhakrishnan). *See* his *The Philosophy of the Upanishads* (1924).

Upāsaka (P. and Sk.) A lay disciple who strives to keep the Five Precepts at all times, and the Eight Precepts on Uposatha days, and who tries to follow the Eightfold Path whilst living in the world. The feminine form is *upāsikā*.

Upasampadā (P.) The ceremony of full ordination for a *Sāmanera* (q.v.) by which he becomes a *Bhikkhu* (q.v.). The Bhikkhu receives a new name with the Robe, but may leave the Sangha (q.v.) on due notice at will.

Upāya (Sk. and P.) (Jap., *Hōben.*) A means, device or method. A Mahāyāna term for a practical means to a spiritual end which, like a raft when the river is crossed, should be in due course laid aside. *Upāya-kausalya*, skill in means.

Upekkhā (P.) Equanimity. Serenity. The fourth of the Brahma Vihāras (q.v.) and their synthesis, the state of mind in which the other three can be practised without attachment. A neutral state. Cp. *Samadhi*.

Uposatha (P.) The 1st, 8th, 15th and 23rd days of the lunar month; i.e. Full Moon, New Moon and the days equi-distant between them. They were kept as fast days in pre-Buddhist times, and were utilized by the early Buddhists as days for special meetings of the Order, and for recitation of *Pātimokkha* (q.v.). They became recognized as 'sabbath' days, for expounding or listening to the *Dhamma*, for keeping special Precepts, etc., and are still recognized for that purpose in most Buddhist lands.

Urga, Grand Lama of *See* **Mongolia.**

Ūrna (Sk.) The jewel or small protuberance between the eyes of a Buddha image representing the 'third eye' of spiritual vision.

Uruvela The place where the Buddha attained Enlightenment under the Bodhi Tree (q.v.).

Ushnisha (Sk.) The protuberance on top of the head of a Buddha image representing the flame of Enlightenment. In some images, notably Siamese, the protuberance is actually in the form of a flame.

Usual Life The Zen master Jōshu, when asked, 'What is Tao?' replied, 'Your every-day life'. This has been interpreted by some to mean that if we just live our usual life we shall gain Enlightenment. This is not the meaning. It means that we shall not find Enlightenment by a study of scriptures and meditation alone, but by a suddenly-acquired awareness that this daily life *is* the Absolute in action and *is* Nirvāna itself, if only it can be seen with the new eyes of enlightenment. To achieve this new vision is the purpose of Zen training, and the training is long and arduous.

Vācā (P.) Speech. Right Speech is the third step of the Noble Eightfold Path (q.v.).

Vacchagotta A wandering ascetic who questioned the Buddha on certain metaphysical problems (the 'indeterminates'), especially those relating to the ego and the state of the *arhat* after death. Related in the *Aggi-Vacchagotta Sutta,* A.P.C. 106.

Vāda (P.) Expression, speech, showing forth. As Musāvāda, lying speech. Hence teaching, as Theravāda, the Teaching of the Elders.

Vagga (P.) A section or chapter in a larger work. So used in A.P.C.

Vahana (Sk.) Vehicle.

Vaipulya (Sk.) A Mahāyāna form of Scripture. A collection of expanded texts, the converse of a digest or summary.

208

Vairocana (Sk.) In Tib. Bsm. the Dhyāni-Buddha (q.v.) of the centre. The central Sun, personifying the Dharma-Dhātu or supreme Wisdom. Being at the centre he is viewed variously in various Schools. In the Shingon (q.v.) of Japan he is Dainichi or Ādi-Buddha. The enormous Buddha-rūpa in Tōdaiji, Nara, erected in 752, is of Vairocana Buddha.

Vajra (Sk.) Tib. Dorje. The thunderbolt symbol used in art and magic of Tibet as representing the force of adamantine Truth. (*See* **Dorje.**)

Vajracchedikā Sutra *See* **Diamond Sutra.**

Vajradhāra (Sk.) The supreme Buddha-hood as viewed by the Gelugpa School of Tibetan Bsm.

Vajradhātu (Sk.) The 'Diamond Element' or positive pole in the manifested universe, of which the negative pole is the Garbhadhātu, or 'Womb Element'. These reflect the Compassion-Wisdom duality of all Mahāyāna writing.

Vajrapāni (Sk.) One of the Dhyāni-Bodhisattvas (q.v.). Wielder of the Vajra, or Diamond Sceptre. The Tibetan name for the Indian God, Indra. Also a title of advanced initiates in Tibetan Bsm.

Vajrasattva (Sk.) The Diamond Being or Essence. One of the many titles given to Ādi-Buddha, the primordial Buddha-wisdom in the Tibetan Schools of Bsm.

Vajrayāna (Sk.) A Tantric school of North Indian and Tibetan Bsm., not to be taken as a name for Tibetan Bsm. as a whole. (*See* **Tantra, Tibet.**)

Vandanā (P.) Salutation, homage.

209

Varada (Sk.)   Generosity. Choice of recipient of a gift.

Vāsanā (Sk.)   Perfuming impression, memory. Important concept in Yogācāra School (q.v.). Discrimination, which prevents Enlightenment, is caused by this habit-energy of memory from past actions. The 'perfuming' of Vāsanā wakes this memory to fresh action and fresh discrimination. *See* Suzuki, *Studies in the Lankavatara Sutra* (1930).

Vassa (P.)   The rainy season. (*See* **Was.**)

Vasubandhu   Famous Indian philosopher and writer (c. 420-500). With his brother Asanga (q.v.) founded the Yogācāra School (q.v.) of Mahāyāna Bsm. His early work, the *Abhidharma-kosa*, is one of the fullest expositions of Abhidhamma teaching of the Hīnayāna School (*see* Stcherbatsky, *The Central Conception of Buddhism* (1923)). Later, on being converted to the M. point of view by his brother, he wrote the *Vijñaptimātra Shāstra*, expounding the doctrine of Mind-Only. For a trans. of the Chinese version *see* Hamilton, *Wei Shih Er Shih Lun*, the Treatise in Twenty Stanzas on Representation-Only (1938).

Vātsīputrīya   *See* **Sammitīya.**

Vāyāma (P.)   Effort. Sammā Vāyāma is the sixth step on the Noble Eightfold Path (q.v.). The Efforts are described as that to destroy such evil as has arisen in the mind, to prevent any more arising; to produce such good as has not yet arisen in the mind, and to increase the good which has arisen. Together these may be described as developing a right Motive (q.v.) for all action.

Vedanā (P.)   Sense reaction to contact. The seventh link in the Chain of Causation (*see* **Nidānas**), producing the craving or thirst for existence. The second of the Five *Skandhas* (q.v.).

Vedānta The end or consummation of the doctrine of the Vedas. One of the six orthodox systems of Hindu philosophy. Teaches the panentheistic doctrine of the Brahman as the Reality unifying all phenomena, and the identity of man's real Self with that ultimate Reality. Nothing Real exists outside Brahman: 'There is One only, without a second'. This doctrine is set forth in a variety of forms in the scriptures called Upanishads (q.v.). Its chief exponent was Sankara c. A.D. 800.

Vicāra (Sk. and P.) Investigation. Sustained mental application, deeper than Vitakka (q.v.). In the first *jhāna* (q.v.) leads on to *Pīti* (q.v.).

Vicikicchā (P.) Doubt, as wavering uncertainty. A hindrance and a Fetter to be removed. (*See* **Four Paths**.)

Vietnam, Buddhism in In 574 a Bhikkhu of south India, returning from China, founded the Ch'an School in North Vietnam. Later Bst. travellers from Ceylon founded the Theravāda, which is the predominant school today.

Vihāra A dwelling-place. Also a state of life or condition (of heart) (*see* **Brahma vihāras**). The houses presented to the Buddha for the use of the Sangha were called *vihāras*, and the name is now usually applied to any Buddhist retreat or monastery. (*See* **Retreat**.)

Vijñaptimātra (Sk.) 'Representation-Only'. Alternative name for the Indian school of Bsm. better known as the Yogācāra or Vijñānavāda School. (*See* **Vasubandhu**.)

Vikalpa (Sk.) Discrimination, as opposed to the intuitive

211

vision which passes beyond it. The false imagination of foolish thinking which imposes a necessary habit of daily life onto the realities of the spirit. Finally, the products of such foolish thinking, subjective forms which the mind believes to be real. Mere appearances. Thus the illusion of a permanent soul, etc. The Mind-Only School of Bsm. regards all forms without exception as Vikalpa in this sense.

Vimalakīrti (Sk.)   The Vimalakīrti Sūtra, in Japanese Yuima Kyō, is a philosophic dramatic discourse written in India about first century A.D., in which basic M. principles are presented in form of conversation between famous Bst. figures and the humble householder, Vimalakīrti. Trans. into Chinese by Kumārajīva in 401, it became immensely popular in China. *See* Suzuki, *Zen and Japanese Culture*, Appendix II (1959).

Vinaya   The Vinaya Pitaka is the first main division of the Tipitaka. It is concerned with the Rules of Discipline governing the Sangha. *See* A.P.C. Eng. trans. S.B.E. vols. xiii, xvii, xx, and S.B.B. vols. x, xi, xiii, xiv and xx, trans. I. B. Horner.

Viññāna (P.) **Vijñāna** (Sk.)   As one of the five *Skandhas*, *Viññāna* is the normal consciousness, the relation between subject and object. It is the empirical mind, the vehicle (*upādhi*) by which one cognizes the phenomenal worlds and gains the experience of life.

Viññāna is also the consciousness which lies below the threshold of normal experience (the subliminal consciousness), in which the experiences of the past are registered and retained, the results of such experience becoming faculties in the next physical birth. This is *Viññāna* as a link in the Chain of Causation, where it is described as arising from the *Sankhāras* (q.v.). (*See* **Bhavanga**.)

212

It is thus a 'Causality Body', a storehouse of causes and effects; a link between personalities. (*See* **Ālaya-Vijñāna**.)

This *viññāna* is no 'soul', for 'that light which shines within thee differs in no wise from the light which shines in thy brother-men'. It is the personality under the illusion of *attavāda*, which says 'my soul and thy soul'. (*See* **Citta, Consciousness, Manas**.)

Vipāka (Sk. and P.) Maturing, ripening. *See* **Kamma-vipāka**, as 'ripe' Kamma.

Vipassanā (P.) Lit. Insight. Intuitive Vision. Also used for a Bst. system of meditation practised in the Theravāda, that of Satipatthāna (q.v.), the Bst. system of developing 'Right Mindfulness'. Cp. *Satori*.

Virāga (Sk. and P.) Non-attachment to pleasure/pain. One of the virtues to be acquired on the Bst. path to self-perfection. The translation as indifference can be misleading, but the reaction, if any, to outward stimulus from sense-objects, is under perfect control.

Virya (Sk.) **Viriya** (P.) Vigour and energy. The fourth of the six Pāramitās (q.v.).

Visuddhi Magga Title of a famous work on Buddhist doctrine by Buddhaghosa (q.v.). Trans. into English by Bhikkhu Ñānamoli as *The Path of Purification* (Colombo, 1956).

Vitakka (P.) Taking hold of a thought. An early process in meditation which deepens into Vicāra (q.v.). Both are technical terms in the Abhidhamma philosophy. Cp. *Vitarka* (Sk.).

Vitarka (Sk.) Deliberation. Speculation. As a Mudrā (q.v.), the gesture of reflection. Cp. *Vitakka* (P.).

Viveka (Sk. and P.) Detachment, either physical, as living in solitude, or mental, mentally detached from being affected by objects of sense. This 'standing aloof from circumstance' (Hui-neng) is not indifference but non-attachment, awareness without clinging or repulsion.

'Voice of the Silence, The'   The title of a book translated by 'H. P. B.' (H. P. Blavatsky, q.v.) from thirty-nine of ninety small treatises comprising the *Book of the Golden Precepts* (q.v.). First published in 1889. The facsimile edition published in Peking in 1927 has a Foreword by the then Panchen Lama. (See **Dzyan, Senzar.**)

Vows   A Bst. takes vows when he takes Pansil (q.v.), but he takes them to himself. Even the more stringent vows taken by a Bhikkhu (q.v.) may be given up on leaving the Sangha. The Bodhisattva vow, taken by many of the M. School, is to work for humanity and to sacrifice all gain for self until that ideal is achieved.

Vulture Peak   A Hill near Rājagriha in N.E. India which was one of the many Vihāras or Retreats given to the Buddha for the use of the Sangha. Here he is said to have expounded many of the esoteric teachings peculiar to the M. School.

Vyūha (Sk.)   Embellishment, a garland or wreath, as in the Ganda Vyūha, a portion still èxtant in Sk. of the Avatamsaka Sūtra (q.v.).

Wabi (Jap.)   A term used in Japanese art to describe a mood of 'spiritual loneliness', manifesting in an aloof serenity of mind which in turn affects technique. A subjective state of poverty. Cp. *Sabi*.

Walk on!   (1) A phrase used first by the Zen master Ummon who, when asked 'What is Tao?' replied, 'Walk on!' Since used to symbolize the 'direct' approach of Zen Bsm. to Reality. (2) The name of a book by Christmas Humphreys (1956).

Wanshi (Jap.) Chin. Huang-chi. 1090-1157. Chinese Zen master in the line of those who formed the Sōtō (q.v.) School of Zen. Creator of Mokushō ('silent sitting') Zen as distinct from Kanna Zen (q.v.). Collected the Sayings of previous Zen masters into the Shōyō Roku (q.v.), comparable with the Hekigan Roku.

Was (Thai) **Vassa** (P.) The rainy season, during which Bhikkhus obey the Rule of their Order not to travel, but to remain in their monasteries for study and meditation. (*See* **Retreat**.)

Wat (Siam.) The Siamese term for a *Vihāra* (q.v.) or temple-monastery.

Watts, Alan English Buddhist now living in California, born 1915. Author of *Spirit of Zen* (1936). Editor of *The Middle Way* (q.v.), 1936-8, when left for U.S.A. Professor of Comparative Philosophy, American Academy of Asian Studies, 1951-57; Dean 1953-56. 1958, Hon. D.D. Univ. of Vermont. Broadcasts and writes on Zen Bsm. and allied subjects. Publications include *The Meaning of Happiness* (1940), *The Wisdom of Insecurity* (1951), *The Way of Zen* (1957), *This is It* (1961) and *In My Own Way* (1972). [Died 1973.]

Wei Lang (Chin.) When the Sūtra of Hui-neng was first trans. into English the translator, Wong Mou-lam, used a Canton dialect for transliteration and rendered the name Wei Lang. The book in English was therefore called *The Sutra of Wei Lang* (1944). In later editions the name Hui-neng was added. The form Wei Lang should now be dropped.

Wesak or **Vesak** (Sinhalese), **Vaisākha** (Sk.), **Vesākha** (P.)
The month corresponding to April-May, on the Full Moon
Day of which is celebrated the Birth, Renunciation, Enlightenment and Parinibbāna of the Buddha. The festival is called
from the name of the month. The Japanese Mahāyāna sects
celebrate the Birth of the Buddha on 8 April. (*See* **Buddha
Day.**)

'Wheel, The' Organ of the British Maha Bodhi Society. A
mimeographed, monthly publication, which replaced the
British Buddhist in January 1935. Publication suspended in
1939.

Wheel of Life (*Bhavacakra*) The Tibetans make great use of
pictures of the Wheel to bring before the mind the nature of
existence. The rim shows Twelve Nidānas (q.v.), its six sections
portraying the different spheres of existence in which the con-
catenation of Cause and Effect operates. The six spheres are:
the Heaven worlds, the *Asura* worlds, the Human worlds, the
Animal worlds, the Purgatorial worlds, and the Hells. It is
noteworthy that in the lowest hell there is an exit, and that
a Buddha is depicted in each of the six worlds, thus indicating
that he is ever ready to aid in whatsoever state one may be. The
Wheel is depicted as being whirled round by a demon, sym-
bolizing the miseries and limitations of existence. In the centre
of the Wheel are shown the three cardinal sins or unwholesome
roots—lust, malevolence, and stupidity-greed—symbolized by
the red cock, the green snake, and the black pig. Outside the
Wheel the Buddha is depicted to symbolize release from the
Wheel as the *summum bonum*, and his attainment thereof.

Wheel of the Law The Buddha set the 'Wheel of the Law'
(Dhammacakka) in motion with his First Sermon (q.v.) in the
Deer Park near Benares (Sarnath). (*See* **Dhammacakka-ppava-
tana Sutta.**)

Will No one Bst. word covers the English term will. The nearest is *Cetanā* (q.v.) meaning mind as inclining to action, hence purpose or intention. (*See* **Chanda, Freewill.**)

Women Bsm. has always aimed at the ideal relationship between men and women. The Sangha was established for women as soon as the time was ripe, and regulations were provided for their protection.

Women played an important part in the spread of early Bsm. both as lay disciples and *bhikkhunīs*. Famous women in early Bsm. were: Bhadda, famous for her discourses, and for her memories of former lives; Visakha, a wealthy patroness of the Order; Ambapālī, a courtesan who became a convert and supported the Sangha; Dhammadinna, the great preacher; Mahāpajapati, the Buddha's foster-mother, who founded the Sangha for women; Khema, the consort of King Bimbisara, renowned for her profound insight; Yasodharā, the wife of Gotama, also entered the Sangha. In later times we have Sanghamitta, the daughter of Asoka, founding the Sangha in Ceylon. *See* Mrs Rh. Davids, *Psalms of the Sisters* (P.T.S. 1909), and Horner, *Women under Primitive Bsm.* (Routledge, 1930).

Won A Korean School of Bsm. founded by So-Tal-San in 1916. Its symbol is a circle. No distinction is made between 'priests' and laity, and the scriptures are in Korean. Regard is paid to social welfare as well as the spiritual life. Won Buddhists are enjoined not to forget their training at any time or place. It has some affinities with Zen, combined with social reform. (*See* **Korea.**)

World Fellowship of Buddhists, The An organization founded at Kandy, Ceylon, in 1950 by Dr G. P. Malalasekera. It promoted the first World Bst. Conference at Colombo in 1951, the second in Tokyo in September 1952, the third at Rangoon in 1954, and others every few years since. Headquarters at Bangkok. Journal, *World Buddhism*.

Wu (Chin.) (1) As pronounced in the 'second tone' is the great 'No' or 'Not' of Jōshu, when asked if a dog had the Buddha-nature. The Absolute Negative. In Jap., Mu. (2) As pronounced in the 'fourth tone', lit. to waken, or understand. In Japanese, *Satori* (q.v.).

Wu Hsin (Chin.) Lit. No-Mind (q.v.).

Wu T'ai Shan (Chin.) Sacred mountain in China, of five hills or terraces, once covered with Bst. temples and inhabited until recent times by a group of Bsts. of great attainment. *See* Blofeld, *The Wheel of Life,* for long account of recent visits.

Wu-Tao-Tzu (Chin.) Jap. Godōshi (700-760). The greatest painter of the T'ang Dynasty. Little of his work survives in China, but the few in Japan are of world rank in painting. His triptych of Sākyamuni, Manjusri and Samantabhadra in Tōfu-kuji, Kyoto, is 'among the most moving religious pictures of the Far East' (Grousset), and with his *Nirvāna* he created a precedent which affected Bst. painting for centuries.

Wu-Wei (Chin.) Lit. Wu, not, Wei action: non-action, as distinct from no action. A Taoist term, which in Bsm. is action karma-less, not bearing fruit for the doer because performed without thought of self; hence purposeless. (*See* **Purposelessness.**) *See* the *Tao Tê Ching,* and Humphreys, *The Way of Action* (1960). (*See* **Kriya.**)

Yab-yum (Tib.) Common term for the figures in Tibetan sculpture and painting of the Vajrayāna School which show a male figure of the Tibetan pantheon in sexual union with his

Shakti (q.v.) or female counterpart. For Tibetans the figures symbolize the primal forces of Reality in manifestation and their intimate and essential unity. They have no gross sexual significance as imagined by Western writers. (*See* **Maithuna, Tantra.**)

Yaksha (Sk.), Fem. **Yakshini, Yakkha** (P.) Nature forces in the Hindu pantheon comparable with minor members of the Deva kingdom. Under different names they appear throughout eastern mythology and art.

Yama The Lord of Death. Cp. *Mara.*

Yana (Sk. and P.) Lit. Career, Vehicle or means of progress. A vehicle of salvation from wheel of Samsara. Thus Mahayana, the larger, and Hina-yana, the smaller vehicle (of salvation). Vajra-yana, Diamond vehicle.

Yantra (Sk.) Symbolic diagram conceived in meditation and used for spiritual development in Tibetan Bsm. In art they are projected as Mandalas and the like.

Yasodhara (Sk.) The wife of Gautama Siddhartha. He won her from all competitors at the age of sixteen in a contest of arms. Her name is elsewhere given as Gopa. Their son was Rahula (q.v.).

Yathabhutam (Sk.) (To see) things as they are, just so. A basic principle of M. teaching. Cp. *Tathata.*

Yellow Hats Members of the Gelug-pa Order of Tibetan Bsm. On special occasions members of this Order, founded in the fourteenth century by Tsong-kha-pa, wear yellow hats as distinct from the red hats worn by other sects.

Yellow Robe The Bhikkhus of the Theravāda School have, since the foundation of the Order by the Buddha, worn three robes of various shades of orange or yellow. Originally these garments were made of rags sewn together and dyed the colour by which the Order has been known for 2,500 years. Besides his robes a Bhikkhu may only, according to the Rules, possess his begging bowl, a needle, a water-strainer and an umbrella. The Zen *Kesa* (q.v.) symbolically represents the Yellow Robe.

Yidam (Tib.) The deity, or aspect of the Absolute, chosen as the protective power for meditation and devotion by Tibetan Bsts. of the Vajrayāna School (q.v.).

Yin-Yang (Chin.) The female and male principles which are the primordial dual forces of the manifested universe. *See* Chap. I and XLII of the *Tao Tê Ching*. The two are symbolised in art as two 'tadpoles' of black and white, each with an eye of white or black, the two involved in a circle. Cp. *S(h)akti, Yab-yum.*

Yoga A word meaning 'yoke', in the sense of 'that which unites', therefore 'union'. The Hindu system of discipline which brings a man to union (with Reality). There are two great systems: Hatha Yoga, psycho-physiological training along ascetic lines, and Rāja Yoga, the development of inner powers by meditation, etc.

Yogācāra School The Mind-Only school of Indian Bsm. founded in the fourth century by the brothers Asanga and Vasubandhu (q.v.). The latter called it the Vijñānavāda, the doctrine of Consciousness-Only. A teaching of subjective idealism, not as speculative belief but as the product of spiritual experience. Developed the doctrine of Ālaya-Vijñāna (q.v.) the 'store-consciousness' which underlies all human consciousness. Leading Scriptures include the Lankāvatāra Sutra

(q.v.), the Avatamsaka Sutra (q.v.), the Awakening of Faith (q.v.) and Vasubandhu's own 'Treatise in Twenty Stanzas on Representation-Only'. The School was refounded in China as the Fa-hsiang by Hiuen-Tsiang (q.v.). Dōsho brought it to Japan as the Hossō School, its most famous temple being Hōryūji (q.v.).

Yongden, The Lama Adopted son of Mme David-Neel (q.v.). The first Tibetan Lama to take up residence in the West. With Mme David-Neel on journey to Lhasa (*see* her *My Journey to Lhasa* (1927)), and co-operated in many more of her works. Lived with her in France until death in 1955. Author of *Mipam* (1938), and other works in French.

'Young East, The' Only Bst. journal published in English in Japan. Founded by Dr J. Takakusu in 1897. Quarterly.

Yuga (Sk.) A specific age or period of time in Hindu chronology. Life on earth passes through cycles of varying lengths, some enormous. The present age is Kali Yuga, the Dark Age. It will last 432,000 years and began in 3102 B.C.

Yūgen (Jap.) An extremely subtle Japanese term used in Zen. It has been called 'the sound of eternal stillness'. It points beyond the finite to the source of finite things.

Yun-Kang Large series of caves to west of Peking cut from cliff-face by Toba Tatars who founded Wei Dynasty in China. Mostly fifth century. Caves contain vast array of elaborately carved Buddha images and other Bst. figures. Original vivid colouring remains. Some figures inches high and some 60 feet. Variety and merit of figures exceeds the later caves of Tun-Huang (q.v.). *See, National Geographical Magazine*, March 1958.

Za-Zen (Jap.) 'Zen-sitting.' Zen meditation, usually in the Zen-dō (q.v.). The correct posture is the Dhyānāsana (*see* **Āsana**), loosely known as the Lotus posture, in which the sole of each foot is upturned on the opposite thigh. The subject in Rinzai Zen monasteries is usually the Kōan (q.v.) given by the Rōshi or Zen master to that pupil. For special periods *see* Sesshin. *See* Suzuki, *The Training of the Zen Buddhist Monk* (1934). (*See* **Mondō, Sesshin, Zen.**)

Zen (Jap.) A Chinese and Japanese school of Bsm. which has been described as the revolt of the Chinese mind against the intellectual Buddhism of India. It evolved from the teaching of Bodhidharma, the Twenty-eighth Patriarch of Bsm., who came to China in A.D. 520. The word Zen is the Japanese equivalent of the Chinese *Ch'an* or *Ch'an-na*, derived from the Sk. *Dhyāna*, usually translated as 'meditation'. This, however, gives an erroneous conception of Zen, which cannot be confined to any particular practice. Although meditation (*see* **Za-zen**) is a part of Zen training, Zen itself includes every possible form of activity. The Chinese mind wished to apply Bsm. to everyday life, asserting that Enlightenment could be found just as much by working in the world as in withdrawing from it.

Zen is described as:

A special transmission (of Enlightenment) outside the
    Scriptures;
No dependence on words and letters;
Direct pointing to the soul of man;
Seeing into one's own nature, and the attainment of
    Buddhahood.

Bodhidharma taught that as all things are Buddhas from the very beginning, the only reason for our not realizing our 'Buddha-nature' is our own ignorance. As man's original nature is this 'Buddha-nature', Zen is the act of discovering oneself.

This teaching cannot be grasped by the intellectual mind, and much of Zen literature seems nonsense to rational understanding. But its illogical technique is a means of jolting the mind out of its ordinary ruts, for purely logical thought leads us in circles.

Zen has had profound influence on Far Eastern culture, and has penetrated into every department of life. It inspired the greatest period of Chinese art and much of the finest art of Japan. It profoundly affected the Japanese military arts of *Jūdō* (v.) and *Kendō* (q.v.), for the 'dynamic immediacy' of its technique appealed to the warrior spirit of the *Samurai* (q.v.). It also sponsored the Tea Ceremony. (*See* **Cha-no-yu**), Flower-Arrangement (q.v.) and Landscape Gardening. *See* Watts, *The Spirit of Zen, and* Humphreys, *Zen Buddhism,* wherein appears a full Biblio. with all the works of the greatest authority, Dr D. T. Suzuki. (*See* **Suzuki**.)

Zen-dō (Jap.) The hall, usually a separate building, used in a Zen monastery for Za-Zen, meditation. The monks have each a mat (Tatami), 6 feet x 3 feet, on which to sit, and they sleep on it at night. The mats are on a platform (Tan) on two sides of the Zen-dō, with a wide space in between. For photographs of a Zen-dō in use *see* Suzuki, *Zen and Japanese Buddhism.*

Zen-ji (Jap.) A teacher of Zen, as Hakuin Zen-ji, the Zen teacher Hakuin. Cp. *Ji* (1) and (3).

Zenkō-ji (Jap.) Group of Bst. buildings near Nagano, Japan. Founded 602. Unique in that it contains in one estate a Tendai monastery and a Jōdo nunnery. Great place of pilgrimage.

Zen Logic Zen training is a process of transcending thought, for the intellect functions in duality, and the 'moment' of Zen experience is in Non-duality. Normal logic is therefore worse than useless to achieve this experience; it binds the mind in the coils of concept. Only when it is seen that A is A *because*

A is not-A is the mind set free. This logic is the fruit of Zen experience and not a means to it. It can be stated, therefore, but not be the subject of intellectual argument. Nevertheless Dr Suzuki for one has described it as far as possible. *See*, for example, his *Introduction to Zen Buddhism*, pp. 46-50.

Zen training in the West   Zen Bsm. was brought to the West by Dr D. T. Suzuki (q.v.) but the training, including long periods of meditation, as applied in Rinzai monasteries, needs either years spent in Japan or the presence of a *Roshi* (q.v.) available in the West in many centres, and in Europe speaking the appropriate language. One solution to the problem thus raised is for the direct training of the Western student's mind towards and after Zen experience, and within the ambit of normal life. As Dr Suzuki wrote 'the Western mind must help the East to construct a new system of thought based upon Zen experience . . . whereby we can present the truth of Zen along the lines already prepared but not fully developed by Western

Zenrin Kushū (Jap.)   A collection of some 6,000 quotations from Bst. Sutras, records of Chinese Patriarchs, and Confucian and Taoist writings, used by Rinzai Zen students in their training. First compiled in Japan in fifteenth century.